Web 2.0 and the Political Mobilization of College Students

Lexington Studies in Political Communication

Series Editor: Robert E. Denton, Jr., Virginia Tech

This series encourages focused work examining the role and function of communication in the realm of politics including campaigns and elections, media, and political institutions.

Recent Titles in the Series

The Perfect Response: Studies of the Rhetorical Personality, by Gary C. Woodward
A Communication Universe: Manifestations of Meaning, Stagings of Significance, by Igor E. Klyukanov
Presidential Campaign Rhetoric in an Age of Confessional Politics, by Brian T. Kaylor
Manipulating Images: World War II Mobilization of Women through Magazine Advertising, by Tawnya J. Adkins Covert
The Politics of Style and the Style of Politics, edited by Barry Brummett
Communication Realities in a "Post-Racial" Society: What the U.S. Public Really Thinks about Barack Obama, by Mark P. Orbe
Politics and the Twitter Revolution: How Tweets Influence the Relationship between Political Leaders and the Public, by John H. Parmelee and Shannon L. Bichard
The Rhetoric of Soft Power: Public Diplomacy in Global Contexts, by Craig Hayden
Coming to Terms: The Collected Works of Jane Blankenship, edited by Janette K. Muir
Reelpolitik Ideologies in American Political Film, by Beverly Merrill Kelley
Media Bias in Presidential Election Coverage 1948–2008: Evaluation via Formal Measurement, by David W. D'Alessio
Gender and the American Presidency: Nine Presidential Women and the Barriers They Faced, by Theodore F. Sheckels, Nichola D. Gutgold, and Diana Bartelli Carlin
The George W. Bush Presidency: A Rhetorical Perspective, edited by Robert E. Denton, Jr.
New Media, Old Regimes: Case Studies in Comparative Communication Law and Policy, by Lyombe S. Eko
Culture, Social Class, and Race in Public Relations: Perspectives and Applications, edited by Damion Waymer
Purpose, Practice, and Pedagogy in Rhetorical Criticism, edited by Jim A. Kuypers
Dark Money, Super PACs, and the 2012 Election, by Melissa M. Smith and Larry Powell
The Rhetoric of Genocide: Death as a Text, by Ben Voth
Studies of Communication in the 2012 Presidential Campaign, edited by Robert E. and Denton, Jr.
Economic Actors, Economic Behaviors, and Presidential Leadership: The Constrained Effects of Rhetoric, by C. Damien Arthur
Image and Emotion in Voter Decisions: The Affect Agenda, by Renita Coleman and Denis Wu
The Four Pillars of Politics: Why Some Candidates Don't Win and Others Can't Lead by James T. Kitchens and Larry Powell
Public Places: Sites of Political Communication, by Carl T. Hyden and Theodore F. Sheckels
Web 2.0 and the Political Mobilization of College Students, by Kenneth W. Moffett and Laurie L. Rice

Web 2.0 and the Political Mobilization of College Students

Kenneth W. Moffett and Laurie L. Rice

LEXINGTON BOOKS
Lanham • Boulder • New York • London

Published by Lexington Books
An imprint of The Rowman & Littlefield Publishing Group, Inc.
4501 Forbes Boulevard, Suite 200, Lanham, Maryland 20706
www.rowman.com

Unit A, Whitacre Mews, 26–34 Stannary Street, London SE11 4AB

British Library Cataloguing in Publication Information Available
The hardback edition of this book was previously catalogued by the Library of Congress as follows:

Library of Congress Control Number: 2016950705
ISBN 9781498538572 (cloth : alk. paper)
ISBN 9781498538596 (pbk. : alk. paper)
ISBN 9781498538589 (electronic)

♾™ The paper used in this publication meets the minimum requirements of American National Standard for Information Sciences—Permanence of Paper for Printed Library Materials, ANSI/NISO Z39.48-1992.

Printed in the United States of America

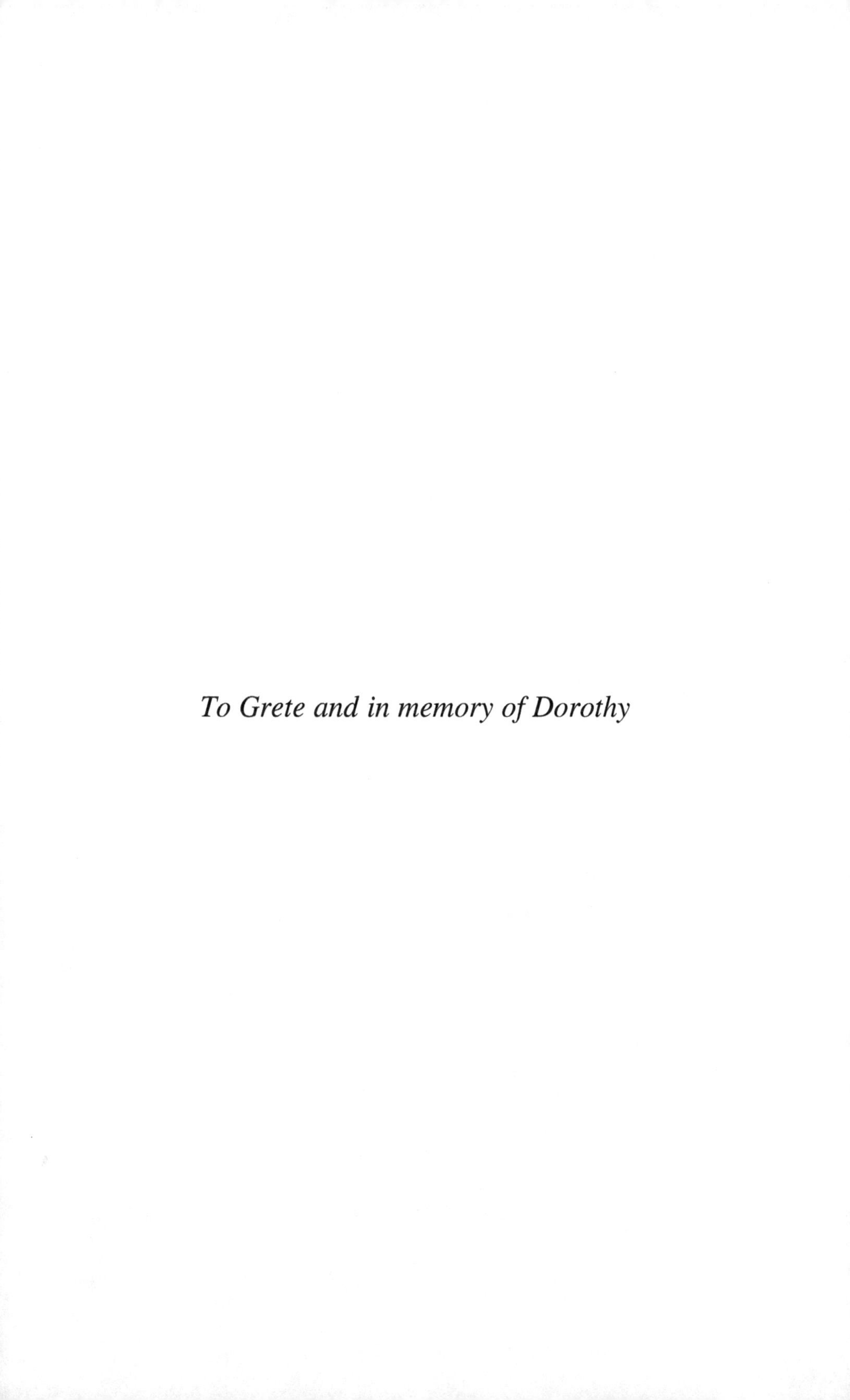

To Grete and in memory of Dorothy

Contents

List of Figures

List of Tables

Acknowledgments

In researching and writing this book, we have benefited immeasurably from the advice and support of others in our discipline. The end result is much improved over what we could ever have written on our own. In particular, we acknowledge two internal sources of financial support from Southern Illinois University Edwardsville: the College of Arts and Sciences Faculty Development Fund and the Department of Political Science Development Fund. We also thank the Office of the Provost at Southern Illinois University Edwardsville for providing each of us with a semester's worth of sabbatical leave: Moffett in Fall 2013, and Rice in Spring 2015. This time allowed each of us to formulate our ideas and complete the writing of this manuscript.

We also thank a number of colleagues within the discipline for their comments on varying portions of the analysis that were presented over multiple years at the annual meetings of the American Political Science Association (2013) and the Midwest Political Science Association (2009 and 2014). In particular, we thank Jessica Feezell, Tom Nelson, Julianna Pacheco, and Claire Smith for their thorough read over the varying analyses that ultimately are incorporated in some form throughout this manuscript. Their feedback made this work much better than it otherwise would have been. We also thank Triniece Cummins for her diligent research assistance. We would be remiss if we did not thank Lynn Maurer and Adam Jadhav who first approached us about conducting a survey in 2008. If they had not encouraged it, then this book would probably not exist. We also thank Ramana Madupalli for his role on our initial survey team.

Finally, we thank the outstanding team at Lexington Press for their belief in our work, and for the collegial, smart, and efficient manner in which they operate. We thank Robert Denton for his initial interest in this manuscript, and for all of his support throughout the publication process.

Nicolette Amstutz expertly shepherded this book through the review process, was very responsive to our many questions, and gave excellent guidance with respect to making revisions that would improve the final product. She is everything that we could ever ask for and want in an Editor. Also, Kasey Beduhn has done a great job with all of our inquiries and has been helpful every step of the way.

Kenneth acknowledges and thanks those who have supported him professionally and personally. In particular, he thanks Scott Ainsworth, Douglas Dion, Brian Harward, Charles Shipan, and Tracy Slagter for all of their insights and for being a sounding board for all manner of research ideas, both good and bad. He also thanks his family, including his parents, Beverly and Vern Bowling, as well as his sister, Becky, and her husband, David. He is grateful for all of their support, love and encouragement no matter what life brings. He thanks his nephew, Boede Mullins, for dutifully reminding him that life exists outside of academic pursuits and for always being a happy presence no matter the setting. He also thanks his grandfather, Wayne Wenzel, for his steadfastness and for encouraging him to keep the "big picture" in mind whenever making any important decision. He thanks his in-laws, Lori and Sam Graf for being the kindest mother and father-in-law that one could ever want.

Most importantly, he thanks his bride, Grete, for all of her love, prayers, encouragement, curiosity, and for being his best friend. She has participated in many adventures with him, including being stranded in Salt Lake City on the way to California to meet most of his immediate family for the first time, and two trips to the state that she most enjoys visiting: Vermont. She has also read more iterations of his scholarly work than he would voluntarily impose on anyone. She is far better to him than he deserves in so many ways. In part, it is for these reasons that his portion of the book dedication is to her.

Laurie would also like to thank those who have supported her professionally and personally. Many of her graduate school professors and mentors helped encourage her interest in and sharpen her thinking about presidential elections and civic engagement – especially Samuel Kernell, Samuel Popkin, and Arthur Lupia. Her friends across fields have helped her to think more broadly than discipline and encouraged her in writing and life. Peter Gent, Denise DeGarmo, and Jean Shen all deserve particular acknowledgment in that respect. She is also deeply thankful for the blessing of a supportive family. She regrets that her grandparents did not live to see this in print, but knows they would not be surprised because they always believed she was capable. Her portion of the book dedication is in memory of her grandmother, Dorothy Rice, who loved her unconditionally, prayed for her daily, and who passed away while this manuscript was still in progress. Finally, she expresses special gratitude to her parents, Larry and Bobbie Rice, who have always surrounded her with love and encouraged her in everything she does, including the writing of this book.

Chapter 1

Participation, Technology, and Age

This book examines the political participation of young adults. A cornerstone of the literature on voting behavior holds that those over the age of 50 vote at far higher rates than those between the ages of 18 and 25 (Miller and Shanks 1996; Teixeira 1987). These same accounts provide considerable evidence that those between 18 and 25 years old are far less likely to participate in politics in other ways, like monetarily contributing to campaigns, volunteering to work on campaigns or for parties, and participating in protests (Miller and Shanks 1996; Teixeira 1987).

If these accounts remain correct and hold over time, the question quickly becomes: why study members of this age group, since they do not vote or participate at very high rates? One answer is that scholars, journalists, and other commentators on this issue might be looking for participation in many of the wrong places. The traditional routes of political participation include activities like contributing money to candidates for office or political parties, contacting or visiting government officials, participating in protests, and attending political events of some kind. If we look solely at these places, then observers are correct that younger people are not participatory in this fashion on a large scale, especially when compared with their older peers.

However, new forms of participation have emerged that are potential game-changers when it comes to investigating this topic. For instance, social networking websites did not exist widely until 2004, and apps did not come into widespread usage until at least 2008 (Curtis 2014). Further, blogging did not become a prominent route by which people express themselves on a wide variety of topics, including politics, until 1998 (Curtis 2014). Moreover, Twitter did not exist prior to 2006, and did not achieve a critical mass of users until after the 2008 presidential election (Curtis 2014). Some studies suggest that these routes appeal disproportionately to younger people over their older counterparts (Dunne, Lawlor, and Rowley 2010).

A second answer to this question is a logical consequence of the first: the new forms of participation that have emerged carry with them a cost calculus that differs from those that preceded them. Consequently, these new forms might appeal to a population that may not have the resources to engage in the more costly forms of participation. For instance, people can "friend" candidates, follow candidates, join online groups, post their thoughts in 140 characters or less (via Twitter) or in a more extended form through a blog, or even message candidates or parties through a wide array of venues. People can do all of these things from any device that is connected to the internet, no matter the location. Thus, people can engage in the political process through mechanisms that may prove tangible yet do not require more formal commitments like going to an event, spending money, or other significant changes in their daily routines. In this way, these routes allow younger people to participate in the political process in ways that are less costly than those faced by previous cohorts.

A third answer is that many policymakers and organizations view low participation among young adults as a problem that needs to be addressed. Several organizations have been created to foster participation in American politics among young people, including Rock the Vote, the Center for Information and Research on Civic Learning and Engagement at Tufts University, and the Dole Center at The University of Kansas. Also, the Pew Charitable Trusts have devoted sizable resources to discovering the civic attitudes of younger people, and where appropriate, to selected campaigns targeted toward increasing civic engagement among younger people.

In addition, Barack Obama's 2008 successful candidacy for president engaged younger voters in ways that were meaningful to them in an effort to gain votes among an overlooked demography. For example, his campaign encouraged donations in small amounts, held campaign events at college campuses on a scale previously not seen, created an app that pushes information to those who have installed it on their smart phones, and used social networking in unprecedented ways (Keeter, Horowitz, and Tyson 2008). In concert with the Democratic Party, his campaign was so successful at these methods that Republicans have bemoaned the "social networking gap" within their own party (Sorenson 2011).

For these reasons, we seek to investigate those factors that affect civic engagement among young adults. To introduce our investigation, we perform several tasks. First, we examine the ways in which young adults systematically differ from their older counterparts with respect to two key indicators of civic engagement: voting and volunteer activity. In this same section, we investigate the ways in which young people differ from their older counterparts in terms of their levels of activity on the internet. In doing so, we make the case for examining young people by themselves, as this subgroup differs from the remainder of the population. Second, we discuss why examining online forms of civic activity might be a better way of examining the civic life of younger people, rather than just examining more traditional forms of civic activity by themselves. Third, we introduce the data that we utilize throughout this book to test our theoretical argument. Finally, we conclude with an overview of the remaining chapters of this book.

CIVIC ENGAGEMENT BY AGE GROUP

Scholarly and media accounts often isolate young adults for particular scrutiny with respect to their civic activity. More specifically, these accounts often depict members of this population as less engaged in civic life than those older than them (Wattenberg 2011), particularly when it comes to voting in elections (Dalton 2008; Wattenberg 2011) and volunteer activity (Wilson 2000). Yet, other accounts portray members of this group as highly adept and agile when it comes to the use of technology, especially when it comes to examining social media (Jones and Fox 2009). We explore these contradictory trends to discern the ways in which young adults systematically differ from their elders. We also explore why these differences matter, and the implications that they carry with respect to the analyses contained in this manuscript.

Young Adults and Civic Activity

In Figure 1.1, we compare the percentage of adults who voted in the 2008 and 2012 elections by age. The vertical axis in this figure is the percentage in each age group who voted, while the horizontal axis denotes the election year. Finally, differing shades of black and gray represent varying age groups.

This figure demonstrates three trends. First, the percentage of young adults who vote is consistently lower than all other age groups. While this percentage increased from 40% in the 2000 election to a height of 51% during the 2008 election (or, by over 27%), it is still lower than that of all other age groups. This trend also held even while turnout remained largely flat among all other age groups over this time period. Second, younger voters differed from those aged 30–44 by 19% in 2000, 13% in 2004, 11% in 2008, and 15% in 2012. Thus, we see a significant gap that only increases as we increase the age difference. Third, younger voters were significantly below the overall average reported turnout among citizens when we consider all ages. More specifically, turnout among younger voters was 33% lower in 2000, 23% lower in 2004, 20% lower in 2008, and 27% lower in 2012.

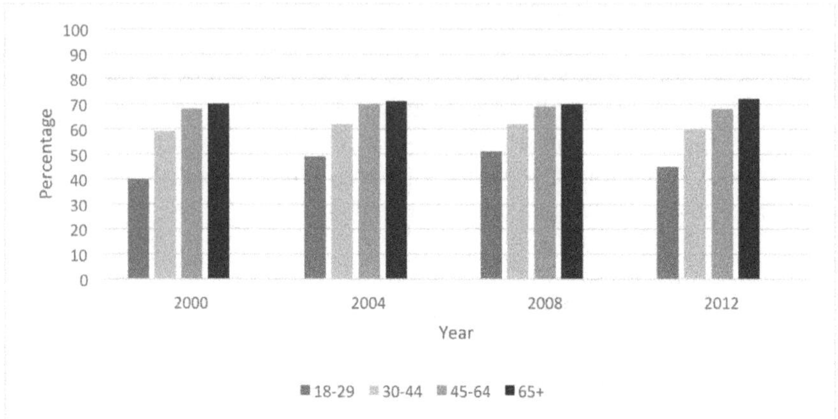

Figure 1.1 Age Groups and Voting among Citizens in the 2000 through 2012 November Elections. *Source*: Center for Information and Research on Civic Learning and Engagement, 2013.

These trends are consistent with the extant political science literature. In particular, Wattenberg (2011) argues that young adults are less likely to vote because they tune out of politics in favor of other entertainment programs. Also, Wattenberg (2011) and Dalton (2008) state that younger people tend to view voting as less of a civic duty than older generations, and that knowledge about public affairs among this same group is lower than that of older cohorts. Dalton (2008) argues that this is part of a larger shift among members of this generation from traditional "citizen duty" norms to "engaged citizen" norms. If Dalton (2008) is correct, then voting might not be the best way to capture civic engagement among young people, and the search for civic engagement should begin elsewhere.

We begin our search by examining the extent to which young people participate in volunteer activity, as this is part of the norms of engaged citizens (Dalton 2008). In Figure 1.2, we compare the percentage of younger people who engage in volunteer activity with those of other age groups. The vertical axis in this figure is the percentage in each age group who volunteered, while the horizontal axis denotes the election year. Moreover, varying shades of black and gray correspond to different age groups.

This figure illustrates two trends. First, those between the ages of 16 and 24 volunteer at the lowest rates, relative to all other age groups despite many high schools and colleges strongly encouraging volunteer activity. More specifically, 22% of those in this age group report having volunteered in 2009, while 31.5% of those between the ages of 35 and 44 report having volunteered. Similarly, 21.8% of those between the ages of 16 and 24 report

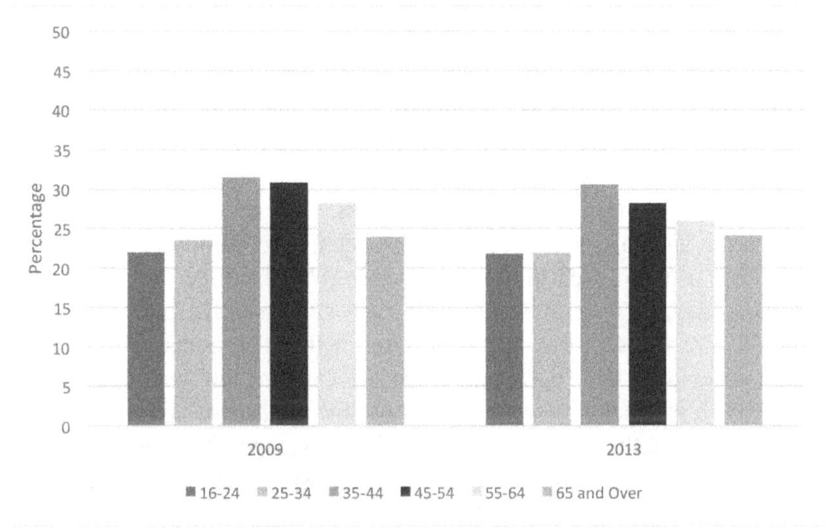

Figure 1.2 Age and Volunteer Activity among Citizens in 2009 and 2013. *Source*: Bureau of Labor Statistics, 2014.

having volunteered in 2013, while 30.6% of Americans between the ages of 35 and 44 report having engaged in volunteer activity. Second, the frequency with which those between the ages of 16 and 24 volunteered was 30% lower in 2009, and 29% lower in 2013, when we compare this group with those between the ages of 35 and 44.

These trends are consistent with the extant literature on volunteering. Smith (1999) points out that young people may volunteer at lower rates because volunteer-involving organizations do not always make themselves attractive to younger age groups. Similarly, Wilson (2000) points out that volunteering decreases among those between the ages of 16 and 24 because of the structure of school-related activities. Moreover, volunteering tends to rise to its peak in middle age (see Herzog, Kahn, Morgan, Jackson, and Antonucci 1989, S134; Menchik and Weisbrod 1987; Schoenberg 1980). If these scholars are correct, then the patterns that we observe here indicate a lower level of engagement for life-cycle-related reasons, more than anything else. Thus, examining rates of volunteer activity might not be the best indicator of civic activity among young adults.

Young Voters and the Internet

However, young adults are quite active with respect to activities related to the internet, especially when we compare them to their older counterparts.

In Figure 1.3, we examine data from the Pew Internet Project about the percentage of those in different age groups that go online at all in 2009 and 2014. The vertical axis is the percentage of each age group that goes online, while the horizontal axis denotes each age group. The dark gray bar corresponds to survey data from December 2009, while the light gray bar is the result from the January 2014 survey.

Figure 1.3 illuminates two trends. First, internet usage among those between the ages of 18–29 is the highest, relative to all other age groups. In 2009, 93% of them used the internet, while 97% used the internet in 2014. Comparatively, 38% of those over the age of 65 used the internet in 2009, while 57% of those in this age group used it in 2014. Second, those in age groups other than the 18–29 age range are catching up to younger adults. Among each group, the percentage who use the internet has grown by at least 10%, and among those over the age of 65, it has grown by over 50%.

We also see some interesting trends when we examine the user base of social networking websites. In Figure 1.4, we examine the extent to which varying age groups used social networking websites. The vertical axis is the percentage of each age group that uses these websites, while the horizontal axis denotes each age group. The dark gray bar corresponds to survey data from April 2009, while the light gray bar is the result from November and December 2012.

Figure 1.4 displays two trends. First, those between the ages of 18 and 29 utilize social networking websites at far higher rates than their older

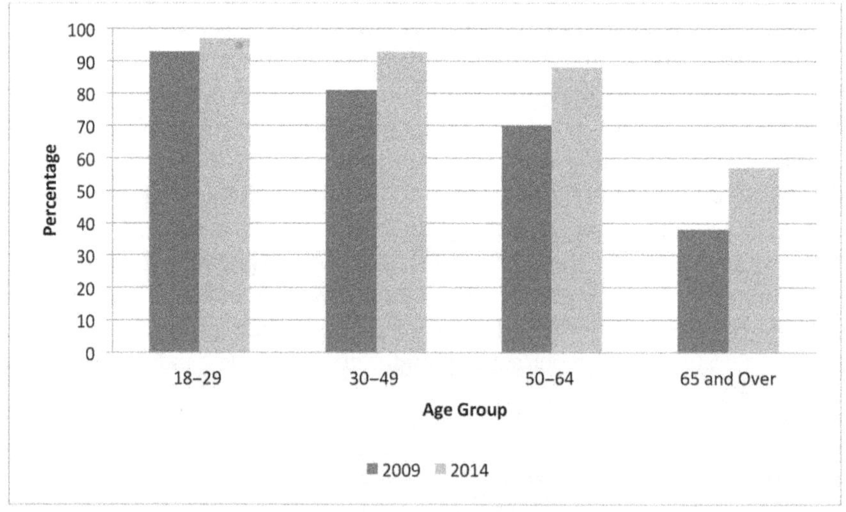

Figure 1.3 Internet Usage by Age Group in 2009 and 2014. *Source*: Lenhart, Purcell, Smith, and Zickuhr, 2010; Pew Internet Project, 2014b.

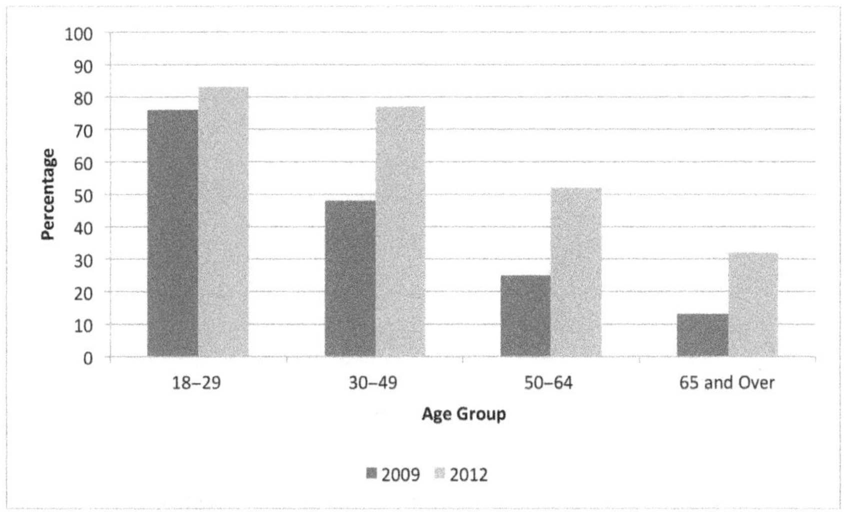

Figure 1.4 Social Networking Site Usage by Age Group. *Sources*: Duggan and Brenner, 2013; Madden, 2010.

counterparts. More specifically, 76% of those in this age group used social networking websites in 2009, while 83% used them in 2013. Conversely, 13% of those ages 65 and over used these websites during 2009, while 32% used them in 2013. Second, older age groups are catching up with their younger counterparts in terms of social networking website usage. Among each age group other than those between 18 and 29, the percentage that use social networking websites has grown by at least 60% between 2009 and 2012.

Jones and Fox (1999) noticed similar trends to those that are identified in Figures 1.3 and 1.4. In particular, they found that over 90% of those between 18 and 24 are internet users. Additionally, Jones and Fox (2009) discovered that those under the age of 32 are disproportionately more likely to perform a wide variety of internet-based activities, including blog reading, blog writing, watching videos online, and using social networking websites.

Put together, Figures 1.3 and 1.4 clearly indicate that younger adults are more likely to utilize the internet, and in particular, social networking websites than those in older age cohorts. However, this observation begets many questions. In particular, which social networking platforms tend to attract young adults? In Figure 1.5, we examine the most popular social networking sites, and identify the demographics of their user base, in terms of age. The vertical axis is the percentage of each age group that uses Facebook or Twitter, while the horizontal axis denotes each age group. In addition, the black bar and varying shades of gray bars correspond to varying social networking sites.

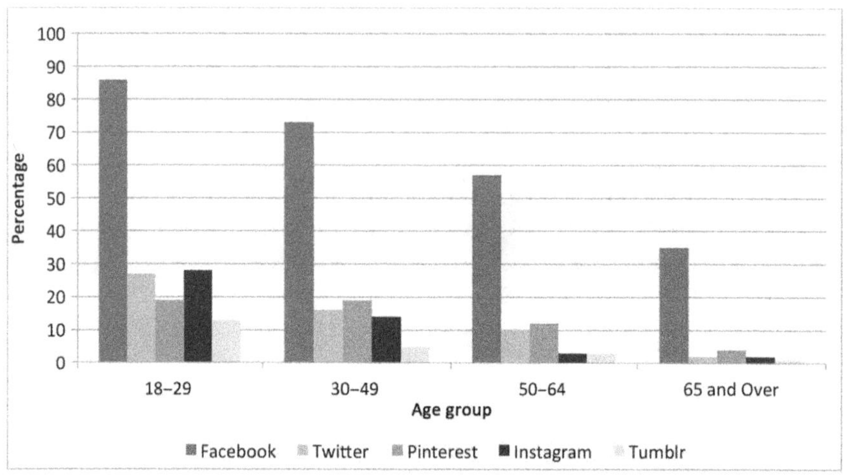

Figure 1.5 Social Networking Site Usage by Age and Site Visited in 2012. *Sources*: Duggan and Brenner, 2013.

This chart illuminates a number of trends. First, those between 18 and 29 years old use all social networking sites, regardless of platform, at far higher rates than their elders. Second, over three times as many people aged between 18 and 29 use Facebook as opposed to any other social networking website. However, the fastest growing social networking platform between the 2008 and 2012 election was Twitter, as by 2012 it was the second largest social networking site after Facebook in terms of the size of its user base (Brenner and Smith 2013). More specifically, 27% of those between the ages of 18 and 29 self-identified as Twitter users in 2012. Because Facebook and Twitter are the largest social media platforms in terms of their user base, and are the most easily usable in a political fashion, we examine the ways in which these two social networks are used and exclude the others.

This section demonstrates that young adults significantly differ from their older counterparts in a number of key respects. More specifically, they vote and engage in volunteer activity at disproportionately low rates relative to their older counterparts. Yet, young adults use the internet and social networking websites at far higher rates than those older than them. In addition, young adults utilize a wide variety of social networking websites, including Facebook and Twitter, at higher rates than their older cohorts.

These trends suggest that the analytic approach that one takes to analyzing the ways in which young adults civically engage should differ from those approaches taken to examine their older counterparts. It is entirely possible that a population that is less active in one area might be more engaged elsewhere. More specifically, traditional forms of civic activity might understate young adults' true levels of engagement, as the internet may be the primary route by which members of this group engage the political process. Taking this approach is consistent with a long line of research in which scholars examine the political behavior of particular subgroups in American politics. For instance, a wide variety of research examines the ways in which Latinos and Latinas view and engage in politics (see e.g., Bedolla 2005; Hero 2000; Pantoja, Ramirez, and Segura 2001; Stokes 2003). Further, a much larger literature investigates the ways in which African Americans engage in civic life, relative to that of other races (see e.g., Dawson 1995, 2003; Hutchings and Valentino 2004; Walton 1985). Because different subgroups behave differently with respect to the political process, it makes sense that young people might diverge in a systematic way from their elders.

ONLINE FORMS OF CIVIC ACTIVITY AMONG YOUNGER VOTERS

The findings from the previous section clearly indicate two trends: (1) younger people vote at lower rates and volunteer less often than their elders, but (2) younger people are far more active online than their elders. This puts them at a potential advantage to make use of the internet in a number of politically relevant ways. In particular, younger people may participate in online forms of civic engagement, including friending or liking candidates or political parties, joining political groups, following political Twitter feeds, or posting or tweeting about politics online. Consequently, we might be better served to primarily focus on online forms of civic activity as opposed to offline forms of activity for four reasons.

First, younger people have grown up in the age of the internet, as the internet itself and particularly, social networking websites have grown and evolved since the 2000 presidential election. In 2000, none of the social networking websites existed when George W. Bush ran for president. LinkedIn and MySpace emerged in 2003, Facebook came onto the scene in 2004, Twitter began in 2006, and Instagram began in 2010 (Curtis 2014). By Fall 2008, Nielsen (2008) reported over 59 million MySpace users, 39 million Facebook users, and nearly 12 million LinkedIn users.

When one breaks down the ages of those who use social networking websites, we discover that younger people use these sites at higher frequencies than their older counterparts. As of January 2014, 89% of those aged between 18 and 29 used any social networking website (Pew Internet Project 2014a). Moreover, 35% of those in this age bracket used Twitter in January 2014 (Pew Internet Project 2014a), while 84% of those in this age bracket used Facebook in September 2013 (Pew Internet Project 2013b). By contrast,

60% of those between the ages of 50 and 64 used Facebook in September 2013, and only 11% of those in this same age group used Twitter in January 2014 (Pew Internet Project 2013b, 2014a).

These statistics also illustrate that younger people utilize social networking websites at very high rates that seemingly indicate that they are adept at doing so. When younger voters utilize social networking sites, they can like different items, comment about these same items, and express their own thoughts in a multitude of ways, among other activities. By using these sites, younger people are able to learn how to appropriately express themselves online (and possibly, help their elders do the same), as well as, acquire additional skills by which to disseminate their views online.

Members of this age group are adept at granulating the ways in which their views are expressed through social networking websites. For example, they know that liking a post, joining a group, or following a tweet are relatively low-cost forms of expressing one's viewpoints. Conversely, composing a tweet or writing a blog are more costly endeavors, as these require some thought before clicking "post" to disseminate them. In particular, blogs are the most costly of the online forms of expression because they are more extended in nature, and for this reason, require a high level of thought to compose. Young adults' accumulation of and aptitude at such skills can easily be applied to participate in civic and political life. We explore this theme further through the empirical tests in this book, as we distinguish between lower and higher cost forms of online participation, and then, compare these with offline forms of civic engagement.

Second, online expression allows for one to express his or her views about politics to a much wider audience than is possible through offline forms of political expression. For example, contributing to candidates for federal office is as costly as the contributor wants it to be (subject to relevant limits as specified by law). However, this same act is often not widely publicized, unless the contributor gives to a candidate for federal office, as his or her name and address is publically searchable on the Federal Election Commission website. Yet, other forms of offline political expression, like participating in protests, changing one's purchasing patterns in response to the behavior of a company, or encouraging friends and family members to participate in the political process are much more localized processes that only have a limited impact.

On the other hand, online forms of expression can be potentially broadcast to a much wider audience, with both positive and negative consequences. For example Brooklyn Reiff, a teenager from Texas, took a picture of another teen named Alex LaBeouf, who was working at a Target on Sunday, October 26, 2014 (Bilton 2014). This picture was retweeted to a friend, with the intent of it being an item that was shared between two friends. Less than ten days later, though, his picture was all over the internet and was the subject of a newly created hashtag (Bilton 2014). Further, on Friday, November 7, 2014, he was on *The Ellen DeGeneres Show* to discuss his newfound fame. In an interview with *The New York Times* on November 13, he stated that he was "kind of scared to go in public" for fear of being accosted (Bilton 2014). The teen who took the picture, Brooklyn Reiff, stated on November 7, "This shows you how fast something can go viral. It's, like, scary. It really is" (Bereznak 2014).

While this is an extreme example of something that can go viral, it indicates that something which was intended for a small audience can be widely disseminated to a much broader audience in a matter of hours, if not days. This artifact carries politically relevant ramifications, as well. In particular, articulating one's views online in any way, be it a share, tweet, blog, friending candidates, or following groups, carries some sort of cost, and can potentially become available for a wider audience to see. This audience can far exceed that of talking about politics with others. In reality, though, there is no guarantee of an audience when one uses online forms of political expression. Nonetheless, expressing one's political views online requires a certain amount of political skill that is fused with those skills gained from using social networking websites. Young people have this unique combination of skills and experiences that differs from, and oftentimes, exceeds that of their elders.

Third, participating in civic life through online activities like friending candidates, joining groups, following politicians or political parties, tweeting about politics, and other forms of online political expression begets additional opportunities to participate in the political process. Through this array of web-based activities, people can find out about different campaign events, have advance notice of a wide variety of campaign opportunities, can interact in other ways with like-minded individuals, and can form relationships that can provide additional opportunities to participate.

For instance, both candidates for the presidency in 2012 used Facebook pages to broadcast events about the campaign, and to provide somewhat targeted news, depending on the location of each Facebook user. However, Michael Scherer (2012) provides a compelling account about the way in which Barack Obama's campaign for reelection uniquely capitalized on some of Facebook's features. This campaign created a Facebook app that appeared to provide another way for voters to connect to the campaign (Scherer 2012). This app, though, gave the Obama campaign permission to look at the friends lists of each of the over one million people who utilized it (Scherer 2012). Instantaneously, this development allowed the campaign to learn the identities of approximately 85% of all of those voters under the age of 30 who had no listed phone number (Scherer 2012). The Obama campaign capitalized on this golden opportunity, and utilized "targeted sharing" to share specified online content with members of this group (Scherer 2012). This happened by blitzing Obama supporters who had downloaded the app with requests to share "specific online content with specific friends by clicking a button" (Scherer 2012). This campaign got more than 600,000 supporters to follow through with more than five million contacts, with requests to do anything from register to vote, give money to the Obama campaign, or to look at videos designed to change their mind (Scherer 2012).

This app worked exactly as designed, as people whose friends sent requests to vote were more likely to vote than those who had not received such requests (Scherer 2012). This finding is borne out in the political science literature on social networking and campaigns, as Bond, Fariss, Jones, Kramer, Marlow, Settle, and Fowler (2012) have found that political mobilization messages from Facebook friends influence voting behavior in precisely this way. Consequently, online participation brought about additional opportunities to participate away from the internet that otherwise would not have been possible and broadened the group of people who participate in politics (see Rice, Moffett, and Madupalli 2013).

Fourth, online civic activity can result in higher levels of offline engagement among those who use it. For example, Shah, Kwak, and Holbert (2001) discover that informational use of the internet among members of Generation X strongly predicts more traditional forms of civic activity. Just as McClurg (2003) uncovers evidence that political discussion in offline social networks yields higher levels of political participation and greater exposure to information about politics, the same may happen in online social networks. Moreover, Min (2007) finds evidence that face-to-face and online deliberation both "have positive impacts on the participants' issue knowledge, political efficacy, and willingness to participate in politics, although the effect of online deliberation on the participation scale turned out to be somewhat smaller."

All forms of online activity discussed thus far are more likely to be used by younger people, as opposed to their older counterparts. Thus, young adults may enjoy a considerable advantage when it comes to political uses of these online tools. We examine this possibility in the remainder of this book. While the reasons provided in this section for examining online activity of young adults presume that all of these forms of civic activity are equally important, and are functionally equivalent to one another, since these activities carry varying costs and can be used toward different aims, it makes sense to disaggregate them when performing our empirical tests. We do so in Chapters 2, Four, and Five of this book.

Three of the reasons provided in this section for examining the online activity of young adults analyze online activity as the dependent variable. Some have dismissed online forms of participation as "slacktivism"—inconsequential activities with both little cost and little impact (Morozov 2009). If true, this investigation might be of little importance. However, the remaining reason we provide for examining the online civic activity of young adults examines it as a possible independent variable that affects offline forms of civic engagement. We argue that online forms of civic activity are connected with higher levels of offline engagement and as the remaining chapters unfold, this becomes one of the major findings from this book. In Chapters 6 and 7, we explore this theme further, and examine issues related to causality with respect to the relationship between online and offline forms of civic engagement.

OUR SURVEYS

To test our primary theoretical expectations about younger voters and civic activity, we utilized two surveys of randomly sampled students between the ages of 18 and 25 in 2008 and 2012 at a single institution: Southern Illinois University Edwardsville. We performed our surveys immediately prior to the 2008 and 2012 presidential elections.[1] This university is located approximately 20 miles from St. Louis, Missouri, and has approximately 14,000 students in attendance.

Our random samples of students in 2008 and 2012 are diverse, yet similar to the overall population of students at this institution. Approximately 5% of students were enrolled in the Reserve Officer Training Corps (ROTC), or were current or former members of the military in 2008, while 6% of students in 2012 had these same attributes. Further, the average age of our students was 20.8 in 2008, and 21.1 in 2012. By comparison, the average age of students at this institution was 22.1 in 2008, and 22.0 in 2012 (Southern Illinois University Edwardsville 2009, 2013).[2]

Our sample is also reasonably representative of students at this institution with respect to race and gender. In 2008, the racial composition of our sample was 85.8% whites, 8.24% African Americans, 1.99% Hispanic, and 1.14% Asian Americans. In 2012, our sample consisted of 84% whites, 8.3% African Americans, 2.6% Hispanics, and 1% Asian Americans. On face value, the racial composition indicates an overwhelming presence of whites in both survey administrations. However, this is consistent with the racial composition at this institution in both years, as whites comprised 84% of the student body in 2008, and 75% of this group in 2012 (Southern Illinois University Edwardsville 2009, 2013). Moreover, our sample consisted of 59.08% females in 2008, and 69.71% of females in 2012. This is relatively consistent with the overall gender composition of students at this institution, as females comprised 54% of the student population in 2008, and 53% of this group in 2012 (Southern Illinois University Edwardsville 2009, 2013).

To establish whether this sample represents the overall population of college students, or the broader public from which it is drawn, one should compare how the Student Election Surveys samples compare with these broader populations. We perform our comparison by examining age, gender, and race. In Fall 2010, the median age of college students at all post-secondary institutions was 19 (U.S. Department of Education 2013). Our sample of students at Southern Illinois University Edwardsville is relatively similar in this respect, as the median ages in 2008 and 2012 were 20.8 and 21.1, respectively. In Fall 2008, the percentage of women enrolled in four-year colleges and universities was 56.2% (U.S. Department of Education 2011). This percentage is very consistent with the gender composition of our sample in 2008, as it was 59% female.

At four-year public colleges and universities, 63% of college students were white, 12% were African American, 14% were Hispanic, and 7% were Asian Americans in Fall 2012 (U.S. Department of Education 2014). While our sample of Southern Illinois University Edwardsville students consists of a higher percentage of whites than other universities in its group, it comes reasonably close with respect to the percentage of its student population who are African American. However, our sample is relatively consistent with the broader population from which it is drawn: residents of Illinois. When we perform this comparison, Illinois consists of 77.7% whites and 14.7% African Americans (U.S. Census Bureau 2014). Conversely, our sample consisted of slightly more than 80% whites, but approximately 8% African Americans.

Thus, we can conclude that our sample is representative of the broader student body from which it is drawn, and is representative with respect to gender and age when compared with the broader population of college students at similar institutions. That said, our sample is only partly representative when compared to this same sample of all four-year public colleges and universities. However, it is reasonably representative of the broader population from which it is drawn when we examine racial characteristics. Thus, we do not foresee any problems in drawing conclusions from this sample, as students at this university should not systematically differ from the broader population of students at similar types of universities.

Nonetheless, we test whether our findings extend beyond the university we surveyed to the broader population. To do so, we supplement our analysis with national survey data from the Pew Research Center. This allows us to determine whether our key findings hold true among 18- to 25-year-olds nationwide and it also allows us to test whether the processes that shape the civic engagement of young adults differs from that of adults as a whole.

PLAN FOR THE BOOK

The theoretical underpinnings that culminate in a discussion about civic engagement among younger voters in this introduction build toward the puzzle to which the rest of this book is devoted to unraveling. Online forms of engagement have recently come into existence, and are disproportionately used by younger voters, relative to their older counterparts. These forms of engagement might unlock answers to a question that has perplexed many scholars and policy practitioners: are younger voters disengaged with the political process?

Exploring the answer to this question is significant because any answer implies a number of normative and theoretical implications. This has been a critical question to many political scientists who study political behavior, and to policy practitioners who have devoted countless hours to increasing engagement among younger people. This question also carries importance to those who study engagement among young people in ways that extend beyond political applications, including service learning and other forms of engagement on college campuses.

Quite often, those who believe that younger voters are not civically engaged articulate their concerns about young people with a broad brush, without looking at specific ways by which this population engages the political process. Since online forms of engagement, like friending candidates or parties, joining online groups, posting on blogs, and utilizing Twitter in multiple ways, are increasingly viable routes by which younger people engage in civic life, it is imperative that we examine these activities. Our objective, then, is to discover whether these activities are meaningful forms of engagement, and the conditions under which younger voters are more likely to engage in these activities.

In Chapter 2, we investigate the impact of political issues on online participation. Although findings on this subject are mixed, students of political behavior frequently focus on issues as one of the primary drivers of who votes, and how people determine for whom they will vote, among other civic activities (Campbell, Converse, Miller, and Stokes 1960; Converse 1964; Downs 1957; Lewis-Beck, Jacoby, Norpoth, and Weisberg 2008). We consider the importance of many issues, as more salient issues should be connected with higher levels of civic engagement, regardless of the form that engagement takes. We discover that issues have differential, and at times, countervailing effects on the civic activities of students.

In Chapter 3, we look at the more traditional forms of civic activity that take place away from the internet. More specifically, we examine activities that range from contributing to campaigns to making purchases based on the conduct of values of a particular company. We investigate the effects of those activities and characteristics that are classically connected with civic engagement. We discover that some of these predictors work well in explaining variance in civic activity among younger voters, while others do not.

That said, examining civic engagement away from the internet might understate the true levels of civic engagement among younger people. In Chapters 4 and 5, we examine varying forms of online activities. In Chapter 4, we investigate friending candidates, joining online groups, and following candidates or groups on Twitter. We group these forms of engagement, since all of them are more passive forms of online engagement that require something of a public component to them. We discover that some of the predictors of offline engagement are also connected with friending, joining, and following activities. Yet, we also learn that some different predictors are also connected with variance in friending, joining, and following activities.

In Chapter 5, we examine more explicit forms of online political expression and tweeting about politics. We examine these forms of engagement in a chapter separate from other online activities because all of them require participants to articulate their thoughts. Twitter, for instance, limits participants to 140 characters while other forms of online political expression allow for a more extended forum in which to express one's opinions about politics. We find that some of the predictors of offline engagement are also connected with online political expression and tweeting. Yet, we also learn that some different predictors are also connected with variance in tweeting and other forms of online political expression.

Chapters 3 through 5 examine varying forms of civic engagement as the dependent variable. If the analysis stopped there, those concerned about young adults and slacktivism might easily be left asking why the analysis matters. Yet, it is likely that these forms of engagement are connected with each other. We argue that among young adults, higher levels of online civic activity (regardless of the form) can result in increases in civic engagement away from the internet. Similarly, we acknowledge that higher levels of offline activities might be associated with increased levels of online civic activity. We examine these possibilities in Chapter 6. When we run these analyses, they begat one question: Do online forms of engagement lead to offline forms, or vice versa? We address this necessary question in Chapter 7, because causality is frequently seen as the "holy grail" in a wide variety of social science research. We consider issues of causality, as well as, online and offline forms of civic activity as primary independent variables. The results should help put concerns about slacktivism to rest.

In Chapter 8, we conclude the book. In this chapter, we review our theoretical argument, along with the major findings of the previous chapters and how they fit together. We test and demonstrate how our key findings generalize to young adults and the broader population. Further, we discuss possible extensions of our findings that can be taken up by other researchers. We then visit some of the empirical and normative implications of this study for political campaigns, college students, and organizations seeking to increase the political participation of young adults in 2016 and beyond. We also discuss some potential long-term trends in online and offline participation among younger voters.

NOTES

1. Hereafter, we refer to these surveys as the Student Election Surveys.
2. We confined our sample and analysis to those aged 25 and under, reducing the average age.

Chapter 2

The Issues That Push Students Online

Political issues can serve as powerful motivators for political activity, particularly when they strike at the heart of self-interest. Take, for example, the protests that erupted in Wisconsin in 2011 after Governor Scott Walker proposed limiting the collective bargaining rights of many state employees. One estimate suggested nearly 40% of the protestors in its early days were local teachers who had called a coordinated sick day in response to the threat to their ability to negotiate wages, pensions, sick days, and working conditions (Altman 2011).

Yet, altruistic concerns or social identification can also increase participation (Fowler and Kam 2007) and mobilize citizens to take action. For example, graduate teaching assistants' collective bargaining rights at the University of Wisconsin were threatened by the budget reform bill but they were joined at the protests by concerned undergraduates, who would bear no direct cost from the bill (Macafee and De Simone 2012).

Issues important to a specific age group can also push members of the age group to participate at higher rates. Look no further than senior citizens' response to threats to Social Security. Threats to Social Security and Medicare benefits in the 1980s led senior citizens to engage in a flurry of letter writing to their elected officials with those most at risk by proposed policy changes most likely to write (Campbell 2003). Such threats continue to trigger higher voting rates among this age group (Campbell 2011).

Young adults in college also face threats unique to their age and their student status such as how they will pay for their degree and if they will be able to get a job afterwards. However, they are far less likely than senior citizens to see letter writing as a natural response to such threats. Instead, they are likely to turn to the online world with which they are familiar and whose tools already form an important part of their everyday lives. In the remainder of this chapter, we identify the issues and views that pushed college students to engage in various forms of online political participation during the elections of 2008 and 2012. This is a necessary first step in an investigation of young adults' engagement as previous research provides inconsistent and somewhat contradictory findings about how issues shape political behavior. We examine the impact of a variety of domestic issues ranging from those that tie to direct self-interest to those that effect particular social groups or the broader society. We also look at broader political views like ideology and the candidate students support. However, before we can do so, it is important to identify which issues students viewed as important each year. The issues prioritized by college students may differ in significant ways from those prioritized by the general public or those emphasized by political campaigns. Fully understanding differences in participation levels requires starting with an examination of issue priorities.

CAMPAIGNS, ISSUES, AND VOTING BEHAVIOR

Different presidential election years bring an array of issues to the forefront. These may be influenced by the current state of the nation, the candidates running, and the stories at the top of the news. Converse (1964) argued that the public is differentiated by varying agendas that might mobilize specific groups. Because most people do not follow politics closely, many only become attentive when issues that are important to the group(s) to which they identify or to them as individuals come to the forefront (Converse 1964). For example, Abramowitz (1995) found that attitudes toward abortion significantly influenced vote choice in the 1992 presidential election. In addition, he found that the effect of abortion on vote choice was stronger than other salient issues at the time, including the death penalty and the Gulf War.

At the same time, others are more skeptical about the effects of issues in aggregate. Carmines and Stimson (1981) discover that issue-based voting rises and falls across particular elections. In addition, they find that "easy" issues tend to be more likely drivers of voting based on issues than ones that require more nuance to understand. Similarly, Macdonald, Rabinowitz, and Listhaug (1995) find evidence that voters consider issues *ad seriatim*, rather than as a combined, monolithic block. Finally, Hawley (2013) has discovered inconsistent evidence that immigration policy affected vote choice during the 2006 midterm elections. While there is no consensus that issues affect vote choice consistently or monolithically, there is also no agreement that issues *never* have an effect on voters. Consequently, we examine the effects of issues because scholars have observed that issues have an effect at least some of the time on voters.

When issues become prominent, candidates seek to demonstrate "issue ownership" by framing the election as being over problems facing the country that they are better suited to solve (Petrocik 1996). Their choices may be slightly constrained as their parties are associated with ownership of different issues (Petrocik, Benoit, and Hansen 2003/2004). Candidates' choice of issues to emphasize also responds to the issues that voters find to be important that particular year (Petrocik et al 2003/2004). Similarly, Fournier, Blais, Nadeau, Gidengil, and Nevitte (2003) find that voters evaluate candidates based on the importance of particular issues, and vote accordingly. Also, Sides and Karch (2008) discover some evidence that emphasizing issues can mobilize certain "issue publics" to vote, especially when those issues appeal to groups that are less participatory.[1]

ISSUE PRIORITIES IN 2008 AND 2012

Despite the presidential candidates' big differences on social issues like abortion and same sex marriage in 2008 and 2012, these issues were overshadowed by other pressing domestic concerns. The Great Recession and its lingering effects brought the economy to the center of the debate in both 2008 and 2012. Its widespread impact meant it was not an issue that candidates could afford to ignore. Candidates also devoted a fair amount of time to discussing alternative energy plans, whether to spur job creation while protecting the environment or to increase domestic security. Health care was also a central object of attention both years among candidates, news media, and voters. In 2008, Barack Obama and John McCain touted competing health care reform proposals. On March 23, 2010, Barack Obama signed the Affordable Care Act into law and in 2012 Obama largely stood by the Affordable Care Act while Mitt Romney called for its repeal.

While the candidates' focus on particular issues may stimulate political participation by mobilizing the party faithful or even appealing to independents, even those issues at the periphery of the debate, when prioritized by individual voters, may lead those individuals to participate at higher rates. When voters care intensely about an issue, they become more likely to participate in politics. For example, those with strong opinions about abortion are more likely to engage in abortion-related participation (Verba, Brady, and Schlozman 1995). The link between issues and participation holds especially true if voters have a direct stake in the outcome (see e.g., Rosenstone and Hansen 1993). For example, Sides and Karch (2008) found that parents in media markets with more campaign advertisements about education were more likely to vote (although campaign advertisements about veterans or entitlement programs failed to boost the turnout of veterans or senior citizens).

Verba et al. (1995) also found that parents of school-aged children were more likely to participate in politics overall and to participate in political activity related to education while those who received means-tested benefits were only more likely to participate in political activity related to these benefits.

Young adults, and particularly college students, may prioritize issues differently than others. For example, in the Vietnam era, young adults tended to be more liberal than their parents on a variety of issues and more politically active (Beck and Jennings 1979). Differences in priorities may stimulate greater participation, especially when these differences are divided by age or social groups. Concentration of an issue priority within a specific group means this group cannot rely on others to advance the issue for them if they want to see progress. The issue is unlikely to get raised unless they do so.

In both 2008 and 2012 we asked students about the importance of nine domestic issues to their vote choice: the economy, health care, abortion, same sex marriage, immigration, energy, the environment, education, and college financing. Some of these issues, such as college financing, strike directly at students' self-interest while others, like the environment, address broader collective goods. Some, like the economy, were a central object of debate, while other issues remained closer to the periphery. Table 2.1 compares the importance of these different domestic issues to the vote choices of college students and of all registered voters in 2008 and 2012.

Extremely large majorities of college students cited both the economy and education as very or extremely important to their vote choice in both 2008 and 2012. College financing and health care were also cited by sizeable majorities both years. The percent citing energy as very or extremely important to their vote choice exhibited the largest drop (20%) from 2008 to 2012 while the environment followed with an 11% point drop. Meanwhile, same sex marriage, immigration, education, and college financing all seemingly grew in importance with respective increases of seventeen, seven, seven, and six percentage points between 2008 and 2012.

In some respects, the issue priorities of college students closely resemble those of registered voters as a whole. Among the questions asked of both groups, overwhelming majorities of both groups in both election years cite the economy as holding great importance for their vote choice. This is consistent with both the economic circumstances at the time and a long line of literature linking the economy to the vote (see e.g., Blais 2000; Godbout and Belanger 2007; Lewis-Beck 1990; Lewis-Beck, Martini, and Kiewiet 2013; Whitten and Palmer 1999). The percentages of college students and registered voters as a whole who state that energy and health care will have a strong influence on their vote also closely track each other.

Meanwhile, the largest gaps between college students and registered voters occur for the importance of education, with far more college students stating

Table 2.1 Importance of Issues to Vote: 18- to 25-Year-Old College Students versus All Registered Voters

	2008 Election		*2012 Election*	
	Student Election Survey (October). 18- to 25-year-olds.(%)	*Pew Research Center Survey of Registered Voters (August)(%).*	*Student Election Survey (October). 18- to 25-year-olds(%).*	*Pew Research Center Survey of Registered Voters (September)(%).*
Economy	93	87	90	87
Education	85	73	92	69
Energy	79	77	59	55
College Financing	78	–	84	–
Health Care	77	73	79	74
Environment	68	–	57	–
Abortion	49	39	52	46
Immigration	40	52	47	41
Same Sex Marriage	34	–	51	–

Notes: First, percentages are rounded up. Second, issues asked about in the Pew survey are only reported if they were also asked about in the Student Election Survey. Third, the percentages in the Student Election Survey correspond to the percentage identifying the issue as very or extremely important to vote. Fourth, the percentages in the Pew surveys correspond to the percentage identifying the issue as very important to vote. Fifth, there were three issues that the Pew survey did not ask about: college financing, the environment, and same sex marriage. Finally, the question wording for each set of surveys is as follows:

Student Election Survey wording: How important are candidates' stances on each of the following issues in influencing your decision about who you will vote for: Not at all important, not very important, somewhat important, very important, or extremely important?

Pew surveys question wording: In making your decision about who to vote for this fall, will the issue of ____ be very important, somewhat important, not too important, or not at all important?

Sources: Table created by authors from Moffett and Rice's Student Election Survey (2008 and 2012), and surveys from the Pew Research Center (2008 and 2012).

it had a strong influence on their vote than registered voters as a whole. This gap was particularly pronounced in 2012. Meanwhile, far fewer college students prioritized immigration as a major influence on their vote than did registered voters in 2008, while in 2012 the gap cut in half but reversed itself in direction. The percentage of college students citing abortion as very or extremely important to their vote was also larger than registered voters in both years but the size of the gap shrunk slightly in 2012. Other issues on which there may be sizeable gaps were not asked of both groups. The Pew Research Center did not ask about college financing, the environment, or same sex marriage in these surveys.

HOW ISSUE IMPORTANCE MAY SPUR PARTICIPATION

All of the issues we asked about were described as very or extremely important to students' vote choice by at least a sizeable minority if not an overwhelming majority in each election year. If these issues are important enough to influence the vote choices of a large number of students, this importance may also motivate students to engage in online political activity. However, some of these issues directly affect college students more than others.

As shown in Table 2.1, 90% or more of college students in 2008 and 2012 identified the economy as very or extremely important to their vote. This percentage was even marginally higher than that of all registered voters. However, statistics showed that college students had good reason to be worried about the economy as unemployment was particularly high among this age group and good jobs were hard to come by upon graduation (Abel, Dietz, and Su 2014). With their self-interest clearly at stake, those concerned about the economy might easily feel mobilized to engage with the political process through online forms of participation.

Table 2.1 also showed that more college students considered education very important than did the general population. This is likely a result of their more direct stake in post-secondary national education policy and their more recent experiences with primary and secondary education than the average voter. Their concerns about education may cause them to take these online.

College financing also strikes at the heart of many students' self-interest. Research by Ozymy (2012) shows that lower income college students who are student loan recipients are more likely to contact government officials about student loans than are those with higher incomes. Whether motivated purely by self-interest or by altruistic concern for their friends, college students who consider the issue of college finances more important to their vote may also be more likely to participate during elections and to turn to online platforms to do so.

The environment and energy policy involve the sorts of public goods that logic might suggest would make participation less likely (Olson 1965). However, college campuses frequently emphasize recycling, energy conservation, and sustainability and encourage concern for the environment. The campus at the focus of our study is no exception. In addition, college students face a longer time horizon of being affected by environmental and energy policy than does the average American. While concern for the environment and energy can be related, they do not have to be. For example, some conservative students concerned about gas prices may say energy policy is extremely important to their vote but might still doubt the causes of global warming and give little importance to environmental policy.[2] Both concern for the environment and concern over energy might spur students to take to online forms of participation.

Health care policy was a central topic in the presidential elections of both 2008 and 2012. Previous research tells us that government policy decisions can mobilize both those who are winners and losers as a result of the policy (Flavin and Griffin 2009). This might suggest that those who say health care is important to their vote choice would participate at higher rates, and especially so in 2012 after the Affordable Care Act was enacted. However, college students routinely receive relatively low-cost health care through their universities and a good part of those in the age group we studied were also eligible to stay on their parents' insurance even before the Affordable Care Act. As a result, they may have been more insulated, and less likely to see themselves as policy winners or losers on this topic. If so, the importance of this issue could be a less important predictor of online political participation than the importance of other issues.

Finally, although the lowest percentages of college students said that abortion, immigration, and same sex marriage were very or extremely important to their vote, students who prioritize these issues may be more likely to participate. This may hold especially true for same sex marriage. National surveys show that young adults, across party lines, are far more supportive of same sex marriage than their elders (Kiley 2014). This large gap in opinion may make college students who prioritize this issue particularly likely to participate online.

Regrettably, we did not ask about students' specific positions on each of these issues so we can only test whether how much priority one gives to each issue pushes students online, not whether views on the issue itself influences online activity. However, other scholars' work suggests that both policy winners and policy losers participate at higher rates in response to government policy (Flavin and Griffin 2009) as do those who give greater priority to an issue (Verba et al. 1995). This suggests that whether someone supports or opposes a policy may be less important to their participation than how much they care about it. In this light, our measures of issue importance should be both appropriate and important when determining the issues that push students online.

BROADER VIEWS AND POLITICAL PARTICIPATION: IDEOLOGY, STRENGTH OF PARTISANSHIP, AND VOTE CHOICE

We did, however, ask students about their broader views including their ideology, their strength of partisanship, and their intended vote choice. These, too, might spur online participation.

Ideology

There is some evidence that particular ideological views may lead to greater political participation. However, the specific ideological views that lead to greater participation have not been consistent over time or across studies. For example, Milbrath and Goel (1977) found conservatives were more likely to participate than liberals while Beck and Jennings (1979) found whether conservatives or liberals participated more varied by election year. In particular, Beck and Jennings (1979) discovered that this variance is partly explained by scenarios in which one of the candidates energizes those who identify with a particular ideological group. In 2008 and 2012, Barack Obama was effective in mobilizing those who self-identify as liberal. Yet, it is possible that his name on the ballot in 2008 also mobilized conservative opposition and engagement. This is more likely, though, in 2012, as Mitt Romney's campaign themes strongly centered around opposition to the Affordable Care Act, and more broadly, to Obama himself.

College students' self-reported ideology differs substantially from that of all adults. In the Student Election Survey, we asked each respondent whether s/he self-identified as a liberal, conservative, or did not know his or her ideology. For those who did not know, we asked a follow-up question asking them to choose between one of these, if they had to do so. In 2008, 35% of college students in the Student Election Survey self-identified as liberal while 22% identified as conservative. In 2012, the percent of college students self-identifying as conservative remained the same while the percent identifying as liberal was 32%.

Gallup polling data by age during this period also support these large gaps. Gallup reported that 18- to 29-year-olds were more likely to identify as liberal and far less likely to identify as conservatives than their elders (Saad 2012). However, Gallup polls also indicated that 22% of adults nationwide self-identified as liberals in 2008 while 37% identified as conservatives; in 2012 the percentage of adults self-identifying as liberal remained at 22% while the percentage self-identifying as conservative was 39% (Saad 2012). These large differences in ideology by age may result in young liberals being more likely to participate online.

More recently, Best and Kruger (2005) found that more liberal attitudes were generally associated with greater levels of online political participation. However, they also found that those with more conservative economic attitudes were also more likely to participate online (Best and Kruger 2005). Similarly, students who identify as liberal or conservative may be more likely to participate online than those who identify as moderates.

Obama Supporters

In addition, some candidates have been credited for energizing those with a particular ideological bent such as Goldwater and conservatives in 1964 or McGovern and liberals in 1972, which may account for the different patterns in participation over time (Beck and Jennings 1979; Finkel and Trevor

1986). We suspect Barack Obama may have done the same for young liberals in 2008 and 2012, as his campaign placed a substantial emphasis on attracting younger voters as part of its overall strategy. In particular, his campaign encouraged young people to volunteer for campaign work and to donate money to support his candidacy in small amounts (Marinucci 2014). Also, his campaign targeted tech savvy people, as it utilized social networking and varying online tools to engage younger voters (Marinucci 2014). Moreover, the Obama campaign's online presence was far superior to that of McCain in 2008 or Romney in 2012. In 2008, Obama became the first presidential candidate to make use of Facebook to help win his campaign (Carr 2008). He had more than two million likes on Facebook, compared to roughly 600,000 for McCain (Dutta and Fraser 2008). In 2012 Obama had more than 20 million Twitter followers while Romney fell far shy of 2 million, and Obama's Facebook likes exceeded 29 million while Romney had roughly 8 million (Wortham 2012). These numbers suggest that Obama supporters should be more active online. Toward this end, we asked each student which presidential candidate s/he intended to support in the upcoming election.

Strong Partisanship

Finally, strong partisans have a greater stake in election outcomes that may motivate them to participate at higher rates. Results from a number of studies of political participation confirm that strength of partisanship is a strong predictor of a variety of forms of political participation offline (see e.g., Campbell et al. 1960; Flavin and Griffin 2009; Rosenstone and Hansen 1993; Verba et al. 1995). There is little reason in general to expect that the mobilizing effect of strength of partisanship would not extend also to the online arena. However, there is some evidence to suggest that the impact of strength of partisanship may be muted among young adults as young adults are more likely to identify as pure independents than other age groups (Dugan 2013). To test this, we asked each student about his or her political party. Then, we asked those respondents who chose either political party whether they strongly or not strongly identified with their chosen party. Based on these responses, we created a binary variable for those students who were strong partisans.

ISSUE IMPORTANCE, BROADER POLITICAL VIEWS, AND ONLINE POLITICAL PARTICIPATION IN 2008

We asked students about two forms of online political activity in 2008: friending or joining an online social network of a candidate, party, or political group and expressing political views online. In 2012, we asked about two additional forms of political activity: following political Twitter feeds and tweeting about politics. In all cases, we used a five-point scale that ranged from never having engaged, to engaging in them rarely, sometimes, frequently, or very often. In Table 2.2, we use ordered logit models to test whether each of the issue importance measures as well as the measures of broader political views is associated with greater levels of engaging in each of these forms of online activity. We employ this technique because our dependent variable operates on a scale. The cut points in these ordered logit models are model coefficients, and effectively act as constants that help estimate the probability of each level of our dependent variable (Fullerton 2009; Greene 2000). To get a better idea of the magnitude of the effects, we also computed the odds ratios associated with each measure.[3] These odds ratios are reported to the right of the results from each model.

The results suggest some evidence that self-identifying as a strong partisan influences the propensity with which students engage in varying online civic activities. First, strong partisans were 246.8% more likely in 2008, and 305.4% more likely in 2012 to engage in higher levels of friending or joining activity. Second, strong partisans were 218.3% in 2008, and 130.8% in 2012 more likely to engage in higher levels of online political expression. Finally, those who self-identify as strong partisans were 288% more likely to engage in higher levels of following political Twitter feeds, and 315.5% more likely to engage in higher levels of tweeting about politics.

Beyond the effects of strong partisanship, there is mixed evidence that ideology and self-identifying as an Obama supporter shaped the propensity with which students engage in a variety of online civic activities. First, being an Obama supporter is connected with higher levels of friending and joining activity in 2008, and with following political Twitter feeds and tweeting about politics in 2012. More specifically, Obama supporters were 142.1% more likely to engage in higher levels of friending or joining activity in 2008, but no more likely than non-Obama supporters in 2012. In addition, supporters of President Obama were 85.5% more likely to engage in higher levels of following political Twitter feeds, and 93.5% more likely to engage in higher levels of tweeting about politics. However, being an Obama supporter had no impact on the propensity to engage in online political expression in 2008 or 2012.

In 2012, students who self-identified as liberal were 50.6% more likely to engage in higher levels of friending or joining activity, 65.1% more likely to engage in higher levels of online political expression, and 62.4% more likely to engage in higher levels of following political Twitter feeds. However, liberals were no more likely than conservatives or moderates to have friended candidates or joined groups, or engage in online political expression in 2008. Interestingly, conservatives were no more likely than moderates to do any of these activities, or tweet about politics, in either 2008 or 2012.

Table 2.2 Issue Importance, Broader Political Views, and the Online Participation of College Students

	2008				2012							
Independent Variable	*Friending or Joining*	*Odds Ratio*	*Online Political Expression*	*Odds Ratio*	*Friending or Joining*	*Odds Ratio*	*Online Political Expression*	*Odds Ratio*	*Following Political Twitter Feeds*	*Odds Ratio*	*Tweeting About Politics*	*Odds Ratio*
Issue Importance												
Economy	0.15	1.16	0.08	1.08	0.32*	1.37	0.28*	1.32	0.25	1.28	0.27	1.31
	(0.20)		(0.20)		(0.15)		(0.14)		(0.20)		(0.20)	
Education	–0.01	0.99	0.14	1.15	0.12	1.13	0.30*	1.34	0.14	1.15	0.15	1.17
	(0.19)		(0.20)		(0.17)		(0.17)		(0.22)		(0.22)	
Energy	0.38**	1.463	0.18	1.20	0.47***	1.60	0.32**	1.37	0.26*	1.30	0.12	1.12
	(0.16)		(0.17)		(0.13)		(0.12)		(0.16)		(0.16)	
College Financing	0.15	1.16	0.05	1.05	–0.07	0.93	–0.24*	0.79	–0.07	0.94	0.12	1.12
	(0.15)		(0.15)		(0.13)		(0.13)		(0.16)		(0.17)	
Health Care	0.01	1.01	0.001	1.00	–0.02	0.98	–0.15	0.86	–0.24	0.79	–0.29*	0.75
	(0.16)		(0.15)		(0.13)		(0.12)		(0.16)		(0.16)	
Environment	–0.21	0.81	–0.07	0.93	–0.37**	0.69	–0.46***	0.63	–0.13	0.88	–0.10	0.90
	(0.16)		(0.17)		(0.12)		(0.12)		(0.14)		(0.15)	
Abortion	–0.06	0.95	–0.21*	0.81	–0.09	0.91	0.04	1.04	0.01	1.01	0.04	1.04
	(0.11)		(0.11)		(0.09)		(0.08)		(0.11)		(0.11)	
Immigration	–0.11	0.89	0.03	1.03	0.14	1.15	0.19*	1.21	0.15	1.16	0.10	1.11
	(0.13)		(0.13)		(0.09)		(0.09)		(0.12)		(0.12)	
Same Sex Marriage	0.24*	1.27	0.18	1.19	0.10	1.10	0.21**	1.24	0.03	1.03	0.15	1.17
	(0.11)		(0.11)		(0.09)		(0.08)		(0.11)		(0.11)	
Control Variables												
Liberal	0.07	1.07	–0.06	0.95	0.41*	1.51	0.50**	1.65	0.485*	1.62	–0.13	0.87
	(0.29)		(0.30)		(0.23)		(0.21)		(0.277)		(0.28)	
Conservative	0.25	1.28	–0.13	0.88	0.33	1.39	–0.08	0.93	0.109	1.12	0.07	1.07
	(0.35)		(0.36)		(0.27)		(0.25)		(0.342)		(0.35)	
Obama Supporter	0.88**	2.42	0.001	1.00	0.32	1.38	0.34	1.40	0.618*	1.86	0.66*	1.94
	(0.31)		(0.30)		(0.23)		(0.21)		(0.285)		(0.29)	
Strong Partisan	1.24***	3.47	1.16***	3.18	1.40***	4.05	0.84***	2.31	1.356***	3.88	1.42***	4.16
	(0.24)		(0.25)		(0.20)		(0.19)		(0.248)		(0.25)	

Source: Moffett and Rice, Student Election Survey

Table 2.2 Issue Importance and Online Participation (Continued)

	2008		2012			
Independent Variable	*Friending or Joining*	*Online Political Expression*	*Friending or Joining*	*Online Political Expression*	*Following Political Twitter Feeds*	*Tweeting About Politics*
Cut Point One	3.26***	2.25**	2.83***	1.71***	2.08***	2.53***
	(1.01)	(1.00)	(0.67)	(0.61)	(0.85)	(0.89)
Cut Point Two	3.76***	2.94***	3.60***	2.67***	2.61***	3.18***
	(1.01)	(1.01)	(0.67)	(0.61)	(0.85)	(0.89)
Cut Point Three	4.59***	3.83***	4.77***	3.72***	3.50***	3.88***
	1.019	(1.02)	(0.69)	(0.62)	(0.86)	(0.90)
Cut Point Four	5.62***	4.31***	5.71***	4.70***	4.30***	4.74***
	(1.03)	(1.03)	(0.71)	(0.64)	(0.88)	(0.92)
N	332	332	513	517	314	313
Log Likelihood	−429.33	−398.71	−608.14	−695.73	−406.53	−394.36
Pseudo R^2	0.08	0.04	0.08	0.06	0.08	0.07
Chi-Square	71.31	32.31	110.09	83.26	66.14	62.33
Prob>Chi-Squared	<0.0001	0.0022	<0.0001	<0.0001	<0.0001	<0.0001

Notes: The coefficients are ordered logit coefficients and the values in parenthesis are standard errors. * denotes $p < 0.05$, ** denotes $p < 0.01$, and *** denotes $p < 0.001$, all one-tailed tests.

Political Issues

Most importantly, the models demonstrate substantial evidence that political issues appear to encourage students to engage in a wide array of politically participatory online activities. These models also show that some political issues have greater impacts than others on the propensity with which students engage in online civic activities. In addition, the results suggest that issue importance played a greater role in promoting online participation in 2012 than it did in 2008. While only three issue importance measures had a statistically significant relationship with either form of participation in 2008, seven of the eight issue importance measures had a statistically significant impact on at least one form of online participation in 2012.

The only political issue that did not have a statistically significant impact in 2012, but had one in 2008 was abortion. We discovered that each unit increase in the importance of abortion to a respondent decreased the odds that favor higher levels of online political expression by 18.8%. However, the importance of abortion had no statistically significant effect on online political expression in 2012. It also failed to exhibit a statistically significant relationship to friending or joining in both years. Further, abortion had no influence on the propensity with which college students engaged in politically-based activities on Twitter.

There were six issues, however, that had statistically significant impacts on at least one form of online civic activity in 2012, but no impact on any online civic activities in 2008: the economy, education, college financing, health care, the environment, and immigration. In 2012, each unit increase in the importance of the economy increases the odds of friending or joining at a higher level by 37.3% and increases the odds of expressing oneself online at a higher level by 31.9%. Each unit increase in the importance of education results in a 34.4% increase in the odds that favor engaging in higher levels of online political expression. Meanwhile, each unit increase in the importance of immigration results in a 21.4% increase in the odds of expressing oneself online at a higher level and each unit increase in the importance of same sex marriage yields a 23.8% increase in the odds of expressing oneself online at a higher level.

In contrast, each unit increase in the importance of college financing decreases the odds that favor engaging in higher levels of online political expression by 21.0%. Each unit increase in the importance of health care produces a 25.3% decrease in the odds of tweeting about politics at higher levels. Finally, each unit increase in the importance of the environment decreases the odds of friending or joining at a higher level by 30.8% and decreases the odds of engaging in higher levels of online political expression by 37.0%.

There were two issues, though, that had an effect across both years, and a variety of forms of online civic activity: energy and same sex marriage.

More specifically, each unit increase in the importance of energy produced a 46.3% increase in the odds that favor higher levels of friending or joining in 2008, and a 59.5% increase in these same odds in 2012. Additionally, a one unit increase in the importance of energy produced a 37.1% increase in the odds that favor higher levels of online political expression, and a 29.8% increase in the odds that favor higher levels of following political Twitter feeds. At the same time, the importance of energy policy had no impact on online political expression in 2008, or tweeting about politics in 2012.

Meanwhile, each unit increase in the importance of same sex marriage yielded a 27.4% increase in the odds that favor higher levels of friending or joining in 2008. Also, each unit increase in the importance of same sex marriage increased the odds that favor higher levels of online political expression by 23.8% in 2012. At the same time, the importance of same sex marriage yielded no change in the odds that favored higher levels of online political expression in 2008, of friending or joining activity in 2012, or any Twitter-based form of online civic activity.

ISSUE IMPORTANCE AND ONLINE PARTICIPATION

In Table 2.3, we consider whether in 2012 the same issue importance and broader political view measures predict greater online participation overall.[4] To do so, we create an index of online participation ($\alpha = 0.83$) with a minimum value of 0 for never having engaged in any of the online forms of participation to 16 for participating in all 4 forms of participation very often. Since the dependent variable takes on a relatively continuous range of values, we estimate our models using ordinary least squares (OLS). Since OLS results allow us to directly interpret the effects of each independent variable, odds ratios are not needed.

The results reveal a slightly different story than when looking at each specific form of online participation separately. Those who placed greater importance on the economy, energy and immigration were more likely to participate online at higher levels. Meanwhile, those who placed greater importance on health care or the environment participated less online. The other issue importance measures failed to exert a statistically significant influence on online participation as a whole. However, liberals, Obama supporters, and strong partisans all participated more online.

Each unit increase in importance of the environment resulted in a 0.757 increase in the online participation index score. In other words, this is equivalent to someone who thought the environment was very important regularly participating in an additional online activity compared to someone who thought the environment was not at all important. Each unit increase

Table 2.3 Issue Importance, Broader Political Views, and Online Political Participation in 2012

Independent Variable	*Online Participation Index*
Issue Importance	
Economy	0.76*
	(0.41)
Education	0.71
	(0.44)
Energy	0.61*
	(0.32)
College Financing	–0.34
	(0.34)
Health Care	–0.65*
	(0.33)
Environment	–0.64*
	(0.30)
Abortion	–0.03
	(0.23)
Immigration	0.45*
	(0.24)
Same Sex Marriage	0.34
	(0.24)
Control Variables	
Liberal	0.96*
	(0.58)
Conservative	0.03
	(0.70)
Obama Supporter	1.30*
	(0.58)
Strong Partisan	3.81***
	(0.51)
Constant	–1.21
	(1.82)
N	293
R^2	0.29
Adjusted R^2	0.26
F	8.94
Prob > F	<0.0001
Standard Error of the Estimate	3.86

Source: Moffett and Rice, Student Election Survey
Notes: The coefficients are OLS coefficients and the values in parenthesis are standard errors. * denotes $p < 0.05$, ** denotes $p < 0.01$, and *** denotes $p < 0.001$, all one-tailed tests.

in importance of energy produced a 0.609 increase in online participation level while each unit increase in importance of immigration produced a 0.447 increase. Someone who thinks these issues are extremely important participates in an additional activity somewhere between rarely and regularly compared to someone who thinks they are not at all important. Meanwhile, each unit increase in the importance of health care and the environment led to respective drops of 0.647 and 0.635 on the online participation index. This is equivalent to dropping from participating in one of the online activities very often to participating in it somewhere between rarely and sometimes. In addition, being a liberal is associated with an increase of 0.962 in online engagement (or moving up almost one level of participation in one activity), being a strong partisan is associated with a 3.806 increase in online engagement (equivalent to participating an additional activity almost very often) and being an Obama supporter is associated with a 1.298 increase in online engagement (equivalent to an increase of just over one level of one form of online activity).

IMPLICATIONS AND CONCLUSIONS: THE ISSUES AND VIEWS THAT PUSH STUDENTS ONLINE

We have demonstrated that issue priorities can and sometimes do push students to engage in online forms of participation. We found that issue priorities played more of a role in spurring students' participation in 2012 than they did in 2008. We also found, consistent with prior research, that the issues that stimulate greater online participation vary across election years. Further, placing greater importance on different issues are associated with increases in specific forms of online participation and this, too, varies across years. This leaves us unable to draw many broad, consistent conclusions about the types of issues that spur online involvement and whether these tend to be tied to self-interest, social group identification, or altruism. However, the results do allow for some interesting insights into the online political participation of college students.

College students may have named education as one of the most important issues to their vote choice, but it only led to an increased likelihood of engaging in online political expression and only did so in 2012. Meanwhile, the issue that struck most clearly at college students' self-interest, college financing, did not yield any increases in most forms of online participation and actually resulted in a decreased likelihood of engaging in online political expression in 2012. Perhaps, if we were able to control for students' income level like Ozmy (2012) or whether students receive financial aid, we would see a positive impact. However, we did not include such measures in our study. While self-interest still may drive college students' political participation, the issues most clearly linked to college students' self-interest failed to exert a clear or consistent impact on their participation in 2008 and 2012.

We suggested that health care, although listed as very or extremely important by 77% of college students in 2008 and 79% of college students in 2012, might not spur the same level of political participation among them as it would the general public because college students are more insulated from health care policy's effects. In fact, its only impacts were a decrease in the likelihood of students tweeting about politics and a decrease in their overall level of online participation.

A number of issues that became more important to more college students in 2012 led to engaging in increased levels of online expression that year. Same sex marriage, immigration, and education exhibited increases in importance ranging from a gain of 7 to 17% points and they also became significant predictors of engaging in increased levels of online political expression in 2012. However, although 6% more students cited college financing as being very or extremely important in 2012 than 2008, its importance led to a decreased likelihood of engaging in online political expression. Energy may have dropped in importance among college students from 2008 to 2012, but it sparked online participation both years. Students who saw it as having greater importance were more likely to engage in friending or joining in 2008, and all online activities except tweeting about politics in 2012.

The state of the economy was a central focus in the elections of 2008 and 2012 and it also exerted a particularly strong impact on college students. Still college students' level of importance placed on the economy only increased their likelihood of friending or joining or engaging in online political expression and only did so in 2012; it also increased their overall level of online participation in 2012.

Some issues that were prioritized by a lower number of college students still produced increases in participation among those who found the issues important. Those who placed high importance on same sex marriage were more likely to engage in higher levels of friending and joining in 2008 and engaging in online political expression in 2012. Meanwhile, those who placed greater importance on immigration were more likely to engage in greater levels of online political expression and engage in greater levels of online participation overall in 2012. The importance of abortion, however, only acted to decrease the likelihood of engaging in online political expression and only did so in 2008.

The potential impact of those issue importance measures that mattered exceeded that of some measures of broader political views. Similar to what Beck and Jennings (1979) found in the Vietnam era, we presented evidence that young adults today self-identify as more liberal than their elders and we also found that young liberals were more likely to participate than young conservatives or moderates. However, increases in the importance of individual issues demonstrated greater potential to increase participation than being a liberal did. We also found that Obama supporters were more likely to engage in certain forms of online participation: friending or joining in 2008, following political Twitter feeds and tweeting about politics in 2012 and overall online participation in 2012. The potential increase in the odds ratios produced by the individual issues that were significant sometimes but not always outweighed the impact of being an Obama supporter.

However, strong partisans were far more likely to engage in greater levels of every form of online political participation we examined in each year. The increase in the odds generated by being a strong partisan outweighed the potential impact of any one issue importance measure. Only large increases in the importance of a combination of issues have the potential to equal the gains in online participation produced by a strong partisan.

In this chapter we have demonstrated how both students' broad political views and the importance they place on specific domestic issues are associated with engaging in greater levels of online participation. However, these are not the only factors known to influence participation. In Chapter 3, we paint a portrait of students' offline participation based on classic predictors of political participation as well as some potential predictors unique to college students. Afterwards, we return to the online world to take a broader look at what drives each of the specific forms of online participation we considered in this chapter: friending or joining, engaging in online political expression, following political Twitter feeds, and tweeting about politics.

NOTES

1. However, not all issues have an equal effect on the public at large, or on the group(s) most affected by those issues.

2. In 2008 the correlation between the importance of energy and the environment was 0.6003 and in 2012 it was 0.6258.

3. We employed the following formula to calculate all of the percentage increase in odds ratios for the ordered logistic regressions:

$$\%OR_{increase} = (e^{\beta} - 1) * 100$$

4. Since we only asked about friending and expressing political views online in 2008, we cannot estimate a comparable model for 2008.

5. We lack measures of individual self-interest to employ. We can only examine the issues most likely to be related to the self-interest of college students as a group.

6. Moving from not at all interested to extremely interested in issues that were significant produces greater increases in odds ratios than does being a liberal.

Chapter 3

A Portrait of Offline Participation

Until recently, the predominant ways by which people engaged in civic life encompassed activities like posting signs in one's front yard and donating money to candidates or political parties. These activities require varying levels of commitment from those who choose to engage in them. For example, participating in a community service activity requires a reasonable level of knowledge and commitment. To begin, a person has to be socially connected enough in a community to know about the different opportunities that exist. Then, the person has to be motivated enough to discover his or her passions. Finally, s/he has to devote time and possibly, financial resources, to the opportunity that s/he has chosen to pursue.

Other traditional forms of civic engagement also require high levels of commitment, and are considered to be more costly in that respect. In this chapter, we investigate young adult engagement in a wide variety of costly offline forms of civic activity that range from participating in community service, wearing campaign shirts, buttons, or other similar items, to contributing money to either a Democratic, or a Republican candidate, or party organization.

For a variety of reasons, young adults may be less willing or able to pay these costs. However, some young adults should be more willing to pay them than others.

In Chapter 2, we examined the political issues that propel friending and joining activities online, expressing one's political views online, and two forms of activity via Twitter.[1] We discovered that issues exert differential effects on civic activity. Here, we examine whether the importance of these issues might also lead to greater levels of offline activity. We build on the insights that we discovered in the previous chapter by considering the effects of these same issues on offline civic engagement as well as test whether traditional predictors of offline activity explain the offline behavior of young adults. We explore offline engagement because the focus of the political science literature on civic activity is centered on *offline* forms of civic activity, as opposed to ones that take place online. These offline activities are seen by some as possessing more value and meaning but young adults have traditionally been underrepresented in this offline world of political activity.

THE UNDERREPRESENTATION OF YOUNG ADULTS IN OFFLINE PARTICIPATION

As with voting, there tends to be an age gap in many forms of offline political participation. For example, Zukin et al.'s (2006) study of participation across generations revealed that only 4% of Dot Nets had reported contributing money to a political group in the past year, compared to 11% of Gen X, and 17% of Boomers and Dutifuls; meanwhile 10% of Dot Nets reported contacting a public official in the last year compared to 16% of Gen X, 20% of Boomers, and 21% of Dutifuls. On other measures, like displaying campaign buttons, stickers or signs, Dot Nets' participation rates exceeded that of Gen X but still paled into comparison to that of Boomers and Dutifuls (Zukin et al. 2006). Older Americans also tend to engage in more political activities than younger ones. Zukin et al. (2006) found that 26% of Dot Nets and Gen X reported engaging in two or more political activities compared to 39% of Boomers and 48% of Dutifuls. Age has been a significant predictor of writing Congress, campaign contributions, and working for campaigns (Rosenstone and Hansen 1993). It is a strong predictor of campaign-related forms of participation and a lesser predictor of community involvement or expression of public voice (Zukin et al. 2006). In sum, older Americans have been more likely to engage in campaign-related activity and younger Americans have been less likely to do so.

Young adults may be underrepresented among those who engage in traditional forms of civic and political activity but they are not unrepresented. For instance, 99.43% of students between the ages of 18 and 25 who responded to our surveys in 2008 engaged in at least one activity on some level. Similarly, 98.83% of students in 2012 report having engaged in at least one activity with some frequency. However, age gaps remain in traditional forms of activities like making campaign contributions. In August 2012, Pew Research Center surveys found that 12% of 18- to 49-year-olds reported having made a campaign contribution, compared to 19% of 50- to 64-year-olds and 27% of those over age 65 (Smith 2013). In the remainder of this chapter, we examine which young adults are most likely to participate offline. To do so, we control for the same factors that we examined in Chapter 2, including issue importance, ideology, being an Obama supporter and strong partisanship. We begin by discussing the other factors that affect levels of offline engagement, starting with the "usual suspects" like interest in politics.

RESPONDENT ATTRIBUTES

Among the general population, interest in politics acts as a strong predictor of traditional forms of civic activity (e.g., Campbell et al. 1960; Verba and Nie 1972; Verba et al. 1995). Since many of the traditional forms of civic activity require high levels of commitment, only those who are sufficiently interested would be expected to engage in them. For instance, the decision to participate in a protest requires a high level of commitment to a particular cause, a desire to act on that commitment in a public way, and a willingness to accept any consequences for having participated in the political process by that route. Thus, we anticipate that higher levels of interest in politics are connected with higher levels of civic activity.

Other factors can also affect the propensity with which individuals engage in offline forms of civic activity. Because of the environment in which many college students are educated, unique social attachments are formed that often endure (Lin 1999; Sullivan 1953). During this life stage, college students have more opportunities to engage with peers within the context of an environment that encourages such connections (Steinfield, Ellison, and Lampe 2008). Consequently, the extent to which an individual's friends are politically engaged may affect whether one participates in civic activity, and if so, how much. Thus, we expect that college students whose friends are highly engaged will themselves be more engaged. Finally, members of the military should have lower levels of civic engagement because of this institution's traditions that discourage public forms of political activity by its personnel (Sarkesian 1981).

INTERNET USAGE

In recent years, online activity has been added to the "usual suspects" that may influence offline participation. Among members of the public, internet access and online skills are connected with higher levels of participatory activity (Best and Krueger 2005). When examining a population of undergraduates, online skills and access should be less of an issue. In 2012, nearly 95% of all 18- to 29-year-olds were internet users (Pew Internet Project 2013a). Also, four out of five 18- to 25-year-olds would feel lost without the internet in 2012 (Bryant 2012). On college campuses, the percentage approaches 100%, as many universities expect students to use university e-mail for many forms of communications.

However, not all students spend an equal amount of time online. If internet usage helps drive offline activity, then among college students, the amount of time spent online, rather than access or skills, should shape offline participation. Consequently, we expect that those students who spend more time online are more likely to engage in offline forms of civic activity. Considerable research connects informational uses of the internet with higher levels of civic participation (Norris 1998; Shah et al. 2001; Shah, Cho, Eveland, and Kwak 2005; Tolbert and McNeal 2003). In particular, Kenski and Stroud (2006) find that two forms of online activity (frequency of reading news online and frequency of reading blogs) yield higher levels of civic engagement. Students who read news online could learn about differing issues, the issue positions of differing candidates for political office, and other forms of information that could foster civic activity. Similarly, students who read politically-oriented blogs may encounter content that encourages civic activities like participating in protests, donating to candidates or parties, or even, community service. For these reasons, we anticipate higher levels of civic engagement among students as the frequencies of political blog reading or online news consumption increase.

DATA AND METHODS

In 2008 and 2012, we asked students about the extent to which they engage in varying offline activities that are connected with civic engagement. In particular, we asked how often each student: (1) "Participated in any community service or volunteer activity? By volunteer activity, we mean actually working in some way to help others for no pay;" (2) "Tried to talk to people and explain why they should vote for or against one of the parties or candidates;" (3) "Made a purchasing decision based on the conduct or values of a company;" (4) "Worked with a group to solve a problem in a community;" (5) "Worn a campaign button or shirt, put a campaign sticker on your car, or placed a sign in your window or in front of your residence;" (6) "Attended any political meetings, rallies, speeches, dinners, or things like that in support of a particular candidate;" (7) "Contacted or visited someone in government who represents your community;" (8) "Participated in political activities such as protests, marches, or demonstrations;" (9) "Worked or volunteered on a political campaign for a candidate or party;" (10) "Contacted a newspaper, radio, or TV talk show to express your opinion on an issue;" (11) "Contributed money to a Democratic candidate or political party;" and (12) "Contributed money to a Republican candidate or political party."

In Table 3.1, we examine the overall distribution of these different forms of participation. We discover that the most common form of civic activity

Table 3.1 Offline Civic Activities among College Students

	2008					2012				
	Frequency of Activity					*Frequency of Activity*				
Offline Activity	*Never*	*Rarely*	*Sometimes*	*Often*	*Very Often*	*Never*	*Rarely*	*Sometimes*	*Often*	*Very Often*
Most Common Activities										
Participated or Volunteered in any Community Service	2.51% (9)	12.29% (44)	45.81% (164)	27.93% (100)	11.45% (41)	4.33% (27)	11.88% (74)	39.00% (243)	25.68% (160)	19.10% (119)
Persuaded Others about Politics	19.78% (71)	17.55% (63)	30.92% (111)	16.71% (60)	15.04% (54)	37.78% (235)	18.65% (116)	24.60% (153)	10.13% (63)	8.84% (55)
Made a Purchasing Decision Based on the Conduct or Values of a Company	41.69% (148)	14.08% (50)	28.17% (100)	9.58% (34)	6.48% (23)	46.52% (287)	15.07% (93)	16.86% (104)	12.64% (78)	8.91% (55)
Less Common Activities										
Worked with a Group to Solve a Problem	52.96% (188)	18.03% (64)	18.59% (66)	7.04% (25)	3.38% (12)	53.06% (329)	16.45% (102)	17.42% (108)	8.06% (50)	5.00% (31)
Wore a Campaign Button or Shirt	62.67% (225)	11.98% (43)	11.14% (40)	5.29% (19)	8.91% (32)	77.40% (483)	9.46% (59)	6.09% (38)	3.69% (23)	3.37% (21)
Attended Political Meetings, Rallies or Speeches	64.89% (231)	14.04% (50)	14.04% (50)	5.62% (20)	1.40% (5)	76.28% (476)	9.94% (62)	8.35% (54)	2.88% (18)	2.24% (14)
Least Common Activities										
Contacted or Visited a Government Official	72.47% (258)	13.76% (49)	8.71% (31)	3.09% (11)	1.97% (7)	71.57% (443)	13.41% (83)	10.02% (62)	3.07% (19)	1.94% (12)
Participated in Protests	82.54% (293)	7.89% (28)	7.04% (25)	1.97% (7)	0.56% (2)	80.71% (502)	9.49% (59)	5.31% (33)	2.89% (18)	1.61% (10)
Worked or Volunteered on a Political Campaign or Party	82.82% (294)	7.89% (28)	6.20% (22)	2.54% (9)	0.56% (2)	85.65% (531)	4.84% (30)	5.00% (31)	2.10% (13)	2.42% (15)
Contacted Newspapers	85.47% (306)	6.15% (22)	5.59% (20)	1.40% (5)	1.40% (5)	89.25% (556)	6.10% (38)	2.89% (18)	1.28% (8)	0.48% (3)
Contributed Money to a Democratic Candidate or Party	84.79% (301)	4.51% (16)	7.89% (28)	1.13% (4)	1.69% (6)	90.05% (561)	5.14% (32)	3.05% (19)	1.28% (8)	0.48% (3)
Contributed Money to a Republican Candidate or Party	90.17% (321)	5.06% (18)	3.65% (13)	0.84% (3)	0.28% (1)	93.92% (587)	3.20% (20)	2.24% (14)	0.32% (2)	0.32% (2)

Notes: All data come from the 2008 and 2012 elections. Also, some percentages may not total to 100% due to rounding.
Source: Moffett and Rice, Student Election Survey.

among students is volunteering or participating in any form of community service. Only 2.51% of students in 2008, and 4.33% of students in 2012 never participated in this activity. In addition, 39.38% of students in 2008, and 44.38% of students in 2012 participated in this activity often or very often. The second most common form of civic activity, though, is one that is definitely more political in nature: persuading others why they should vote for or against one of the parties or candidates. More specifically, 31.75% of students in 2008, and 18.97% of students in 2012 participated in this activity often or very often. There are other activities, too, that are reported by a sizable minority of students including working with a group to solve a problem, wearing campaign buttons or shirts, and attending political rallies or speeches. That said, other forms of civic activity were less common, including giving to candidates from either political party, or contacting newspapers or other media outlets. There is one other noteworthy item across the varying forms of civic activity: students were more active in 2008 than in 2012. This makes sense because the Obama campaign made a more concentrated effort toward targeting young people in 2008 as opposed to 2012.

Issue Importance

Numerous factors affect civic activity among young people. In particular, we begin our statistical analysis with the primary variables of interest from our last chapter: issue importance. We asked each student about how important they consider a candidate's position on each issue when deciding for whom s/he will vote. Using separate questions, we asked about the level of importance that each student places on the economy, education, energy, college financing, health care, the environment, abortion, immigration, and same sex marriage. Zero points were allocated when a student thought an issue was not at all important; one point for "not very important," two points for "somewhat important," three points for "very important," and four points for "extremely important."

Online Activities

Since younger voters are more adept with technology than their elders, they might use web-based resources as sources of information over more traditional resources like watching televised newscasts or reading newspapers. We analyze whether these activities are associated with greater offline activity by utilizing two measures of online activities: (1) how frequently s/he read web-based blogs about politics and current events and (2) how frequently s/he read web-based news about politics and current events. Both items that were used to measure each concept were answered on a five-point scale for which zero points are allocated to "not at all," and four points for "very often." We anticipate a positive sign for both coefficients in 2008 and 2012.

Figure 3.1, displays the propensity with which students read web-based blogs about politics, as well as how frequently students read web-based news about politics. The solid lines note trends from 2008, while the dashed lines note trends from 2012. Also, black lines correspond to blog reading, while gray lines represent web-based news. Among those who read web-based blogs in 2008, 32.95% never did, 28.94% rarely did, 20.34% did sometimes, 11.46% did regularly, and 6.30% did very often. In 2012, 32.9% never did, 24.19% rarely did, 21.13% did sometimes, 10.97% often did, and 10.81% read blogs very often. Among those who read web-based news in 2008, 6.57% never did, 16.29% rarely did, 26.86% did sometimes, 24.86% did regularly, and 25.43% did very often. In 2012, 10.84% never did, 15.37% rarely did, 29.29% did sometimes, 23.46% often did, and 21.04% read web-based news very often. These descriptive statistics indicate that students read blogs on a regular basis in both 2008 and 2012, and that a plurality get their news about politics often or very often from web-based sources.

Respondent Attributes

We employed five sets of variables to investigate the effects of respondent characteristics on offline engagement. First, each respondent was asked about the extent to which s/he was interested in politics. We used a four point scale

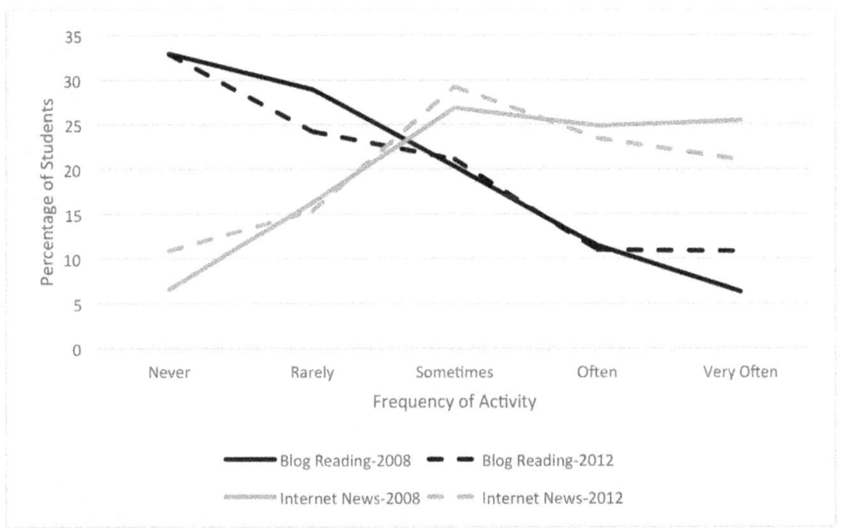

Figure 3.1 Online Activities among Students in 2008 and 2012. *Source*: Moffett and Rice, Student Election Survey.

for this question, where three points were allocated to "Very Interested," two points for "Somewhat Interested," one point for "Not Very Interested," and zero points for "Not at all Interested."

Second, we considered strength of partisan attachment, as many (e.g., Verba et al. 1995; Rosenstone and Hansen 1993) have discovered evidence that this predicts most traditional forms of political activity. We used three questions to measure the degree of partisan attachment among students. First, each person was asked whether s/he self-identifies as a Democrat, Republican, independent or something else. Using two questions with substantially similar wording, each respondent who self-identified as a Republican or Democrat was asked whether s/he strongly or not strongly identified as a Republican or Democrat, respectively. From this data, we constructed a binary variable for strong partisans.

To investigate the effects of peer civic experiences on offline engagement, we used three questions in our surveys that allowed us to construct an index that examined the degree to which the friends of each student engaged in a series of activities. We asked about the extent to which each student's friends: (1) are active in volunteer work in their community; (2) vote in elections; and (3) encourage the respondent to express his or her opinions about politics and current events, even if those opinions differ from the friends' views. Each of these items were answered on a five-point response scale for which zero points were allocated to "strongly disagree," one point for "disagree," two points for "neutral," three points for "agree," and four points for "strongly agree" ($\alpha = 0.65$, 2008; $\alpha = 0.70$, 2012).[2]

Fourth, we asked whether each student is a political science major through a binary variable constructed based on a question about student major(s) in the surveys. Finally, each respondent was asked whether s/he has or is currently serving in the United States military, the National Guard, military reserves, or in an ROTC program. We used this to create a dummy variable for those who are currently serving or have formerly served in the military.

Political Attributes

We used three variables to control for the effects of political characteristics on online engagement. First, we examined the effects of ideology by asking each respondent whether s/he self-identifies as a conservative, moderate, liberal, other, or did not know. If the respondent replied, "don't know" or "unknown," then we followed up with a question about whether that respondent self-identifies as a liberal or conservative. Based on replies to both questions, we created dichotomous variables for liberals and conservatives.[3] For example, the dummy variable for liberals is coded one when a respondent replied that s/he was a conservative or self-identified as a liberal in the follow-up question that was directed to those who did not know their ideology.[4] Finally, we considered support for Barack Obama by asking each respondent who s/he plans to vote for in the upcoming presidential election. From here, we constructed a binary for those who intended to vote for Barack Obama.

RESULTS

Table 3.2 displays our results. The model in the second column corresponds to the 2008 election, while the model in column three is connected with the 2012 elections. We discovered some evidence that the level of importance that students attach to various issues on their vote choice provides limited explanatory leverage when it comes to explaining patterns of offline civic activity for three reasons. First, there is no issue that exerts a statistically significant effect in both 2008 and 2012. Second, the majority of political issues do not exert statistically significant effects in either year.

Third, the issues that do exert statistically significant effects do so in an inconsistent manner. More specifically, each unit increase in a student's stated importance about education yielded a 1.36 point increase in his or her civic engagement score in 2008. Put differently, a shift from education being "not at all important" to being "extremely important" increased civic engagement by a single activity being engaged in very often, plus another activity being engaged in at one higher level than it was previously. In addition, each unit increase in a student's stated importance about health care in 2012 decreased his or her civic engagement score by 0.72 points. Also, each unit increase in a student's stated importance about immigration in 2012 yielded a 0.56 point increase in his or her civic engagement score.

Beyond the effects of issues, the political attributes of respondents exert very little influence on offline engagement in 2008 and 2012. We found no relationship between ideology and offline engagement, and only found a relationship between supporting Barack Obama and offline civic activity in 2012, but not in 2008. More specifically, we found that supporting Barack Obama in 2012 is connected with a 1.29 point increase in each student's offline engagement score.

Respondent Attributes and Offline Civic Activity

However, we discovered much more evidence that connects respondent attributes to offline engagement. On average, we found that being a strong partisan was connected with a 2.39 point increase in civic activity in 2008, and a 1.54 point increase in this activity in 2012. Further, we discovered that

Table 3.2 Offline Engagement Prior to the 2008 and 2012 Elections

Independent Variable	*2008*	*2012*
Issue Importance		
Economy	–0.13	–0.41
	(0.60)	(0.49)
Education	1.36*	–0.45
	(0.62)	(0.56)
Energy	0.72	0.37
	(0.54)	(0.41)
College Financing	–0.55	0.47
	(0.47)	(0.42)
Health Care	–0.17	–0.72*
	(0.47)	(0.41)
Environment	–0.56	–0.29
	(0.50)	(0.40)
Abortion	–0.11	0.17
	(0.38)	(0.30)
Immigration	–0.21	0.56*
	(0.41)	(0.31)
Same Sex Marriage	0.21	0.25
	(0.34)	(0.29)
Online Activities		
Frequency of Blog Reading	1.08**	0.68**
	(0.34)	(0.28)
Online News Consumption	0.88**	0.15
	(0.37)	(0.34)
Respondent Attributes		
Interest in Politics	–1.86***	2.16***
	(0.55)	(0.47)
Strong Partisan	2.39***	1.54*
	(0.79)	(0.68)
Peer Civic Experiences	0.45**	0.60***
	(0.18)	(0.12)
Political Science Major	6.00***	5.76***
	(1.86)	(1.29)
Military	1.12	1.37
	(1.55)	(1.91)
Political Attributes		
Liberal	0.36	–0.68
	(0.90)	(0.73)
Conservative	–1.76	0.10
	(1.09)	(0.89)
Obama Supporter	–0.15	1.29*
	(0.91)	(0.73)
Constant	2.72	–1.07
	(3.62)	(2.04)
N	281	459
R^2	0.38	0.31
Adjusted R^2	0.34	0.28
F-Statistic	8.46	10.36
Prob>F-Statistic	<0.0001	<0.0001
Standard Error of the Estimate	5.58	6.07

Notes: The values in parenthesis are standard errors. Also, * denotes $p < 0.05$, ** denotes $p < 0.01$, and *** denotes $p < 0.001$, all one-tailed tests.
Source: Moffett and Rice, Student Election Survey

political science majors are more apt to be engaged offline, as identifying in this way was connected with a 6.01 point increase in offline civic activity in 2008, and a 5.76 point increase in offline civic engagement in 2012. This is not surprising, since those who actively pursue their interests in studying politics are also among the most active in higher-cost forms of political activity.

Moreover, we found that the civic experiences of peers also affect the propensity with which college students engage offline. More specifically, we discovered that a one unit increase in the civic experiences of one's peers is associated with a 0.45 point increase in offline civic activity in 2008, and a 0.60 point increase in this activity in 2012. Put differently, an increase in the civic experiences of one's peers from no engagement to maximum engagement (or, from zero to twelve), results in an average increase in offline civic activity of 5.4 points in 2008, and 7.2 points in 2012. Conceptually speaking, this is the equivalent of going from never performing one offline activity to performing that activity very frequently, *plus* performing an additional offline activity at one higher level than it was performed previously in 2008. Using the 2012 data, this is the equivalent of going from never performing two offline activities to performing one of those activities very often, and the second of those activities often.

To perform a more finely-tuned analysis of these results, we used CLARIFY to compute the change in offline civic activity for each unit increase in peer civic activity.[5] The figure on the left corresponds to 2008, while the figure on the right corresponds to 2012. In both illustrations, the vertical axis denotes the change in offline civic engagement, while the horizontal axis is the frequency of peer civic activity. Moreover, the solid line denotes the change in civic activity, given different levels of peer civic engagement, while the dashed lines denote the 95% confidence intervals around these expected

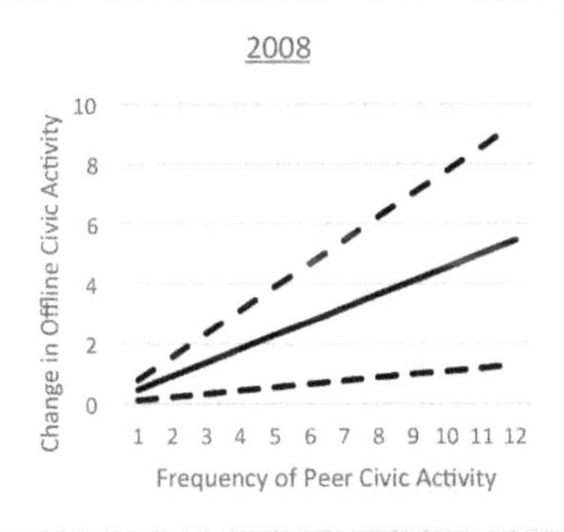

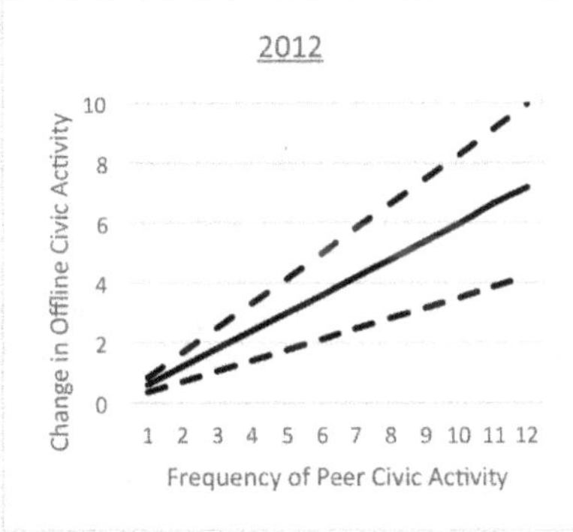

Figure 3.2 Peer Civic Engagement and Changes in Offline Civic Activity in 2008 and 2012. *Source*: Moffett and Rice, Student Election Survey.

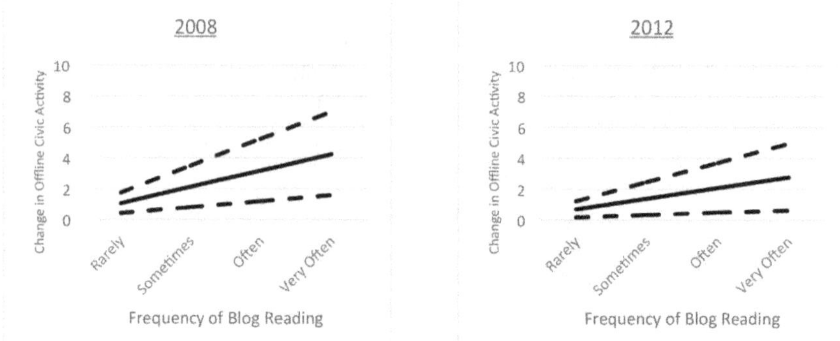

Figure 3.3 Blog Reading and Changes in Offline Civic Activity in 2008 and 2012. *Source*: Moffett and Rice, Student Election Survey.

values. As Figure 3.2 depicts, an increase in the level of peer civic activity in 2008 corresponds to an expected increase in civic activity from 0.46 points (when going from never performing any activity to performing a single activity rarely) to 5.47 points (when going from never performing any activity to performing all activities very often). In 2012, an increase in the level of peer civic activity is connected with an expected increase in civic activity from 0.60 points (when going from never performing any activity to performing a single activity rarely) to 7.18 points (when going from never performing any activity to performing all activities very often).

Yet, we uncovered mixed evidence with respect to the effects of interest in politics on offline engagement. In 2008, we found that each unit increase in interest in politics is connected with a decrease in offline engagement of 1.86 points. At the same time, though, we discovered that each unit increase in interest in politics in 2012 was associated with an increase in offline engagement by 2.16 points. In 2008, interest in politics was much higher, as was the incidence of many other forms of civic activity. In part, this was higher because of an emphasis on younger voters by the Obama campaign. When viewed in this light, it makes sense that interest in politics might be connected with a decrease in offline engagement in 2008. When many of these factors were removed or reduced in 2012, interest in politics had the expected, positive relationship. Finally, we found no evidence that being a current or former member of the military is connected with offline engagement.

Online Activities and Offline Civic Engagement

Most importantly, we discovered substantial evidence that online activities are connected with higher levels of offline engagement. We found that each unit increase in online news consumption in 2008 was connected with a 0.88 point increase in offline civic activity. On average, we also found that each unit increase in the frequency of blog reading was connected with a 1.08 point increase in offline engagement in 2008, and a 0.68 point increase in this activity in 2012.

To perform a finer-grained analysis of these results, we used CLARIFY to compute the change in offline civic activity for each unit increase in blog reading. The figure on the left corresponds to 2008, while the figure on the right corresponds to 2012. In both illustrations, the vertical axis denotes the change in offline civic engagement, while the horizontal axis is the frequency of blog reading. Moreover, the solid line denotes the change in civic activity, given different levels of blog readership, while the dashed lines denote the 95% confidence intervals around these expected values. As Figure 3.3 depicts, an increase in the level of blog reading in 2008 corresponds to an expected increase in civic activity by 1.06 points for rarely reading blogs, 2.12 points for sometimes reading blogs, 3.18 points for reading blogs often, and 4.24 points for reading blogs very often. Further, an increase in the level of blog reading in 2012 is connected with an expected increase in civic activity by 0.70 points for rarely reading blogs, 1.39 points for sometimes reading blogs, 2.09 points for reading blogs often, and 2.79 points for reading blogs very often.

CONCLUSION

So far, we have demonstrated a strong link between college students' online activities and their civic activity offline. More specifically, higher levels of blog reading and online news consumption are connected with higher levels of civic activity. Also, we discovered that strong partisans and political science majors are also associated with higher levels of civic engagement. Finally, we discovered that students whose friends are more engaged in political activity will themselves be more civically engaged. In this way, we examined those forms of engagement that political scientists consider to be costly and found evidence that is consistent with parts of the literature on civic activity.

On the other hand, though, we found very little evidence that political issues, political attributes, or interest in politics exert any kind of consistent effect on offline civic activity. The factors that drive the offline activity of college students do not perfectly mirror those that have been found to drive the activity of the general public. Some factors unique to college students such as their major and the civic experiences of their peers have a strong relationship with their level of offline engagement. Meanwhile, interest in politics does not consistently drive students' offline engagement even though it has traditionally been one of the strongest predictors of political activity. However, these offline activities are not the only political activities in which young adults engage. Many online activities carry far less cost and may attract additional young adults to the political process. To explore this possibility, we examine other forms of civic activity in Chapters 4 and 5: friending and joining activities, online political expression, and two newer forms of online political expression via Twitter. It is to that task that we now turn.

NOTES

1. We will explore the factors that affect friending and joining activities, expressing one's political views online, and two forms of activity via Twitter in Chapters 4 and 5.
2. These were the only questions asked about peer civic experiences in both surveys. Some respondents replied that they did not know for these questions. We coded values for these variables as missing for the purposes of index construction. Thus, no peer civic engagement score exists for those who answered "don't know" for at least one of the questions.
3. Unfortunately, our survey does not contain a measure that allows us to determine the strength of ideological attachment. That said, considering ideology in the manner that we do in this analysis allows us to determine the effect of ideological direction on civic engagement.
4. We coded the dummy variable for conservatives in the same manner.
5. To compute the change in the expected value of offline civic engagement for Figures 3.2 and 3.3, we generally assume that the values of all continuous variables are held at their mean, and that all binary variables have a value of zero. To compute this change, we alter the value of peer civic activity in Figure 3.2 from zero to each value for this variable until we have reached its maximum. For Figure 3.3, we alter the value of blogging from zero to each value for this variable until we have reached its maximum.

Chapter 4

Friending and Following as a Pathway for Political Participation

With a limited amount of time for activities, people often make decisions based on benefits and costs. The more interesting they find an activity, the more benefit expected. The more time, money, or effort it takes to engage in an activity, the greater its costs. For example, a couple on a weekend trip to New York City with little interest in art is unlikely to choose to take a cab across town to visit an art museum with a $25 admission fee. However, a different decision might be reached if one sufficiently reduces the costs and efforts involved. If the art museum is instead across the street from their hotel and has no entry fee, that couple becomes more likely to at least make time for a brief visit. Drawn in by the convenience and the lack of cost, they may discover they like art more than they thought.

Similarly, many traditional forms of civic or political activity, like those examined in Chapter 3, require relatively high costs. Some of these costs can be monetary such as those associated with making campaign contributions. However, many instead involve significant investments of effort or time like devoting nights or weekends volunteering for a campaign or spending several hours at a political meeting or campaign rally. Even waiting in line for 15 minutes at the polls might be perceived as a nontrivial cost to someone already short on time. For someone with little interest in politics, these costs represent significant barriers to entry.

However, advances in technology offer new forms of political participation with dramatically reduced "entry fees" and much greater convenience. We consider two in this chapter: liking, friending, or otherwise joining an online social network that is political in nature and following political Twitter feeds. For both, the entry fee is little more than signing up for an account, and then, clicking a mouse or tapping a smart phone or tablet. While someone not very interested in politics is unlikely to drive across town to attend a political party meeting or a campaign rally, s/he might take the few seconds necessary to like a party or friend a candidate online or even follow their Twitter feed. That simple click of a mouse or a smart phone or tablet then leads to greater exposure to campaign politics, which may prove more interesting than once thought. In the remainder of this chapter, we examine who takes advantage of this convenient and low-cost form of participation. We begin with the political use of online social networking through Facebook, LinkedIn and other similar sites and then turn to following political Twitter feeds.

MAKING FRIENDS WITH POLITICS

Mark Zuckerberg launched what became Facebook at Harvard University just as the 2004 presidential primaries were getting underway. However, its use at the time was largely confined to university students. It quickly spread off campus though, and by Fall of 2006, Facebook joined its competitors MySpace and LinkedIn as social networking platforms accessible to anyone who registered with an e-mail address. While no longer confined to college campuses and high schools during the 2008 election, its users were still disproportionately made up of young adults. A Pew Internet and American Public Life survey the month after the election showed that 35% of all online adults used social networking sites (Jones and Fox 2009). This average hid a sharp age bias in usage—just over two-thirds of those ages 18 to 32 reported using social network sites compared to only 36% of Generation X, 20% of young baby boomers, and an average in the single digits for those over age 55 (Jones and Fox 2009).

Given young adults' historically low participation rates, Barack Obama's decision to meet with a Facebook board member in February 2007 about how social networking might be used in political campaigns (Carr 2008) might have easily been dismissed at the time by many campaign experts as futile. However, his campaign's early efforts and success meant that candidates at every level soon scrambled to develop a social media presence. By the time of the November election, Obama had amassed well over 2 million Facebook supporters in the United States alone; McCain had just over 600,000 (Dutta and Fraser 2008).

By 2012, social networking platforms were an accepted campaign essential. By late September 2012, Obama had amassed over 28.8 million likes compared to Romney's nearly 7.2 million (Felix 2012). While usage of online social networks increased across all age groups in 2012, much of the bias in age usage remained. 83% of those ages 18–29 reported using social networking sites compared to 77% of 30- to 49-year-olds, 52% of 50- to 64-year-olds, and 32% of those over age 65 (Duggan and Brenner 2013).

Historical trends involving more traditional forms of political participation would suggest that despite their strong presence on online social networking sites, few young adults would use them to foray into the political world. However, online social networking, as a form of political participation, is fundamentally different in terms of costs. Instead of having to venture out into unfamiliar forms of participation, social networking brought a low-cost entry point into politics directly into a world that young adults already heavily populated. In a matter of seconds, with little more than a click or tap, they could add a candidate, political party, or other political group to their already wide social networks. A form of political participation with hardly any "entry fee" became incredibly convenient to young adults. One decision to like or friend might easily lead to others. And, with each political addition to their social networks, came further exposure to the world of politics. This exposure might cause some to realize they had more interest in politics or at least the election than they previously thought. The generation that "nobody asks" (Rosenstone and Hansen 1993) became the generation best poised to receive invitations extended via social networks to participate through other more traditional means (Rice, Moffett, and Madupalli 2013).

A fairly large percentage of students in our surveys reported using online social networks to friend, like, or otherwise join an online social network of a candidate, party, or political group in both 2008 and 2012. In 2008, about 50% of students surveyed reported some level of this activity. More specifically, 10.06% reported doing so rarely, 15.36% reported doing so sometimes, 12.85% reported doing so regularly, and 11.45% reported doing so very often. In 2012, the percent reporting engaging in some level of campaign-related social networking shrunk ever so slightly. Still, 14.78% reported doing so rarely, 16.17% reported doing so sometimes, 7.30% reported doing so regularly, and 6.09% reported doing so very often.

Clearly, a number of students added at least some political dimension to their social networks during the 2008 and 2012 campaigns. But, were these the same students already more inclined to participate or did online social networking help draw more young adults into the world of political participation? Rice, Moffett, and Madupalli (2013) discovered that some of the traditional predictors of political activity, like interest in politics, failed to help predict whether young adults engaged in campaign-related friending or joining in 2008. Here, we expand this analysis by examining what predicts campaign-related online social networking in 2008 and 2012. Specifically, we investigate how the respondent characteristics and domestic issue priorities that predicted traditional forms of offline activity in Chapter 3 may differ from those that predict whether students add politicians or political groups to their online social networks.

If campaign-related online social networking only appeals to those already likely to participate, then, for the same reasons provided in Chapter 3, those with greater consumption of political news and political blogs, interest in politics, and strength of partisanship should all be significantly more likely to engage in this activity. The same holds true for political science majors. All of these are characteristics of political buffs already highly prone to participate in politics. As in Chapter 3, we expect that those who have civically engaged friends should also be more likely to join online political social networks. Not only is having civically engaged friends associated with greater levels of traditional, offline forms of political participation, it also should make it easier to expand one's social network into the political realm. If, instead, the ease of expanding one's social network to political candidates or groups draws in a broader circle of young adults, then these will not all be significant predictors of campaign-related online social networking.

We also control for issue priorities as our results in Chapters 2 and 3 suggest different issues push students online than drive students offline. Finally, we control for the same additional respondent characteristics as we did in Chapter 3—military service, liberal and conservative, and support for Obama. Table 4.1 presents the results of ordered logit models for both 2008 and 2012. It also reports odds ratios in order to interpret the magnitude of the effects.

Some of the respondent characteristics associated with engaging in traditional forms of political activity also predict friending or joining campaign-related online social networks. In 2008, higher information consumption in the forms of reading both internet news and political blogs was associated with greater levels of friending or joining activity. Each unit increase in the frequency of reading internet news increases the odds that favor engaging in higher levels of friending and joining by 27% and each unit increase in the frequency of reading political blogs increases the odds that favor higher levels of friending and joining by 37%. Strong partisans and political science majors are also more likely to engage in more campaign-related social networking. Strong partisans were 187% more likely to engage in higher levels of friending or joining activity while political science majors were 505% more likely to do so. However, greater interest in politics or having more civically engaged friends failed to make a significant difference.

The results here suggest Obama's efforts to successfully leverage Facebook in his campaign bore fruit as his supporters were 188% more likely to engage in higher levels of political social networking in 2008. We also find that those who put greater priority on the issue of same sex marriage were more likely to friend or join online political social networks. Each unit increase in the importance of same sex marriage yields a 27% increase in the odds that favor higher levels of friending or joining activity. This is consistent with our

Table 4.1 Young Adults and Campaign-Related Social Networking

Independent Variable	*Friending or Joining (2008)*	*Odds Ratio (2008)*	*Friending or Joining (2012)*	*Odds Ratio (2012)*
Issue importance				
Economy	0.15	1.16	–0.02	0.99
	(0.22)		(0.18)	
Education	–0.16	0.85	0.24	1.28
	(0.21)		(0.20)	
Energy	0.23	1.26	0.27*	1.31
	(0.19)		(0.14)	
College Financing	0.13	1.14	0.06	1.07
	(0.16)		(0.15)	
Health Care	–0.06	0.94	–0.10	0.90
	(0.18)		(0.14)	
Environment	–0.09	0.92	–0.12	0.89
	(0.17)		(0.14)	
Abortion	–0.05	0.95	–0.10	0.91
	(0.14)		(0.10)	
Immigration	–0.09	0.91	0.12	1.12
	(0.14)		(0.11)	
Same Sex Marriage	0.24*	1.27	0.08	1.08
	(0.13)		(0.10)	
Information Consumption				
Internet News	0.31**	1.37	0.19	1.21
	(0.13)		(0.12)	
Political Blogs	0.28**	1.33	0.27***	1.31
	(0.11)		(0.09)	
Respondent Characteristics				
Peer Civic Experiences	0.05	1.06	0.09**	1.10
	(0.06)		(0.04)	
Political Science Major	1.80***	6.05	–0.11	0.89
	(0.64)		(0.41)	
Military	–0.08	0.93	0.40	1.49
	(0.50)		(0.65)	
Interest in Politics	–0.15	0.86	0.80***	2.22
	(0.20)		(0.18)	
Liberal	0.12	1.12	–0.04	0.97
	(0.32)		(0.25)	
Conservative	0.23	1.26	0.20	1.22
	(0.39)		(0.30)	
Obama Supporter	1.06***	2.88	0.15	1.16
	(0.35)		(0.26)	
Strong Partisan	1.05***	2.87	1.15***	3.14
	(0.27)		(0.22)	
Cut Point One	3.48		4.92	
	(1.29)		(0.85)	
Cut Point Two	4.07		5.80	
	(1.29)		(0.86)	
Cut Point Three	4.93		7.17	
	(1.31)		(0.89)	
Cut Point Four	6.08		8.26	
	(1.33)		(0.91)	
N	288		439	
Log Likelihood	–357.49		–491.00	
Pseudo R^2	0.1231		0.1512	
Chi-Square	100.42		174.89	
Prob>Chi-Square	<0.0001		<0.0001	

Notes: The coefficients are ordered logit coefficients and the values in parenthesis are standard errors. * denotes $p < 0.05$, ** denotes $p < 0.01$, and *** denotes $p < 0.001$, all one-tailed tests.
Source: Moffett and Rice, Student Election Survey.

findings in Chapter 2. However, in this fuller model, the importance of energy no longer predicts greater levels of friending or joining.

In 2012, a slightly different process was at work. Unlike in 2008, in 2012 greater interest in politics and more civically engaged friends did help predict greater levels of campaign-related social networking. Each unit increase in interest in politics produces a 122% increase in the odds that favor engaging in higher levels of this activity while each unit increase in the level of civically engaged friends produces a 10% increase in these odds. However, frequency of internet news consumption or being a political science major did not. As in 2008, strong partisans and those who read political blogs more frequently were more likely to engage in friending or joining. Strong partisans were 214% more likely to engage in higher levels of friending or joining and each unit increase in the frequency of reading political blogs produced a 31% increase in the odds that favor higher levels of this activity. In 2012, Obama supporters were no more likely to engage in this activity. And, unlike in the simpler model of friending in Chapter 2, only prioritizing energy positively predicts friending in 2012. Each unit increase in the importance of energy produces a 31% increase in the odds that favor higher levels of friending or joining.

So far, we have found that while some of the "usual suspects" that drive political participation also predict campaign-related social networking, not all of them do. This certainly suggests that in both years, online social networking helped draw in some students who would not otherwise participate. We return to this topic later in the chapter but first we turn to the similarities between friending and following political Twitter feeds.

FOLLOWING POLITICS

Like Facebook, when Twitter first emerged on the scene in 2006 and asked users to send short messages in response to the question "what are you doing?" it was not an obvious forum for political expression. It also failed to match the rapid explosive growth enjoyed by Facebook. In May 2008, 6% of internet-connected American adults reporting using Twitter and by the time of the 2008 election, this number had grown to nine (Lenhart and Fox 2009). Its users were small enough in number that we didn't think to ask about it in 2008. While both candidates used Twitter they did not attract a large number of followers. John McCain had less than 5,000 followers on Twitter and while Obama had significantly more, they still numbered under 120,000 (Dutta and Fraser 2008). However, in between the 2008 and 2012 presidential elections, many campaigns began to add Twitter into their campaign arsenal. In 2010, congressional challengers who used Twitter to control information flow did better at the polls (Gainous and Wagner 2014). Campaign tweets in 2010, particularly by challengers, were most likely to be positive in tone and those that included url links helped predict victory (Parmelee and Bichard 2012).

By 2012, politics and elections provided much fodder for tweets. In fact, Wilkinson and Thewall (2012) found politics to be the third most tweeted about subject among tweets that use the English language. With a little over a month to go before the 2012 election, Obama had amassed nearly 20 million followers on Twitter and Romney had yet to reach 1.2 million (Felix 2012). Still, Twitter usage was not as widespread as that of Facebook. Only 16% of internet users reported using Twitter in 2012 and they were disproportionately made up of those ages 18 to 29 (Duggan and Brenner 2013)[1], an age range that has been historically less likely to participate in politics.

Following a Twitter feed is a relatively low-cost endeavor, since it requires little more than a click of a mouse or a tap on a smart phone or tablet. By following the Twitter feed of a candidate for office, a political party, or an interest group, a user can gain information on the status of a race for office, candidates' or groups' political positions, and opportunities for involvement. Candidates for office and political leaders use Twitter to communicate to their supporters, followers, and constituents. For example, members of Congress most frequently use Twitter to advertise their activities or take positions on issues (Lawless 2012). Both major presidential candidates had active Twitter accounts during the 2012 election with followers numbering in the millions (Wortham 2012). Their followers were provided with information about the campaign in 140 characters or less.

Twitter can potentially draw more young adults into the political world. As they reach their first opportunity to vote in a presidential election, young adults' high familiarity with Twitter may make it a natural, easy source for both political information and expression. Like Facebook, it has a lower "entry fee" to young adults. The particularly low-cost nature of Twitter, as opposed to more traditional sources of political information or forms of political participation, may facilitate greater levels of political involvement among young adults.

51.8% of students we surveyed in 2012 reported having a Twitter account. Just under half of these students reported following the Twitter feeds of presidential candidates, political parties, or other politically-oriented groups. While 51.71% of those students with a Twitter account reported never following political twitter feeds, 10.57% reported doing so rarely, 15.43% reported doing so sometimes, 9.71% reported doing so regularly, and 12.57% of students reported doing so very often.

There is good reason to think that not everyone finds political information equally desirable. Followers may be made up primarily of those already most interested, engaged, and informed about politics—a group of people who might be labeled political buffs. If following political Twitter feeds is confined to those who are already interested and engaged in politics, then those with greater consumption of political news and political blogs, interest in politics, and strength of partisanship should all be significantly more likely to follow politics on Twitter, as should political science majors and those with more civically engaged friends. However, signing up to follow a candidate or political group's Twitter feed requires little more than a click of a mouse or a tap on a smart phone and thus is particularly low in cost compared to other potential sources of political information.

Young adults' greater familiarity with Twitter may make it a natural place to turn for political information. If the ease of adding candidates or political groups to those one already follows on Twitter helped widen the circle of young adults following politics, then these will not all be significant predictors of following political candidates or groups on Twitter. Students with weaker or no partisan affiliation may turn to Twitter feeds for information because they are short, easy to access, and require less time to read than other information sources. Likewise, because of Twitter's easy accessibility and familiarity to young adults, following political figures or groups on Twitter may require less interest in politics than would information gathering from more traditional and more time consuming sources. Further, political buffs are likely to consume multiple sources of political information while political novices, attracted by a familiar web 2.0 application, may turn only to Twitter. Thus, we compare who follows political figures or groups on Twitter to two alternate venues for information seeking: online political news and political blogs. If only students highly informed about politics already are the ones who decide to follow the Twitter feeds of political figures, then those who consume more political blogs and internet news would also be more likely to follow political figures on Twitter. However, if political Twitter feeds are attracting more students into the political world, then neither consumption of internet news or political blogs may predict following.

We also control for issue priorities as different issue priorities can foster different forms of participation. Since Obama had far more Twitter followers than did Romney, Obama supporters may be more likely to follow political Twitter feeds. Finally, we control for the same additional respondent characteristics as we did previously—military service, liberal, and conservative. Table 4.2 provides the results of this ordered logit model along with odds ratios for easier interpretation of effect size.

First, we note that the results of this fuller model of following political Twitter feeds depart notably from that in Chapter Two in several ways. When we control for interest in politics and other respondent characteristics, liberals and Obama supporters are no longer any more likely to follow political

Table 4.2 Young Adults and Following Political Twitter Feeds in 2012

Independent Variable	*Following Political Twitter Feeds*	*Odds Ratio*
Issue Importance		
Economy	–0.21	0.81
	(0.22)	
Education	0.12	1.13
	(0.24)	
Energy	0.02	1.02
	(0.18)	
College Financing	0.35*	1.42
	(0.20)	
Health Care	–0.35**	0.71
	(0.18)	
Environment	0.05	1.05
	(0.17)	
Abortion	0.11	1.11
	(0.12)	
Immigration	0.05	1.06
	(0.13)	
Same Sex Marriage	–0.14	0.87
	(0.13)	
Information Consumption		
Internet News	0.16	1.18
	(0.15)	
Political Blogs	0.09	1.10
	(0.11)	
Respondent Characteristics		
Peer Civic Experiences	0.08	1.09
	(0.05)	
Political Science Major	–0.98	0.38
	(0.62)	
Military	–0.72	0.49
	(0.80)	
Interest in Politics	1.29***	3.65
	(0.25)	
Liberal	–0.31	0.73
	(0.32)	
Conservative	–0.31	0.74
	(0.39)	
Obama Supporter	0.29	1.33
	(0.33)	
Strong Partisan	1.26***	3.52
	(0.27)	
Cut Point One	3.76	
	(1.04)	
Cut Point Two	4.37	
	(1.04)	
Cut Point Three	5.45	
	(1.07)	
Cut Point Four	6.39	
	(1.09)	
N	269	
Log Likelihood	–325.70	
Pseudo R^2	0.1489	
Chi-Square	113.98	
Prob>Chi-Square	<0.0001	

Notes: The coefficients are ordered logit coefficients and the values in parenthesis are standard errors. * denotes $p < 0.05$, ** denotes $p < 0.01$, and *** denotes $p < 0.001$, all one-tailed tests.
Source: Moffett and Rice, Student Election Survey.

Twitter feeds than others. Further, those who give greater priority to energy are also no more likely to follow political Twitter feeds. Instead, those who place greater priority on college financing are more likely to follow political Twitter feeds while those who place greater importance on health care are less likely to follow political Twitter feeds. Each unit increase in importance of college financing is associated with a 42% increase in the odds that favor higher levels of following political Twitter feeds while each unit increase in the importance of health care is associated with a 29% decrease in the odds that favor higher levels of following.

More importantly, two of the characteristics most strongly associated with greater offline participation also predict following political Twitter feeds: interest in politics and strength of partisanship. Strong partisans have a 252% increase in the odds that favor engaging in higher levels of following political Twitter feeds. Each unit increase in interest in politics is associated with a 265% increase in the odds that favor engaging in higher levels of following political Twitter feeds. However, none of the other respondent characteristics are statistically significant predictors of following political Twitter feeds. Most notably, being a political science major, levels of peer engagement, or the frequency with which one reads political blogs or consumes internet news, does not affect the extent to which one follows political Twitter feeds. This implies that while political information on Twitter appeals strongly to those with high interest or stakes in politics, it also potentially draws in some who might not otherwise participate in politics or consume political information.

FRIENDING AND FOLLOWING AS PATHWAYS TO PARTICIPATION

Friending and following certainly appeal to those who care about politics. We have found that strong partisans were more likely to friend in both 2008 and 2012 and were also more likely to follow. Yet, other factors typically associated with greater political participation do not always predict these newer, low-cost forms of participation already familiar to young adults. Interest in politics did not foster friending in 2008 but it was associated with greater friending and following in 2012. Frequency of blog consumption was associated with greater friending both years but not with greater following. Frequency of internet news consumption and political science major was only associated with greater friending in 2008. These findings leave room for the possibility that friending and following also attract those who do not care much about politics.

We have argued that the low "entry fees" and convenience associated with friending and following may attract those who might not otherwise participate. We now perform a more finely grained analysis through employing CLARIFY to compute the predicted probabilities of friending and following tweets among avid political buffs and complete political novices.[2] We define an avid political buff as a respondent who reads political blogs very often, consumes online news very often, is highly interested in politics, is a political science major, and is a strong partisan. Figure 4.1 displays the predicted probabilities of avid political buffs engaging in each level of friending in 2008 and 2012 and of each level of following in 2012.

a. Friending in 2008

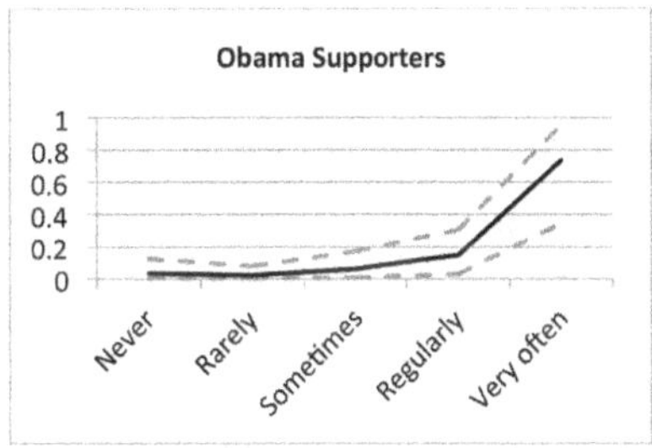

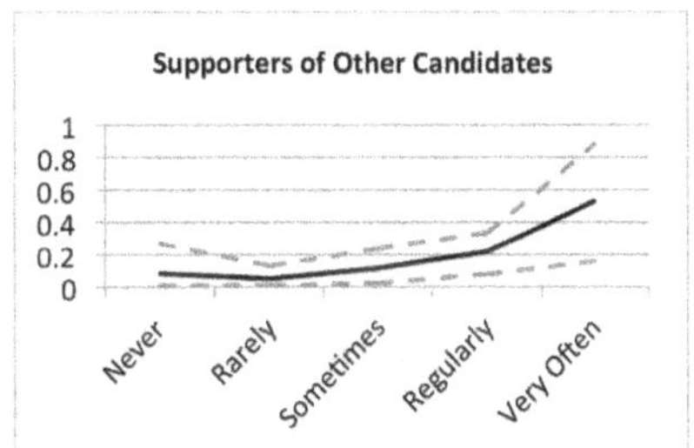

b. Friending in 2012

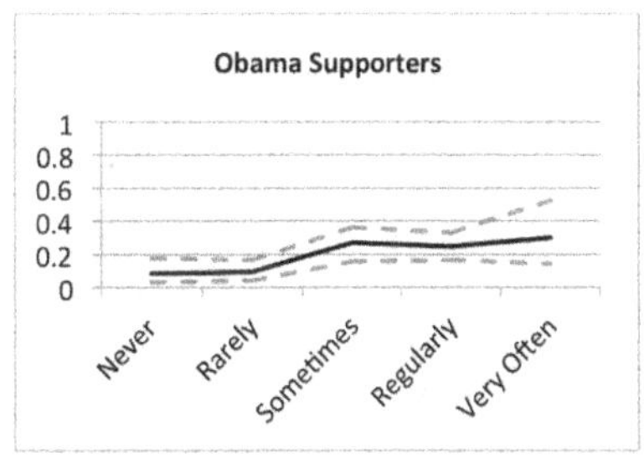

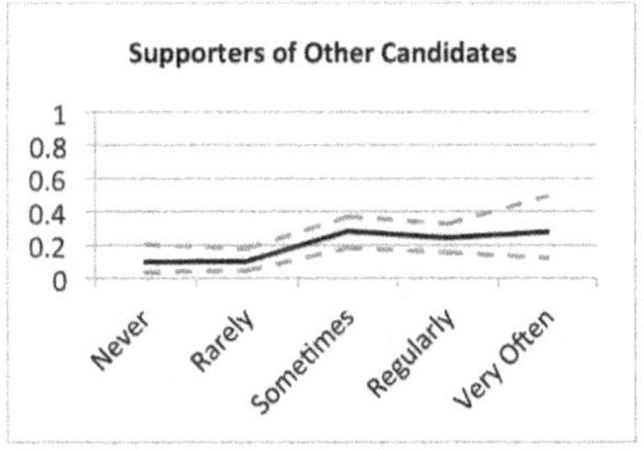

c. Following in 2012

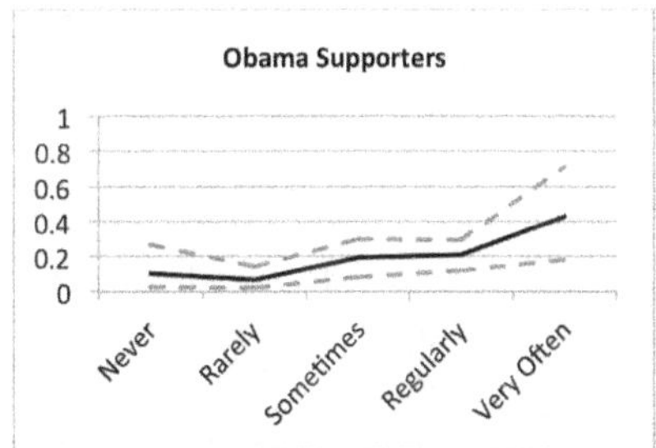

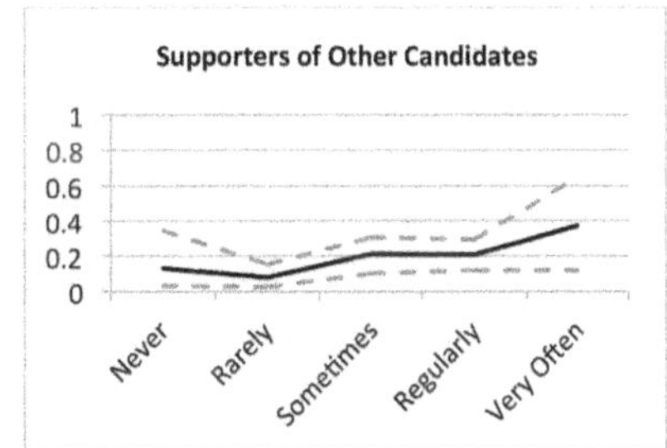

Figure 4.1 The Probability of Friending and Following among Political Buffs. *Source*: Moffett and Rice, Student Election Survey.

Clearly, political buffs have a very high probability of engaging in at least some level of friending and following. As Figure 4.1 shows, political buffs had a much higher predicted probability of friending in 2008 than they did in 2012. In 2008, political buffs who intended to vote for Obama had a 74.4% predicted probability of friending very often, a 14.9% probability of friending regularly, a 6.1% probability of friending sometimes, a 2.3% probability of friending rarely and only a 3.2% predicted probability of never friending. Meanwhile, among political buffs intending to vote for McCain or minor party candidates, the predicted probability of friending very often was 53.1% while the predicted probability of friending regularly was 22%, sometimes 11.6%, rarely 5.1% and never 8.3%.

In 2012, the predicted probabilities of political buffs friending candidates or political groups very often dropped dramatically. Obama supporters had a 30.7% predicted probability of friending very often, a 24.9% probability of friending regularly, a 26.8% probability of friending sometimes, a 9.3% probability of friending rarely and a 8.3% probability of never friending. Supporters of Romney or minor party candidates had predicted probabilities of friending of 27.8% very often, 24.3% regularly, 28.1% sometimes, 10.3% rarely and 9.6% never. Political buffs also had a higher predicted probability of following than they did friending in 2012. Political buffs intending to vote for President Obama had a 42.3% predicted probability of following very often, a 20.9% probability of following regularly, a 19.1% probability of following sometimes, a 6.7% probability of following rarely and a 10.4% probability of never following. For political buffs supporting Romney or candidates from minor parties, the respective predicted probabilities of following were 36.9%, 20.8%, 21.1%, 8%, and 13.2%. However, this predicted probability of political buffs following political Twitter feeds in 2012 was still much smaller than their predicted probability of friending in 2008.

If Facebook and Twitter's low entry fees helped also draw in those who would not normally participate, then complete political novices should also have a nonzero likelihood of friending and following. Here, we define a complete political novice as one who never reads political blogs, never consumes news online, is not at all interested in politics, is not a political science major, and is not a strong partisan. Figure 4.2 displays the predicted probabilities of complete political novices engaging in each level of friending in 2008 and 2012 and of each level of following in 2012.

In 2008, complete political novices who intended to vote for Obama had a 72.1% predicted probability of never friending and a 9.8% probability of friending rarely a 9.4% probability of friending sometimes, a 5.7% probability of friending regularly and a 3.1% probability of friending very often. Complete political novices supporting McCain or other candidates had predicted

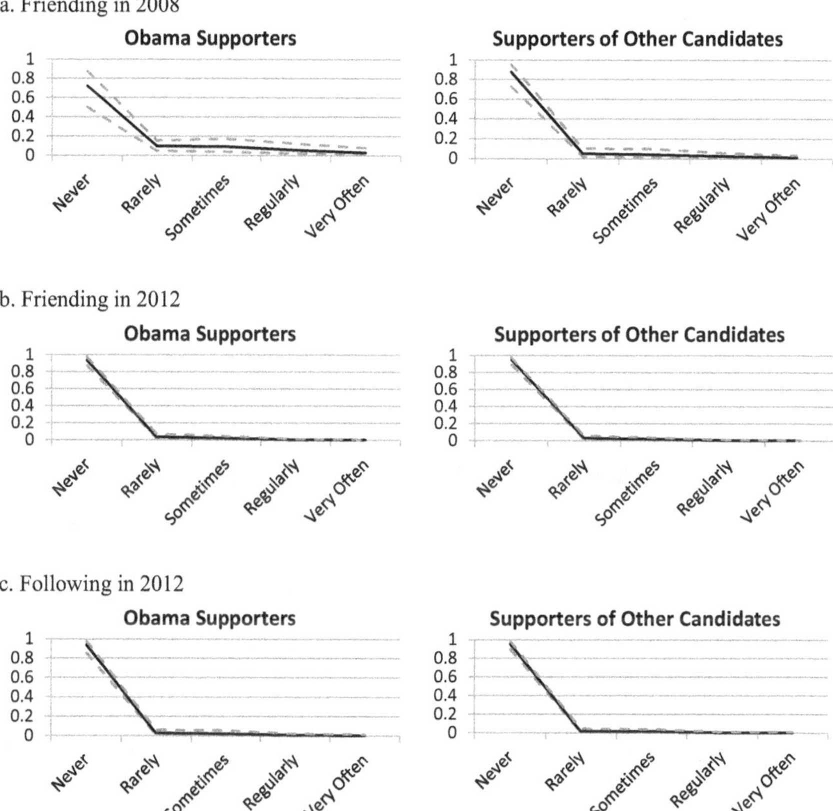

Figure 4.2 The Probability of Friending and Following among Complete Political Novices. *Source*: Moffett and Rice, Student Election Survey.

probabilities of 87.6%, 5%, 4.1%, 2.2%, and 1.1%, respectively. In 2012, complete political novices who supported Obama instead had a predicted probability of never friending of 93.6%, while supporters of Romney or minor party candidates had a predicted probability of never friending of 94.4%. The predicted probability of friending rarely was under 4% regardless of candidate supported, with the probabilities shrinking dramatically for each level higher of friending. Complete political novices who supported Obama had a 93.9% predicted probability of never following political Twitter feeds in 2012 compared to a 95.4% probability for supporters of other candidates. The remaining probabilities were clustered largely in the rarely and sometimes categories. Complete political novices do have a nonzero predicted probability of engaging in some level of each activity but this probability was very close to zero for friending and following in 2012 and only a bit higher in 2008. This evidence suggests the low entry fee for friending and following is not drawing in large numbers of complete political novices.

However, the average young adult is neither an avid political buff nor a complete political novice. What about the likelihood of those with average levels of interest in politics and average levels of information consumption engaging in political friending or following? Is there evidence that the low-cost nature of political uses of Facebook and Twitter draws them in? In 2008, the average level of self-reported interest in politics was only a two on a scale of one to four. Respondents at this level report being "not very interested" in politics. On a scale of zero to four, the average level of internet news consumption was a 2.46 (midway between sometimes and regularly) and the average level of political blog consumption was 1.29 (just slightly more than rarely). In 2012, the mean level of interest in politics was 1.79 on a scale of zero to three, or a little less than "somewhat interested." On a scale of zero to four, the average level of internet news consumption in 2012 was 2.29 and the average level of political blog consumption was 1.43. Compared to 2008, self-reported interest in politics was up, internet news consumption of our sample was down some, and political blog reading was slightly up. Clearly, based on these measures, the average student had marginal political interest at best in 2012 and even less in 2008. These are exactly the sort of individuals who might be swayed to participate by friending and following's convenience and low entry fees. Figure 4.3 displays the predicted probabilities for those with mean levels of interest in politics and mean levels of internet news and political blog consumption.

In 2008, Obama supporters with average levels of political interest and information consumption had a 49.8% predicted probability of never friending, a 14.1% probability of rarely friending, a 16.8% probability of sometimes friending, a 12.1% probability of regularly friending, and a 7.2% probability of friending very often, while comparable supporters of McCain or third party candidates had predicted probabilities of 73.7%, 9.6%, 8.9%, 5.2%, and 2.7%, respectively. In 2012, Obama supporters with average levels of political interest and information consumption had a 60.5% predicted probability of never friending, an 18% probability of friending rarely, a 14.9% probability of friending sometimes, a 4.3% probability of friending regularly and a 2.3% probability of friending very often. For comparable supporters of Romney or other candidates these probabilities were 63.9%, 17%, 13.4%, 3.7%, and 2%, respectively. When it came to following political Twitter feeds instead, those with average levels of political interest and information consumption who supported Obama had a 46.2% predicted probability of never following, a 14.7% probability of rarely following, a 21.1% probability of sometimes following, a 9.9% probability of regularly following, and an 8.1% probability

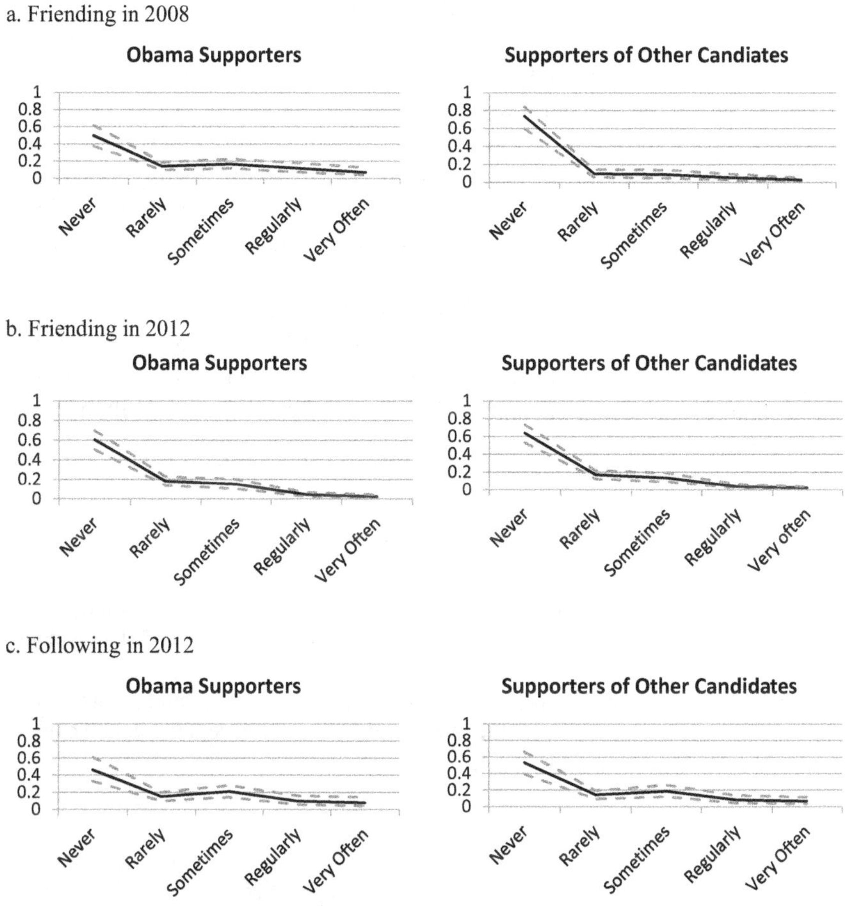

a. Friending in 2008

Obama Supporters

Supporters of Other Candiates

b. Friending in 2012

Obama Supporters

Supporters of Other Candidates

c. Following in 2012

Obama Supporters

Supporters of Other Candidates

Figure 4.3 The Probability of Friending and Following among Those with Average Interest and Information. *Source*: Moffett and Rice, Student Election Survey.

of following very often. For comparable supporters of Romney or third party candidates, these predicted probabilities were 52.9%, 14.2%, 18.5%, 8.1%, and 6.3%, respectively.

CONCLUSION

While avid political buffs may be far more likely than others to friend or follow a political candidate, political party, or other political group, they are not the only ones who do so. The average young adult may possess only marginal interest in politics but they had predicted probabilities of engaging in some level of friending or following that ranged from 26% to 54%. This certainly suggests that the low entry fee and convenience of friending and following is successfully drawing in a broader swath of young adults than might otherwise participate in politics. These simple, low-cost actions have potentially far broader ramifications on young adults' participation. Young adults who choose to friend or follow receive exposure to political information and invitations to get involved via other, more traditional means. And once they do, they may discover they are more interested in campaigns and politics than they once thought. This may result in branching out into a variety of other more traditional forms of political participation. We return to this possibility in Chapter 6, but first we turn to how two other familiar online activities—blogging and tweeting—may attract more young adults to express themselves politically.

NOTES

1. 27% of 18- to 29-year-olds reporting using Twitter compared to 16% of 30- to 49-year-olds, 10% of 50- to 64-year-olds, and 2% of those over age 65 (Duggan and Brenner 2013).

2. To compute the predicted probabilities for each figure, we hold friends' civic experiences and issue priorities at the mean, and military service, liberal, and conservative at a value of zero.

Chapter 5

Blogging and Tweeting as Attractors to Political Participation

Compared to friending or following candidates and political organizations, expressive forms of civic engagement like blogging, posting, and tweeting about politics carry greater cost. Formulating views and taking the time to put them in writing for others to see requires considerably more engagement than clicking a mouse or tapping a smart phone or tablet. This might suggest that only young adults highly interested in politics would take to the political blogosphere or to Twitter to share their political views. After all, why take the time to craft and post an opinion about something that holds little interest to you? It might also suggest that young adults would be underrepresented in the political blogosphere. They are, after all, less likely to find politics interesting than their elders.

Yet, young adults have greater familiarity with the online world of which these activities are a part. Blogging is a form of participation that has been around since the earliest memories of college students in 2008 and 2012 and while Twitter emerged on the scene later, its users in 2012 were disproportionately made up of those under 30 (Duggan and Brenner 2013). This greater familiarity may lower the perceived cost. If college students see blogging and tweeting as normal ways of sharing their views, regardless of the subject, then less interest in politics and other traditional predictors of costly political activity is required. In this chapter, we consider which young adults are most likely to blog, post, or tweet about politics and how these forms of participation may help expand young adults' civic engagement. We begin with blogging and posting and then turn to tweeting.

COLLEGE STUDENTS AND THE POLITICAL BLOGOSPHERE

College students play an integral role in the history of blogging. In fact, many credit Justin Hall, a student at Swarthmore College, with beginning one of the first of what would later become known as a blog in 1994 (Thompson 2006). What started as chronicles of life events soon became forums for expression about all sorts of topics, including politics.

This expression does not occur in a vacuum, as others can read what is posted and respond accordingly. However, the political blogosphere also represents a heavily polarized world where those on opposite sides of the aisle rarely communicate. Several studies have found that blogs written from one partisan perspective rarely link to those of other party affiliations or to more moderate blogs (Hargittai et al. 2008; Meraz 2013). What Sobieraj and Berry (2011) label "outrage writing" makes up an overwhelming percentage of the discourse on the most popular liberal and conservative blogs. However, even these polarized rants cannot be dismissed as inconsequential forms of participation, as their readers trust them and turn to them as an information source (Armstrong and McAdams 2011; Johnson and Kaye 2004).

While such blogging bypasses traditional institutions (Schlozman, Verba and Brady 2012), they sometimes resemble traditional media content. Researchers characterize the relationship as a "high-speed, two-way street" where the blogosphere simultaneously responds to traditional media coverage, drives traditional media coverage, and at times, has no relationship to this coverage (Wallsten 2007). It was not long before the effects of the political blogosphere began to ripple through mainstream politics. For example, the outrage on the blogosphere generated by then-Senate Majority Leader Trent Lott's comments about Strom Thurmond garnered attention from mainstream media and led to Lott's eventual resignation in 2002 (Bloom 2003; Wallsten 2007).

Blogs made their official entrance into presidential campaigning during the 2004 Democratic presidential primaries when Howard Dean employed his Blog for America to share information and foster greater support and involvement (Kerbel and Bloom 2005). Yet even before then, individuals took to the blogosphere with their views on political candidates. In both 2008 and 2012 the presidential campaigns remained a popular subject of discussion. Delli Carpini, Cook, and Jacobs (2004) argue that researchers should take the long view with respect to such discussion about politics, and count it alongside other, more traditional forms of participation (c.f., Bennett, Flickinger, and Rhine 2000).

As the blogosphere took shape, young adults remained at its forefront. By 2006, the majority of blogs were written by someone under the age of 30 and politics served as bloggers' second most blogged about subject (Lenhart and

Fox 2006). This age gap in the blogosphere has persisted over time. By 2009, those under age 32 were still far more likely to read and write blogs than older generations (Jones and Fox 2009). In 2008, about 42% of students surveyed in the Student Election Survey reported having engaged in some level of blogging or posting about politics. More specifically, 15.08% reported doing so rarely, 12.85% reported doing so sometimes, 4.47% reported doing so regularly, and 9.78% reported doing so very often. In 2012, the percentage reporting blogging or posting about politics grew to just under 55%. 20.93% of students reported doing so rarely, 17.47% reported doing so sometimes, 8.82% reported doing so regularly, and 7.61% reported doing so very often.

Students who engage in this costly activity must form an opinion, put it in writing, and typically make it available for anyone (or no one) to see. Although it is possible to hide one's identity when sharing political views in this manner, minimizing potential personal costs of expression such as loss of friendships, blogging remains a costly activity that requires a certain amount of political skill. This would ordinarily suggest that blogging would draw in the same sorts of people who already participate heavily in more traditional forms of political activity—those with high levels of interest in politics. However, as a whole, young adults tend to have far less of this than their elders. On the other hand, young adults possess far greater familiarity with blogs and blogging than their elders. If young adults view blogs as a natural forum to express their views on all sorts of topics, they may turn to posting about politics online during the excitement of a presidential campaign. Might their familiarity and ease with expressing views online help counteract their predispositions to be unengaged? We consider the relationship between blogging or posting and the same set of variables we examined in our models of friending and following in Chapter 4. However, some of our expectations differ.

We expect that the information consumption variables may be particularly important for understanding who blogs. First of all, blogging about politics requires familiarity with blogs. Our measure of frequency of political blog reading serves as a measure of blog fluency and we expect that those with greater familiarity with blogs should have greater proclivity to blog. More importantly, though, political blog reading itself should promote blogging about politics. Consuming others' opinions and political information on blogs should promote developing political opinions of one's own and may also spur the desire to share them. Whether angered by someone else's opinion or emboldened by the discovery that others agree, political blog reading may empower readers to become authors of their own posts.

Some research suggests that young adults turn to blogs for information as a substitute for traditional news sources (Armstrong and McAdams 2011). And, frequent blog readers tend to find blogs to be more credible than other information sources (Johnson and Kaye 2004). If young adults read blogs about politics primarily to gain information, prior research suggests that also should make it associated with higher levels of blogging (Kenski and Stroud 2006; Lewis 2011). Thus, we expect that those who read political blogs with higher levels of frequency should be much more likely to blog about politics.

Previous research disagrees about whether young adults are more heavily represented among readers of political blogs. Lewis (2011) found that political blog readers are younger while Lawrence, Sides, and Farrell (2010) and Pew (2010) find that despite young adults higher level of blog reading in general, readers of political blogs are slightly older.[1] Regardless, we expect that those young adults who read political blogs are more likely to blog or post about politics.

Several studies reveal that reading news online is associated with higher levels of political participation (Kenski and Stroud 2006; Norris 1998; Shah et al. 2001; Shah et al. 2005; Tolbert and McNeal 2003). Like reading political blogs, reading political news might easily provide the raw material needed to write a blog entry or post a comment about an article. One's level of online news readership also serves as another indicator that an individual spends more time online and is more familiar with the internet's mechanisms for sharing one's views. However, young adults' news consumption preferences differ dramatically from their elders with young adults consuming far less news, even from their favored online sources (Pew 2012; Zukin et al. 2006). Thus, although we expect that online news consumption would help foster blogging or posting about politics among the general population, we have less confidence it will influence whether young adults post their views about politics online.

Some respondent characteristics are likely to have a strong relationship with who engages in blogging or other online political expression. In particular, we expect strong partisans to be more likely to engage in this behavior. Strong partisans tend to have a greater vested interest in the outcome and may be more likely to share their views. Previous research shows that strength of party identification, how much one cares about the election outcome, and overall feelings about parties and presidential candidates are among the strongest predictors of trying to persuade others how to vote (Rosenstone and Hansen 1993). These same motivations are likely to help drive individuals to attempt to shape others' votes through what they post online. Likewise, interest in politics may encourage posting political views online. Certainly interest in politics may make it more worthwhile for someone to devote the time to drafting a political blog post or comment. Those with greater interest in politics are also likely to know more about politics and have more to say about the subject. Prior research into talking about politics in the offline world found that those with greater interest in politics and stronger partisanship were both more likely to engage in political discussion (Verba et al. 1995). We expect some of these same patterns to carry over online.

However, interest in politics may not be required in order to post one's political views online. Greater familiarity with blogging potentially lowers the cost of engaging in this activity. The more normal someone sees the online world as a venue for sharing opinions, the more likely they will use it themselves. If someone already uses blogs or other online forums to share their views on all sorts of issues, then they may also turn to these to share their views about politics in the midst of a presidential campaign without being particularly interested in politics in general. Familiarity lowers the cost such that high levels of interest in politics are not required to make posting one's views online worthwhile.

The relative importance students place on various issues is also likely to influence whether they blog or otherwise post their views about politics online. Those who place high priority on specific issues clearly have opinions about them and these issue priorities provide potential topics for online political expression. Previously, in Chapter 2, we found that, especially in 2012, viewing a number of different issues as important to vote choice was associated with being more likely to engage in online expression. We expect that a number of these issue priorities will continue to influence whether students blog in this more complete model of engaging in online political expression. Finally, we also control for the same additional respondent characteristics as we did in the previous two chapters: peer civic experiences, political science major, military service, Obama supporters, liberals, and conservatives. Table 5.1 presents the results of these ordered logit models of blogging or posting about politics in 2008 and 2012.

As the results show, one of the strongest predictors of how likely students are to blog about politics is their frequency of reading political blogs. Each unit increase in frequency of political blog readership increases the odds of engaging in higher levels of posting about politics by 207% in 2008 and by 30% in 2012. This suggests that posting one's political views online is driven in part by consumption of others' political views. It also suggests that greater familiarity with blogs leads to greater use of this vehicle for political expression which can potentially draw more young adults into the blogosphere than would otherwise participate.

Strong partisanship also exerts a significant influence on frequency of posting about politics. Strong partisans had an odds ratio of engaging in higher levels of posting about politics of 142% in 2008 and 83% in 2012. In this manner, who engages in blogging resembles who engages in other more traditional forms of participation and expression. Also, in both years, those that attached greater importance to the issue of same sex marriage were also more likely to post their political views online at higher levels. Each unit increase

Table 5.1 Young Adults and Blogging or Posting about Politics

	Blogging or Posting (2008)	*Odds Ratio (2008)*	*Blogging or Posting (2012)*	*Odds Ratio (2012)*
Issue importance				
Economy	0.17	1.18	0.01	1.01
	(0.24)		(0.16)	
Education	0.17	1.18	0.39*	1.48
	(0.24)		(0.19)	
Energy	−0.09	0.91	0.12	1.13
	(0.21)		(0.14)	
College Financing	0.01	1.01	−0.17	0.85
	(0.19)		(0.14)	
Health Care	−0.22	0.81	−0.26*	0.77
	(0.19)		(0.13)	
Environment	0.09	1.09	−0.35**	0.70
	(0.20)		(0.14)	
Abortion	−0.23	0.80	0.11	1.12
	(0.15)		(0.09)	
Immigration	0.07	1.07	0.23*	1.26
	(0.16)		(0.10)	
Same Sex Marriage	0.27*	1.31	0.22*	1.25
	(0.15)		(0.10)	
Information Consumption				
Internet News	−0.13	0.88	0.22*	1.25
	(0.15)		(0.11)	
Political Blogs	1.12***	3.07	0.27**	1.30
	(0.14)		(0.09)	
Respondent Characteristics				
Peer Civic Experiences	0.04	1.04	0.05	1.05
	(0.06)		(0.04)	
Political Science Major	0.02	1.03	−0.08	0.93
	(0.68)		(0.39)	
Military	−1.10	0.33	−0.30	0.75
	(0.68)		(0.65)	
Interest in Politics	−0.69**	0.50	0.67***	1.95
	(0.22)		(0.16)	
Liberal	−0.07	0.93	0.11	1.11
	(0.35)		(0.23)	
Conservative	−0.62	0.54	−0.45	0.64
	(0.41)		(0.28)	
Obama Supporter	−0.27	0.77	0.04	1.04
	(0.36)		(0.24)	
Strong Partisan	0.88**	2.42	0.60**	1.83
	(0.30)		(0.21)	
Cut Point One	1.30		2.98	
	(1.38)		(0.75)	
Cut Point Two	2.28		4.09	
	(1.39)		(0.76)	
Cut Point Three	3.49		5.35	
	(1.40)		(0.78)	
Cut Point Four	4.09		6.41	
	(1.41)		(0.80)	
N	288		442	
Log Likelihood	−286.25		−554.60	
Pseudo R^2	0.2034		0.1271	
Chi-Square	146.14		161.48	
Prob>Chi-Square	<0.0001		<0.0001	

Notes: The coefficients are ordered logit coefficients and the values in parenthesis are standard errors. * denotes $p < 0.05$, ** denotes $p < 0.01$, and *** denotes $p < 0.001$, all one-tailed tests.
Source: Moffett and Rice, Student Election Survey

in importance in the issue of same sex marriage was associated with a 31% increase in the odds of posting at higher levels in 2008 and a 25% increase in the odds of posting at higher levels in 2012.

Aside from frequency of reading political blogs, strength of partisanship, and the importance of same sex marriage to vote choice, it is clear that different processes were at work influencing who was more likely to blog in 2008 compared to 2012. First, and most strikingly, interest in politics played opposite roles across these two election years. In 2008, interest in politics was associated with reduced likelihood of posting about politics while in 2012 it was associated with greater likelihood of posting about politics. In 2008, each unit increase in interest in politics decreased the odds of engaging in higher levels of blogging or posting about politics by 50%, while in 2012 each unit increase in interest in politics increased the odds of engaging in higher levels of posting by 95%.

While we cannot fully confirm the reason for this with our data, we suspect differences in the underlying nature of the two elections may be contributing factors. In 2008, there was no incumbent seeking reelection. It was a historic election leading to the election of the nation's first black president and it generated more discussion than most. Further, it excited many who do not typically participate, including young adults. In this environment, even, and perhaps especially, those with typically little interest in politics were drawn to this election and they took to the familiarity of the blogosphere to share their opinions. In 2012, that same level of excitement was lacking. History had already been made and political expression seemingly fell back to the "usual suspects."

In 2008, only the importance of same sex marriage, political blog readership, strength of partisanship and interest in politics had a statistically significant relationship with students' level of posting about politics. Those more familiar with blogs who cared more about the outcome and who desired policy change were more likely to post their views online. However, those with less overall interest in politics were more likely to take to the internet to share their political views.

In 2012, more issues shaped the propensity to blog about politics as did students' level of internet news consumption. Students who placed greater importance on education and immigration were more likely to post their political views online while students who placed greater importance on health care and the environment were less likely to post their views online. These results suggest that college students had a slightly different focus than did the candidates. Each unit increase in the importance of immigration was associated with a 25% increase in the odds of engaging in higher levels of posting activity while each unit increase in the importance of education was associated with a 48% increase in the likelihood of engaging in posting more frequently.

In contrast, each unit increase in the importance of health care was associated with a 23% decrease in the odds that favor higher levels of posting about politics and each unit increase in the importance of the environment was associated with a 30% decrease in these odds. In an election that focused largely on health care policy, college students who placed more importance on that issue were actually less likely to share their political views online. Note, also, that these results on issue importance differ some from the results in Chapter 2. Once we consider the role of interest in politics, internet news consumption, political blog readership, and other respondent characteristics, the importance of the economy, energy, and college financing are no longer significant predictors of engaging in online political expression.

In sum, our results in 2008 suggest blogging drew in some who would ordinarily be less likely to participate while in 2012 who blogged more closely resembles who already participates through other vehicles. However, the issues associated with engaging in increased online political expression were not always the same ones at the center of the mainstream political debate. This also suggests that blogging may be drawing fresh voices into political expression. We will return to the question of whether blogging expands political expression among young adults later in the chapter but first we examine a newer form of online political expression.

COLLEGE STUDENTS AND TWEETING ABOUT POLITICS

Tweeting about politics, also known as microblogging, is a form of expressive participation that requires formulating political views, expressing them in 140 characters or less, and making them available for anyone to see. However, Twitter did not start out as an obvious forum for political expression when it first emerged in 2006 and asked its users to send short replies to the question "what are you doing?" Its role in the 2008 presidential election was quite limited. Four years later, though, the presidential elections provided much fodder for tweets, setting a number of records beginning with President Obama's acceptance speech at the Democratic National Convention (Sharp 2012a), continuing through the debates (Sharp 2012b), and culminating on election night when election-related tweets hit a fever pitch of 327,452 per minute (Sharp 2012c). Altogether, the hashtag #election 2012 was part of some 20 million tweets on Election Day 2012 (Zhang, Seltzer and Bichard 2013).

In fact, that same year Wilkinson and Thelwall (2012) found politics to be the third most tweeted about subject among English language tweets. By its sixth anniversary in 2012, Twitter users posted an average of 340 million tweets per day. The following year, the bastion of the English language, the Oxford English Dictionary, recognized tweet as part of the official lexicon, violating its own rule that a word be in use for ten years before its inclusion (Simpson 2013).

These short statements known as tweets are far from meaningless. Researchers have found that the content of tweets can be used to track spread of the flu (Cheng, Sun, Hu, and Zeng 2011), coordinate responses to national disasters (Bruns, Burgess, Crawford, and Shaw 2012; Cheong and Cheong 2011), help coordinate protests and share information during revolutions (Bruns, Highfield, and Burgess 2013; Eltantawy and Wiest 2011), and even predict the results of federal election results in Germany (Tumasjan et al. 2011). In the American political context, congressional challengers in 2010 who used Twitter to control information flow did better at the polls (Gainous and Wagner 2014) and campaign tweets that included url links helped predict victory (Parmelee and Bichard 2012). However, political Twitter use is not confined to candidates or elected officials. Twitter was a venue for expression about the 2011 gubernatorial elections (Bekafigo and McBride 2013), and it was also used by college students as a forum for expression about the Budget Repair Bill protests in Madison, Wisconsin in 2011 (Macafee and De Simone 2012). Twitter usage in all of these events was easily eclipsed by the number of tweets generated about the 2012 presidential election.

Young adults made up a disproportionate share of the 16% of Americans who used Twitter in 2012 (Duggan and Brenner 2013). They may also make up a disproportionate share of those who use it to tweet about politics. Bekafigo and McBride (2013) found that few who tweeted about politics were over age 40. However, not all young adults have a Twitter account and fewer students reported tweeting about politics in 2012 than did posting about politics. 45.84% of students in our Student Election Survey with a Twitter account reported having engaged in some level of tweeting about politics in 2012.[2] 13.47% reported doing so rarely, 11.46% reported doing so sometimes, 9.74% reported doing so regularly, and 11.17% reported doing so very often.

Compared to blogging about politics, tweeting about it may be lower in cost. After all, tweets are shorter, and should be less time consuming to write than longer posts. However, tweeting is still costlier than the more passive forms of participation of friending and following considered in the previous chapter. Both interest in politics and strength of partisanship are likely to encourage students to take to Twitter to share their political views. Finding politics interesting likely makes the costs associated with tweeting about politics seem more worthwhile. Also, to the extent that stronger partisanship is associated with heightened political interest, greater perceived stake in the election, and stronger political views, it is also likely to generate increased likelihood of tweeting about politics. Previous research into tweeting about the 2011 gubernatorial elections found that strength of partisanship predicted tweeting about politics (Bekafigo and McBride 2013). We expect the same pattern to be present during the 2012 presidential elections.

Students who tweet about politics also need raw material to trigger the contents of their tweets. While interest in politics or strong partisanship may make possessing this more likely, consuming other online sources of information also provides political information that could inspire a tweet. Reading online political news regularly during a presidential election means exposure to news about the current status of the "horse race." It may involve exposure to specific political issues, current happenings in Congress, or the outcome of the latest presidential debate. All of these can provide students material for future tweets. However, as discussed previously, many young adults seem to prefer blogs as a source of political information. Reading political blogs is also likely to foster tweeting about politics. After all, a synonym for tweeting is micro-blogging. Twitter offers a slightly lower cost method of responding to the information read on political blogs.

We also control for the same series of personal characteristics employed in the models in the previous chapter: issue importance variables, peer civic experiences, political science majors, military service, liberal and conservative, and Obama supporters. Of these, the only variables with slightly different expectations for explaining tweeting about politics are those involving ideology and candidate supported. Scholars have found a partisan imbalance in tweeting by members of Congress (Lawless 2012; Peterson 2012) that could also be reflected among college students. If so, it may result in a link between ideology and tweeting about politics with liberals less likely to tweet than conservatives.

Also, if Republican politicians adopt Twitter usage at a much higher rate than Democratic ones, this pattern could trickle down into their supporters as well. However, the behavior of the presidential candidates seems to be an exception to the rule since Obama Twitter followers outweighed Romney Twitter followers by more than 19:1 (Wortham 2012). This could make Obama supporters more likely to tweet about politics.

Finally, we add one additional variable to our model. Several studies suggest African Americans may be more likely to be Twitter users and particularly to tweet than members of other racial and ethnic groups (Bekafigo and McBride 2013; Duggan and Brenner 2013; Hargittai and Litt 2011). We test whether young African Americans are also more likely to tweet about politics in particular.[3] If so, Twitter is drawing in more students who might otherwise be unlikely to participate, as political scientists have consistently found differential participation patterns between whites and African Americans (see e.g., Dawson 1995, 2003; Hutchings and Valentino 2004; Walton 1985).

Table 5.2 presents the results of this ordered logit analysis. Model One provides the results of the full model while Model Two drops military service from the analysis.[4]

Table 5.2 Young Adults and Tweeting about Politics in 2012

	Tweeting about Politics (Model One)	*Odds Ratio (Model One)*	*Tweeting about Politics (Model Two)*	*Odds Ratio (Model Two)*
Issue Importance				
Economy	−0.07	0.94	−0.11	0.90
	(0.22)		(0.22)	
Education	0.14	1.15	0.14	1.15
	(0.24)		(0.24)	
Energy	−0.08	0.93	−0.10	0.90
	(0.19)		(0.18)	
College Financing	0.25	1.29	0.30	1.35
	(0.20)		(0.20)	
Health Care	−0.39*	0.68	−0.42*	0.66
	(0.17)		(0.17)	
Environment	0.06	1.06	0.06	1.06
	(0.18)		(0.18)	
Abortion	0.07	1.07	0.06	1.06
	(0.13)		(0.13)	
Immigration	−0.02	0.98	0.04	1.04
	(0.13)		(0.13)	
Same Sex Marriage	0.05	1.06	0.08	1.08
	(0.13)		(0.13)	
Information Consumption				
Internet News	0.12	1.13	0.14	1.15
	(0.16)		(0.15)	
Political Blogs	0.23*	1.25	0.22*	1.25
	(0.11)		(0.11)	
Respondent Characteristics				
Peer Civic Experiences	0.01	1.01	0.00	1.00
	(0.05)		(0.05)	
Political Science Major	−0.53	0.59	−0.40	0.67
	(0.59)		(0.59)	
Military	−15.23	–	–	—
	(709.99)			
Interest in Politics	0.96***	2.61	0.91***	2.48
	(0.24)		(0.24)	
Liberal	−0.88**	0.42	−0.87**	0.42
	(0.33)		(0.33)	
Conservative	−0.21	0.81	−0.21	0.81
	(0.40)		(0.40)	
Obama Supporter	0.29	1.34	0.30	1.35
	(0.34)		(0.34)	
Strong Partisan	1.18***	3.27	1.18***	3.26
	(0.28)		(0.28)	
African American	0.77*	2.16	0.83*	2.28
	(0.42)		(0.42)	
Cut Point One	2.74		2.68	
	(1.02)		(1.02)	
Cut Point Two	3.52		3.44	
	(1.03)		(1.03)	
Cut Point Three	4.37		4.28	
	(1.05)		(1.04)	
Cut Point Four	5.40		5.30	
	(1.07)		(1.06)	
N	269		269	
Log Likelihood	−324.38		−328.76	
Pseudo R^2	0.1367		0.1250	
Chi-Square	102.73		93.97	
Prob>Chi-Square	<0.0001		<0.0001	

Notes: The coefficients are ordered logit coefficients and the values in parenthesis are standard errors. * denotes $p < 0.05$, ** denotes $p < 0.01$, and *** denotes $p < 0.001$, all one-tailed tests.
Source: Moffett and Rice, Student Election Survey.

As the results show, both level of interest in politics and strength of partisanship was associated with tweeting at higher levels. In this respect, who tweets about politics resembles who traditionally participates, as well as who posted about politics in 2012. Each unit increase in one's level of interest in politics was associated with a 148% increase in the odds that favor higher levels of tweeting about politics. Meanwhile, strong partisans had a 226% increase in the odds that favor higher levels of tweeting about politics. The results also indicate that consuming higher levels of political blogs fosters higher levels of tweeting about politics but consuming internet news has no statistically significant effect. Each unit increase in the frequency of consuming political blogs resulted in a 25% increase in the odds that favor engaging in greater frequency of tweeting about politics.

While we did not find evidence that conservatives were more likely to tweet about politics than anyone else, the results do suggest that liberals are less likely to tweet about politics. Liberals have decreased odds of issuing a greater frequency of political tweets. Being a liberal is associated with a 58% decrease in the odds of doing so. Also, only one issue importance variable had a statistically significant relationship with tweeting about politics. Each unit increase in the importance of health care to vote choice was associated with a 44% drop in the odds that favor engaging in higher levels of tweeting about politics. This contrasts some with the pattern seen in Congress in the years leading up to the election where Republican members of Congress made more use of Twitter than Democrats and the most frequently tweeted about issue was health care (Lawless 2012).

We also confirmed that African American college students were more likely to tweet about politics. Being African American was associated with a 128% increase in the odds ratio that favors higher levels of tweeting. This is consistent with research on overall patterns of Twitter usage (Bekafigo and McBride 2013; Duggan and Brenner 2013; Hargittai and Litt 2011) but builds on it in an important way by establishing that young African Americans are also more likely to tweet about politics in particular. In this respect, Twitter appears to be helping to broaden who participates in politics. None of the other variables we examined had a statistically significant relationship with tweeting about politics.

BLOGGING AS A PATHWAY TO PARTICIPATION

Like friending and following, blogging appeals to those who care about politics. Strength of partisanship was associated with higher levels of blogging about politics in 2008 and 2012 and tweeting about politics in 2012. So was reading political blogs. However, while interest in politics fostered greater levels of blogging in 2012, it was actually associated with lower levels of blogging about politics in 2008. This provides strong evidence that blogging attracted those who would not otherwise participate in 2008. However, other characteristics usually associated with greater political participation, like majoring in political science or having more civically engaged friends, failed to explain engaging in these expressive forms of participation. This leaves room for the argument that these forms of participation appeal to those who might not otherwise participate.

We now perform a more nuanced analysis through making use of CLARIFY to compute the predicted probabilities of blogging about politics among avid political buffs and complete political novices.[5] This comparison helps identify the breadth of these forms of participations' appeal. We define an avid political buff as a respondent who reads political blogs very often, consumes online news very often, is highly interested in politics, is a political science major, and is a strong partisan. Figure 5.1 displays the predicted probabilities that political buffs, political novices, and those with average interest in politics engage in each level of posting or blogging in 2008 and 2012.

In 2008, avid political buffs had an 82% probability of engaging in some level of blogging or posting about politics. While they were most likely to report blogging about politics very often (a 31% predicted probability of doing so), they are not steadily more likely to engage in each greater level of activity, with a 18% predicted probability of doing so never, 15% of doing so rarely, 25% of doing so sometimes, and 11% of doing so regularly. In 2012, avid political buffs had a 93% probability of engaging in some level of blogging or posting about politics and only a 7% predicted probability of never posting. Their predicted probability of posting successively increased across most levels of activity with an 11% probability of posting rarely, a 25% probability of sometimes, a 24% probability of regularly, and a 32% probability of doing so very often. Overall, avid political buffs are highly likely to blog or post about politics, and they were more likely to blog or post about politics in 2012 than they were in 2008.

If young adults' familiarity with blogs helped attract those who would not normally participate, then complete political novices should have a nonzero likelihood of blogging about politics. Consistent with our definition in Chapter 4, a complete political novice is one who never reads political blogs, never consumes news online, is not at all interested in politics, is not a political science major, and is not a strong partisan. Complete political novices had a predicted probability of never posting of 73% in 2008 and 86% in 2012. In 2012 their predicted probability of engaging in each successive level of activity dropped, while in 2008 the probability of posting very often was a slight exception to this pattern. While complete political novices were not highly likely to engage in posting, they clearly had a nontrivial likelihood of doing

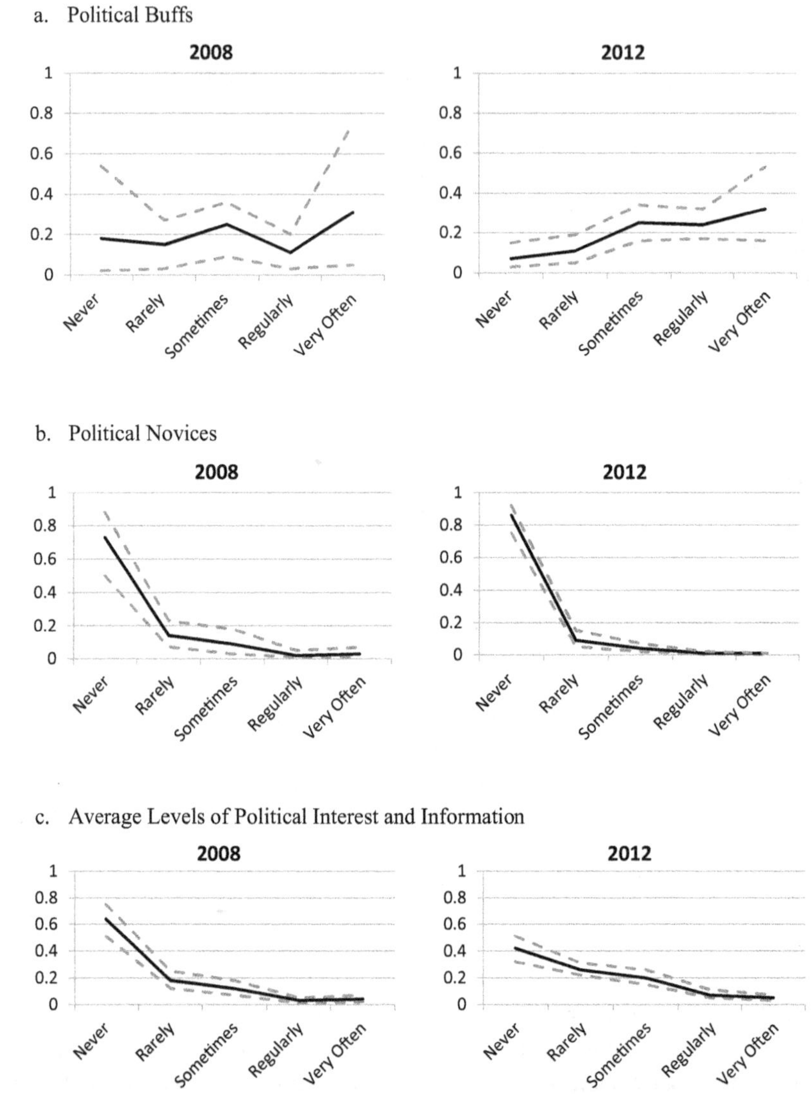

a. Political Buffs

b. Political Novices

c. Average Levels of Political Interest and Information

Figure 5.1 Blogging about Politics by Interest Level in Politics. *Source*: Moffett and Rice, Student Election Survey.

so that was stronger in 2008 than it was in 2012. This pattern of predicted probabilities is consistent with blogging and posting drawing young adults in who would not ordinarily participate.

However, the average young adult is neither an avid political buff nor a complete political novice. Thus, we consider the likelihood of those with average levels of interest in politics and average levels of information consumption engaging in blogging about politics. Students with average interest and information levels had a much greater likelihood of engaging in some level of posting about politics in 2012 than they did in 2008. In 2012, they had a 58% probability of engaging in some level of blogging or posting about politics, but in 2008 this probability was only 36%. Specifically, students with average interest and information levels in 2012 had a 42% probability of doing so never, a 26% probability of doing so rarely, a 20% probability of doing so sometimes, a 7% probability of doing so regularly, and a 5% probability of doing so very often. Their probabilities of doing so in 2008 were 64%, 18%, 12%, 3%, and 4%, respectively. Despite the difference across years, these probabilities suggest that a significant number of students with average interest and information levels were drawn to participate through expressing their views about politics online.

AFRICAN AMERICANS, INTEREST IN POLITICS, AND TWEETING ABOUT POLITICS

In the previous section, we found that the propensity to blog about politics depends on the level of interest in politics. In this chapter, though, we have uncovered a second significant finding that we should explore further: Twitter may help expand the participatory base by fostering tweets about politics among African American college students. We explore this finding by comparing levels of tweeting about politics in 2012 among African Americans and all other groups, at the different levels of interest in politics in the previous section (political buffs, political novices, and those with average levels of interest and information consumption). Figure 5.2 displays the results of this analysis.

African American avid political buffs had a 93% predicted probability of engaging in some level of tweeting about politics in 2012, with a 7% predicted probability of doing so rarely, a 13% probability of doing so sometimes, a 22% probability of doing so regularly and a 52% probability of doing so very often. Avid political buffs who are not African American had slightly lower predicted probabilities of tweeting about politics, with an 85% predicted probability of doing so at some level. More specifically, they had a 11% predicted probability of doing so rarely, an 18% predicted probability of doing so sometimes, a 23% probability of doing so regularly, and a 33% probability of doing so very often.

African Americans who were complete political novices had an 80% predicted probability of never tweeting about politics in 2012 and a 20% predicted probability of engaging in some level of tweeting about politics, with a 9% probability of doing so rarely, a 6% probability of doing so sometimes, a 3% probability of doing so regularly, and a 2% probability of doing so very often. Other complete political novices had a 90% probability of never tweeting about politics and only a 10% predicted probability of

a. Political Buffs

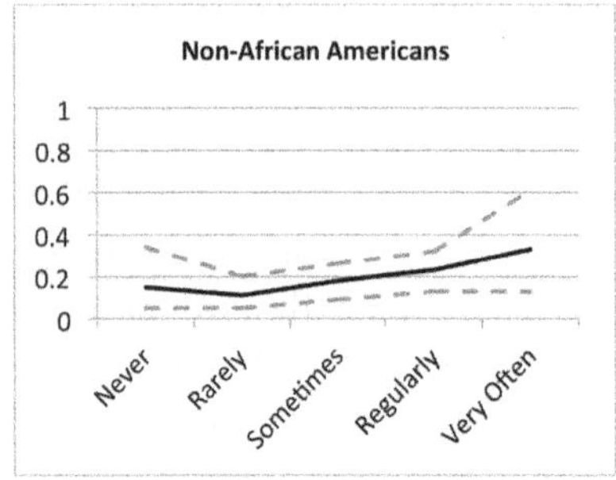

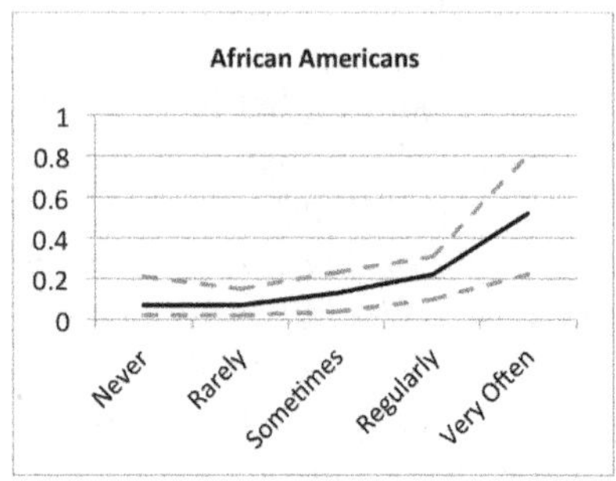

b. Political Novices

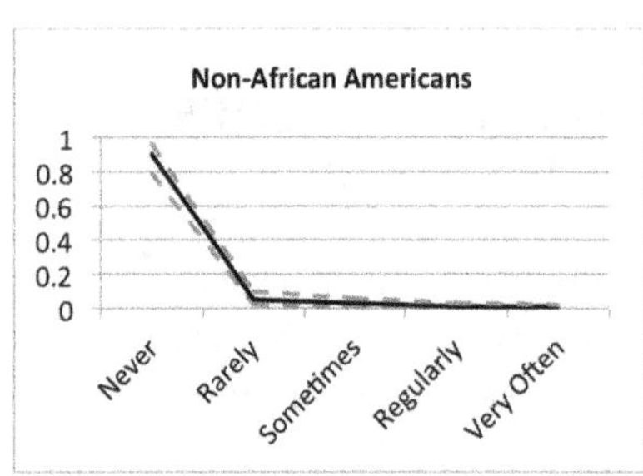

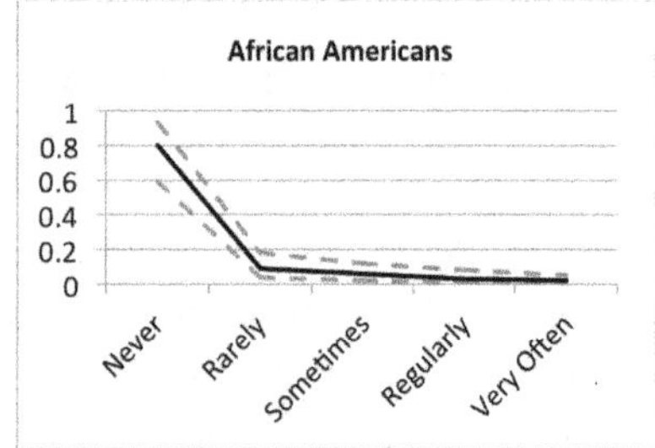

c. Average Political Interest and Information Consumption

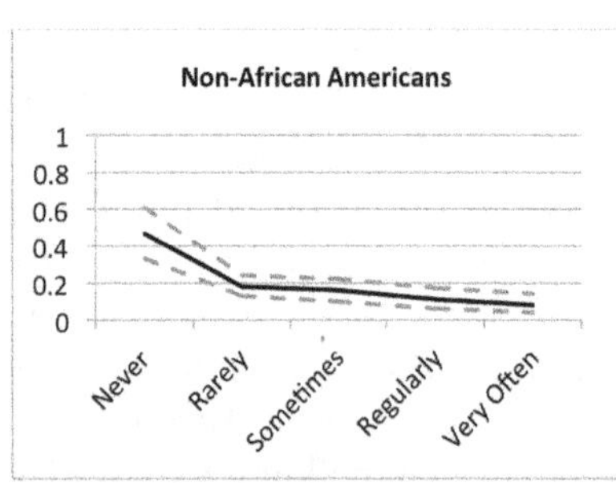

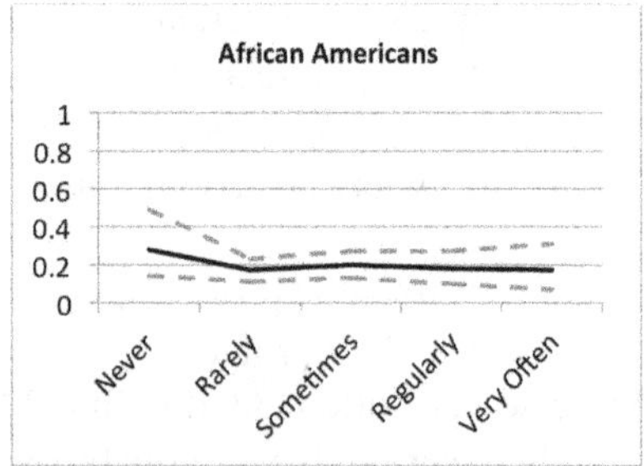

Figure 5.2 Tweeting about Politics among African Americans by Interest Level in Politics. *Source*: Moffett and Rice, Student Election Survey.

engaging in some level of tweeting about politics, with a 5% probability of doing so rarely, a 3% probability of doing so sometimes, and a 1% probability of doing so regularly or very often. While the odds of never tweeting about politics were very high for complete political novices, they did have some chance of tweeting about politics, particularly if they were African Americans. The results leave at least some room for some complete political novices to be drawn to participate through Twitter.

The evidence also suggests that Twitter drew in a significant number of students with average levels of interest and information. African Americans with Twitter accounts and average levels of interest and information consumption had a 72% predicted probability of engaging in some level of tweeting about politics, with a 28% probability of doing so never, a 17% probability of doing so rarely, a 20% probability of doing so sometimes, an 18% probability of doing so regularly and a 17% probability of doing so very often. Members of other race and ethnic groups with average levels of interest and information consumption had a 53% predicted probability of engaging in some level of tweeting about politics, with a 47% probability of doing so never, an 18% probability of doing so rarely, a 16% probability of doing so sometimes, an 11% probability of doing so regularly, and an 8% probability of doing so very often. Altogether, those with Twitter accounts and average levels of interest and information were more likely than not to tweet about politics.

CONCLUSION

The odds are overwhelmingly in favor of avid political buffs blogging, posting, and tweeting about politics and they are overwhelmingly against complete political novices engaging in these activities. While those with higher levels of interest and information seem more willing to pay the costs of political expression, the analysis presented in this chapter reveals that they are not the only ones who do so. Even complete political novices with Twitter accounts have anywhere between a 10 and 20% chance of engaging in some level of tweeting about politics. Complete political novices also have between a 14 and 27% chance of blogging or posting about politics. These odds, while small, are clearly nonzero. More importantly, considerable evidence suggests that the typical college student is likely to engage in political expression. We found that the odds are stacked in favor of those students who have average levels of political interest and information consumption and Twitter accounts using them to tweet about politics. The odds also favor those with average levels of interest and information posting about politics, especially in 2012.

When students, regardless of their interest or information levels, decide to blog or tweet about politics, this indicates the presence of some level of political efficacy. Whether opinions are well-grounded in facts or not, sharing them requires a certain amount of self-confidence. The decision to post one's views about politics online may build the confidence necessary to branch out into other less familiar forms of political participation. In Chapter 6, we explore how engaging in political uses of friending, following, posting, and tweeting can lead to engaging in other more traditional offline forms of participation.

NOTES

1. These scholars also disagree about whether there is a gender bias in political blog readership. Lewis (2011) found that blog readers are more likely to be male while Lawrence et al. (2010) found no difference in political blog reading based on gender. We found no evidence that gender is related to whether college students blog about politics.

2. We did not ask about Twitter in 2008.

3. When this variable was included in each of our previous models in prior chapters, it was not significant and had no effect on the signs or significance of other variables in the model. In light of this and a lack of theoretical expectations that race or ethnicity should help explain other forms of political expression, we chose to only include it in our model of tweeting about politics.

4. There was insufficient variation when this independent variable was included resulting in six fully determined observations and questionable standard errors. Thus, all of the results discussed below are for Model Two.

5. To compute these predicted probabilities, we hold friends' civic experiences and issue priorities at the mean, and military service, liberal, and conservative at a value of zero. Since candidate supported was not statistically significant, the figures displayed are for Obama supporters.

Chapter 6

Going Offline? Online Participation's Mobilizing Effects

If young adults with limited interest in politics are going to participate, the costs of doing so need to be sufficiently low to entice them in. For young adults who grew up in an online era, online forms of political participation may carry lower costs than traditional forms. Participating through online means does not require learning new technological skills, it simply requires extending them into the realm of politics. We found in previous chapters that while political buffs with the highest levels of preexisting interest in politics are still most likely to engage in online political activity, they are not the only ones who do so. For that matter, even complete political novices had nontrivial likelihoods of engaging in this form of political activity. Once they do, they may discover they have more interest than previously thought and pursue additional opportunities, with greater entry fees, to further this new-found interest. Further, they may also now receive invitations to participate via other, otherwise more costly means. Thus, participating in the online world may make participation in the offline world both more appealing and more accessible.

In the analyses throughout this chapter, we examine whether online participatory forms constitute "slacktivism" (see e.g., Morozov 2009), or whether these participatory forms also lead into the offline world. We begin by reviewing prior research on the movement of online participation offline and establish why friending and following are likely to offer different pathways to offline participation than would blogging and tweeting. Then, we revisit the model of offline engagement presented in Chapter 3 and expand it to include political usages of friending, following, blogging, and tweeting. We also consider how each of these forms of online engagement may lead to use of others and whether offline engagement might also produce greater online participation.

PREVIOUS RESEARCH AND MOVING OFFLINE

Previous research has focused more on whether online participation leads to offline participation than why and while it generally finds one form of online participation leads to other forms of online participation (Baumgartner and Morris 2010; Best and Kruger 2005; de Zuniga, Puig-i-abril, and Rojas 2009; Vitak et al. 2011), it is divided over whether greater online engagement leads to greater participation in the offline world. Informational uses of the internet have frequently been found to lead to greater levels of participation (Kenski and Stroud 2006; Norris 1998; Shah et al. 2001, 2005; Min 2007; Tolbert and McNeal 2003; Towner 2013; Towner and Dulio 2011), as has online discussion (Shah et al. 2005). However, Best and Kruger (2005) found that attempts at online mobilization failed to successfully extend to offline participation.

Previous research also reflects some disparity in findings with respect to the types of online participation that lead to greater offline participation. In a study comparing the mobilizing impact of a wide range of information sources, Towner (2013) found that those who paid more attention to information about the campaign for president on Twitter were more likely to participate offline at higher rates while attention paid to the campaign on Facebook failed to exert a statistically significant effect on offline participation. Supporting concerns about slacktivism, Baumgartner and Morris (2010) also discovered that social networking users were no more likely to participate than users of other media. However, Vitak et al. (2011) found that political uses of Facebook were associated with greater levels of offline participation, and Rice, Moffett, and Madupalli (2013) found that those who joined campaign-related social networks were more likely to engage in greater offline participation.

The research literature on blog use also provides conflicting conclusions. De Zuniga et al. (2009) and Towner (2013) found that blog use promoted online participation but failed to generate greater offline participation while Kenski and Stroud (2006) and Lawrence et al. (2010) found that political blog readers participated offline at higher rates. Although there has been less study of political bloggers, those who cite extrinsic motivations as reasons for blogging have been found to be more likely to participate offline at higher rates (Ekdale, Namkoong, and Fung 2010). Given these conflicting findings, it is particularly important to establish why specific forms of online participation are not simply slacktivism and should be expected to lead to greater offline participation.

FRIENDING AND FOLLOWING AS PATHWAYS TO OFFLINE PARTICIPATION

In some respects, who friends and who follows strongly reflect those already more likely to participate. After all, we found that strong partisans are more likely to engage in both activities and interest in politics predicts both activities in 2012 but not friending in 2008. We also discovered slightly different precursors to friending and following. Different issue priorities drove involvement across activities and years. Also, a number of characteristics were associated with greater friending in 2008, 2012, or both election years but not with greater following, such as political blog readership, intending to vote for Obama, or peer civic experiences.

While who friends and who follows vary some, we found in Chapter 4 that both have similarly low costs that draw in some young adults who might not otherwise participate. Depending on candidate supported, complete political novices had roughly a 12% to 28% chance of engaging in some level of political friending in 2008 and about a 6% chance in 2012. Further, complete political novices who had Twitter accounts in 2012 had between a 4.6% and 6.1% chance, depending on candidate supported, of following political Twitter feeds. Meanwhile, those with average levels of political interest and information had between a 26.3% and a 53.8% chance of engaging in these activities, depending on the candidate supported and the year.

Friending and following are activities of similar low cost to college students. Young adults are most likely to already have the social networking accounts necessary to engage in these activities and once they do, expanding one's social network to include candidates, political parties, and other political groups requires little more than the click of a mouse or a tap on a smartphone or tablet. Deciding to friend or follow candidates results in exposure to campaign-related information and can include appeals for further action. In 2008 connecting with candidates via Facebook opened the door to invitations to participate in other activities, both online and offline. By Election Day these went out to at least 2 million Obama supporters and 600,000 supporters of McCain (Dutta and Fraser 2008). Young adults were disproportionately likely to be on Facebook, thus bringing these opportunities for mobilization to a group of people historically less likely to participate in politics (Rice, Moffett, and Madupalli 2013).

By 2012 these appeals had broader reach. With a little over a month to go before the election, Obama had amassed over 28.8 million likes while Romney attracted nearly 7.2 million (Felix 2012). Use of Facebook in the campaign grew increasingly sophisticated as well. In 2012, the Obama campaign built on its 2008 Facebook success and developed a Facebook app that, when downloaded, gave the Obama campaign access to one's friend list and resulted in requests from the campaign for the user to share appeals for registration, votes, campaign contributions, and other forms of activity with specific friends (Scherer 2012).

Both campaigns took to Twitter as well. By late September 2012, Obama had gathered nearly 20 million followers on Twitter and Romney had a little under 1.2 million (Felix 2012). The Obama campaign in particular issued appeals to register to vote via Twitter that were targeted at specific states and voter groups and issued requests to retweet campaign appeals or otherwise share information with friends (Twitter 2015). While his opponents' Facebook and Twitter efforts may not have been quite as developed or sophisticated, appeals for votes were common on both candidates' Facebook pages in 2012 (Groshek and Al-Rawi 2013) and previous research reveals that those who receive appeals to vote via Facebook are more likely to vote (Scherer 2012; Bond et al. 2012). This suggests that appeals for other forms of offline involvement issued via Facebook or Twitter may also make friends or followers more likely to engage in these activities.

Appeals for action lower the cost of offline engagement and increase the accessibility of these forms of involvement. In Rosenstone and Hansen's (1993) landmark study, one of the chief reasons they uncovered for lack of electoral participation was "nobody asks." However, campaign-related social networking can change this for young adults. The decision to follow or friend can open the door to numerous invitations and requests for help. Those who reported some level of friending or joining in our 2008 pre-election Student Election Survey were more than twice as likely to report in our post-election survey that they had "been contacted by someone personally to work for or contribute money to a candidate, political party, or any other organization that supports candidates" since October 1, 2008 than those who did not engage in campaign-related social networking. In 2012, those who friended were more than three times more likely to report both being personally contacted and being contacted online since October 1, 2012 than those who did not friend.[1] Those who followed political Twitter feeds of presidential candidates, political parties or other politically-oriented groups were more than twice as likely to report both being personally contacted and being contacted online to work for or contribute money to a candidate, party, or other organization that supports candidates since October 1, 2012 than those who did not use their Twitter accounts to follow politics.

Invitations issued via social networking also supply the information needed to participate. Instead of having to seek out information about how to register to vote, where to get a campaign button or sign, how to volunteer for a political campaign or donate money, or when and where the next political party meeting or campaign rally will be, this information may appear in the tweets or posts someone signs up to receive. These recipients may not have been seeking out these opportunities or invitations, but they begin to come to them nonetheless. Suddenly, the offline political world becomes more accessible and less mysterious.

Other information supplied in Facebook posts or tweets may spark greater interest in the campaign, increasing the desire to get involved in other ways. Perhaps a campaign post or tweet focuses on an issue some of its readers find particularly important. While they do not care much for politics, they may care a lot about same sex marriage, energy policy, or college financing. When the campaigns speak out about these issues via Facebook or Twitter, suddenly the outcome of the election may become more important in these readers' eyes. They may now have a desire to participate that they previously lacked.

Social networking sites also foster a sense of personal connection with candidates (Twitter 2015). Instead of seeing candidates as distant talking heads that appear periodically on television, social media more easily results in personal attachments with candidates. Seeing a candidate as a "friend" rather than just someone who wants your vote, may mobilize followers to take action to help get them where they want to be. After all, friends in need of help may more readily inspire taking costly, otherwise unappealing action than strangers would.

BLOGGING AND TWEETING AS PATHWAYS TO OFFLINE PARTICIPATION

Like friending and following, we found that who blogs and tweets about politics also bears some resemblance to who is already more likely to participate. However, while friending and following focus on messages received, blogging and tweeting involve messages expressed. Strong partisans were more likely to express their political views online, as were those who read political blogs more frequently. Although greater interest in politics was associated with greater levels of both forms of online political expression in 2012, in 2008, greater interest in politics was associated with lower levels of blogging about politics. Different issues prompted young adults to take their political views online across the two election years. The two activities also had a few varying precursors—African Americans were more likely to tweet about politics but no more likely to blog about politics than others while liberals were less likely to tweet about politics in 2012 but no less likely to blog about it than others.

While who blogs about politics and who tweets about politics vary some, they share similarities as expressive forms of participation. We found evidence in Chapter 5 that this online political expression is not just confined to those with high stakes or interest in politics. Complete political novices had a predicted probability of engaging in some level of posting of 27% in 2008 and 14% in 2012. Further, complete political novices, depending on ethnicity, had between a 10% and 20% predicted probability of engaging in some level of tweeting about politics. Meanwhile, students with average interest and information levels had, depending on the year, between a 36% and 58% chance of engaging in some level of blogging or posting about politics. And, in 2012, those with twitter accounts and average levels of interest and information had, depending on ethnicity, between a 53% and 72% predicted probability of engaging in some level of tweeting about politics. A number of young adults who might not otherwise be predisposed to participate in politics take their political views online during presidential elections.

Expressive forms of participation offer a different potential pathway to greater offline participation. Taking the step of sharing one's political views online may help boost political efficacy. As young adults begin to share their political views online, they may gain confidence in their ability to both understand and influence politics. If so, this mirrors the progression among some of America's most popular political bloggers. In Ekdale et al.'s (2010) study of popular political bloggers, they found that bloggers who started out with intrinsic motivations for blogging like organizing one's thoughts or letting off steam became increasingly motivated over time by extrinsic motivations like influencing others and boosting a party or cause (Ekdale et al. 2010). Other research suggests this effect is not limited to those with wide audiences. Experiments suggest that when online political expression is part of an online deliberative conversation, it can boost both political efficacy and participation (Min 2007).

In Table 6.1, we provide some support for the argument that blogging and tweeting boosts efficacy. While we did not ask about efficacy in our Student Election Surveys conducted prior to the elections, we did ask those completing a brief post-election survey multiple questions about efficacy. From that we create an index adding together their answers for seven different measures of efficacy ($\alpha = 0.77$ for 2008 and $\alpha = 0.76$ for 2012). These add together how strongly they agreed with each of three statements "I feel that I have a pretty good understanding of the important political issues facing our country," "I consider myself well-qualified to participate in politics," and "I think that I am better informed about politics and government than most people," and how strongly they disagree with four statements "My vote doesn't matter," "Public officials don't care much what people like me think," "People like me don't have any say about what the government does," and "Sometimes politics and government seem so complicated that a person like me can't really understand what's going on." The minimum possible score for this index of efficacy is seven and the maximum possible score is 35.

Table 6.1, compares the averages of the answers given by those who said they blogged or tweeted about politics in the Student Election Survey conducted prior to the election (those who did so early), those who never blogged or tweeted about politics at all, and those who had not posted or tweeted in the pre-election survey but posted or tweeted just prior to the election (those who did so late). We expect that those who blog or tweet will have greater efficacy than those who do not. However, if blogging and tweeting increases

Table 6.1 Efficacy and Online Political Expression

	2008		2012	
Form of Expression	*N*	*Mean Efficacy Score*	*N*	*Mean Efficacy Score*
Timing of Blogging Activity				
Never	108	23.43	156	22.65
Early	74	26.66	246	25.81
Late	14	25.21	21	23.91
Timing of Tweeting				
Never	–	–	112	22.92
Early	–	–	104	26.44
Late	–	–	15	23.53

Source: Moffett and Rice, Student Election Survey

efficacy then those who blogged or tweeted late should have greater efficacy scores than those who never did so at all.

The results suggest that online political expression increased efficacy and confirm that those who engage in online expression possess greater efficacy than those who do not. A number of studies have linked higher levels of political efficacy to greater levels of participation through traditional offline forms (see e.g., Rosenstone and Hansen 1993; Verba et al. 1995). More specifically, college students with greater efficacy have been found to be more civically and politically engaged (Zukin et al. 2006). Thus, to the extent posting one's views online via blogs or Twitter helps increase efficacy, as it did for America's most popular political bloggers (Ekdale et al. 2010), it should help foster greater offline participation as well.

ASSESSING MOVEMENT OFFLINE

Having established why we might expect friending, following, blogging, and tweeting to all increase offline participation, we now test whether this is true. Table 6.2 adds these online activities to the model of offline engagement presented in Chapter 3.

Through the analysis contained in Table 6.2, we discovered very limited support for the importance of issues. Once we considered the varying internet-based ways by which college students can engage, we discovered no evidence that the importance of the economy, energy policy, college financing, health care, the environment, abortion, immigration, and same sex marriage affected offline engagement. We only found evidence that views on education increased civic engagement, as in 2008, each unit increase in the importance with which one viewed education yielded an increase of 1.14 units in civic activity. Put differently, going from assigning education no

Table 6.2 Effects of Online Modes of Engagement on Offline Civic Activity

Independent Variable	*2008*	*2012*
Online Civic Activity		
Friending and Joining	1.57***	1.62***
	(0.24)	(0.36)
Blogging	1.43***	–0.05
	(0.29)	(0.37)
Following on Twitter	–	0.50
		(0.36)
Tweeting about Politics	–	0.81*
		(0.38)
Issue Importance		
Economy	–0.24	–0.59
	(0.52)	(0.70)
Education	1.14*	–0.86
	(0.54)	(0.75)
Energy	0.40	0.35
	(0.47)	(0.56)
College Financing	–0.61	0.55
	(0.41)	(0.58)
Health Care	0.16	–0.19
	(0.41)	(0.55)
Environment	–0.27	–0.31
	(0.44)	(0.52)
Abortion	–0.06	0.003
	(0.33)	(0.38)
Immigration	–0.23	0.36
	(0.35)	(0.40)
Same Sex Marriage	0.06	0.42
	(0.29)	(0.40)
Information Consumption		
Internet News	0.59*	0.02
	(0.32)	(0.47)
Political Blogs	–0.002	0.54
	(0.33)	(0.35)
Respondent Characteristics		
Peer Civic Experiences	0.36*	0.57**
	(0.15)	(0.16)
Political Science Major	4.20**	8.09***
	(1.63)	(1.99)
Military	1.91	5.06*
	(1.35)	(2.44)
Interest in Politics	–1.25**	0.70
	(0.49)	(0.71)
Liberal	0.01	0.10
	(0.79)	(0.97)
Conservative	–1.07	0.06
	(0.95)	(1.20)
Obama Supporter	–0.63	0.53
	(0.81)	(0.98)
Strong Partisan	0.64	–1.13
	(0.71)	(0.91)
Constant	2.86	0.63
	(3.14)	(3.03)
N	278	243
R^2	0.54	0.48
Adjusted R^2	0.51	0.42
F-Statistic	14.51	8.63
Prob>F-Statistic	<0.0001	<0.0001
Standard Error of the Estimate	4.82	5.65

Notes: The coefficients are OLS coefficients and the values in parenthesis are standard errors. * denotes $p < 0.05$, ** denotes $p < 0.01$, and *** denotes $p < 0.001$, all one-tailed tests.
Source: Moffett and Rice, Student Election Survey.

importance to assigning it a maximal level of importance increases offline civic activity by approximately 5 points (or one additional activity that was not performed at all, but now, performed very often).

Similarly, we uncovered limited evidence that information consumption affected offline civic activity, but more evidence that respondent characteristics affected these activities. We discovered that the frequency with which one reads political blogs, ideology, being a supporter of Barack Obama, or self-identifying as a strong partisan did not affect offline civic activity. However, we found that those who read news online on a regular basis were more likely to be engaged offline in 2008, as each unit increase in online news readership is connected with a 0.58 point increase in offline civic activity. If a person shifted from never reading news online to doing so very often in 2008, s/he should be expected to have a two point increase in his or her offline civic activity (or, going from never performing an activity to doing it sometimes). In addition, those who are or were currently in the military are connected with a 5.06 point increase in offline civic activity in 2012. During this year, members of the military should be anticipated to have performed an additional offline civic activity that was otherwise not performed very often, *and* a higher level of frequency with an additional activity than their nonmilitary counterparts.

We discovered our strongest, most consistent evidence for the effects of two respondent characteristics: peer civic experiences and being a political science major. Each unit increase in peer civic experiences is connected with between a 0.36 and 0.57 point increase in offline civic activity. Put differently, a shift from peers who are never engaged (nor encourage it) to those who encourage all forms of engagement as much as possible is associated with an increase in offline civic activity of between 4.27 and 6.80 points. At a minimum, this shift results in an additional activity that was not performed to now being performed very often.

Not surprisingly, being a political science major results in higher levels of offline civic activity. We found that being a political science major is connected with an increase in offline civic activity by between 4.2 and 8.09 additional points. Those who become political science majors are expected to engage in between one and two additional offline activities very often. Equally important, these activities would otherwise not have been performed. This is not surprising in that political science majors choose this major because of an innate interest in government and politics, and the opportunities that it provides in terms of engaging in a wide variety of civic activities.

Online Activities and Offline Engagement

We turn now to the main question we set out to answer: does engaging in various online forms of activity lead to greater offline engagement? We theorized two different routes to greater offline participation—one through the more passive forms of friending and following and the other through the more expressive forms of blogging and tweeting. In Table 6.2, we found evidence that both routes can be connected with increased offline engagement. More specifically, we found that each unit increase in friending and joining activity is connected with between a 1.57 and 1.62 point increase in offline civic activity. If we shifted from never friending to friending very often, we would expect to see an additional activity being performed very often (that otherwise would not be performed at all), *and* a second activity being performed sometimes, when it would not have occurred. This clearly suggests that friending can serve as a pathway to greater offline engagement.

We also discovered that those who tweeted about politics during 2012 were also more likely to engage in higher levels of offline activity. More specifically, each unit increase in tweeting about politics is connected with a 0.81 point increase in offline civic activity. If one went from never having tweeted about politics to performing this activity very often, s/he would be expected to have about a 3.2 point increase in his or her offline civic activity index. This is the equivalent of shifting from rarely performing an offline civic activity to doing that same activity very often. Tweeting also appears to offer a pathway to greater offline participation.

Yet, we discovered inconsistent evidence that blogging is connected with higher levels of offline engagement. In 2008, we found that each unit increase in blogging resulted in an increase in offline civic activity of 1.43 points. Yet, in 2012, this effect evaporated, as we uncovered no statistically significant connection between offline civic activity and blogging. It is possible that the rise of Twitter between 2008 and 2012 changed the ways in which those who blogged now engage. We suspect that some of these same people shifted their online expressive activity from blogging to tweeting about politics.[2] Finally, we found no relationship between following politicians or political parties on Twitter and offline civic activity. One form of passive online participation—friending—has a strong positive relationship with offline engagement while following does not. Both forms of expressive online participation have strong positive relationships with offline engagement in at least one year. However, of the online activities we studied in both 2008 and 2012, only friending and not blogging has a consistent, positive, and significant relationship with offline engagement.

While these results demonstrate that online civic activities can yield higher levels of offline civic activity, they do come with a few caveats. In particular, we have yet to establish a causal direction of the relationship between these online and offline activities. The causal arrow could potentially run from online to offline, from offline to online, or in both directions. While many of the online activities have significant, positive relationships with offline engagement (which we uncovered in Table 6.2) one can ask whether online activity has a causal relationship with offline activity or whether higher levels of offline activities lead to additional online activities. This caveat is significant because our theories only receive confirmation if other, alternative causal arrow directions have been ruled out. For example, if we discover that the causal arrow provides a stronger indicator that offline activities cause online activities (rather than the converse), then this raises real questions about our main theoretical arguments and the results that have been obtained to this point.

Second, we have yet to disentangle how the different online activities may be connected to each other. This question is important because answering it allows us to investigate one of the stated aims of this book: to discover how civic activities relate to one another. Up until Table 6.2, we have examined online activities in a largely *ad seriatum* manner. Now that we have unveiled these results, we need to press further on them by determining, to the extent possible, how online activities relate to one another.

The remainder of this chapter is devoted to beginning to address both of these caveats. We start by addressing one aspect of the first one: is there also evidence that engaging in offline activity is associated with higher levels of online forms of civic activity? Then, we begin to address the second caveat: how do the online activities connect with one another? By addressing these caveats, we seek to accomplish two goals. First, we hope to unravel the relationships between these different variables to determine how they work together. Second, we hope to generate some unique findings that allow us to speak to the different scholarly debates about offline, and especially, online civic activity. It is to these tasks that we now turn.

ONLINE AND OFFLINE CIVIC ACTIVITIES

The results in Table 6.2 seemingly indicate that online activities can lead to offline engagement. However, they do not eliminate the possibility that offline engagement leads to higher levels of online activities. To investigate this, we need to examine whether offline engagement, as an independent variable, has positive relationships with each of the online forms of participation as dependent variables, while controlling for the remaining independent variables that were used in Table 6.2. To begin such an analysis, we used each of our online variables as separate dependent variables, and controlled for all of the remaining independent variables that were a part of the model in Table 6.2. Thus, friending and joining activity, blogging, and the two Twitter-based activities are each dependent variables in separate models. Where applicable, we have included models for 2008 and 2012 as well.

Table 6.3 Online and Offline Civic Engagement in 2008 and 2012

	Friending and Joining Activity				*Blogging*							
Independent Variable	*2008*	*Odds Ratio*	*2012*	*Odds Ratio*	*2008*	*Odds Ratio*	*2012*	*Odds Ratio*	*Following on Twitter (2012)*	*Odds Ratio*	*Tweeting (2012)*	*Odds Ratio*
Civic Activity												
Friending and Joining	–	–	–	–	0.32**	1.37	0.51***	1.67	0.23*	1.25	–0.09	0.91
					(0.12)		(0.12)		(0.13)		(0.14)	
Blogging	0.32**	1.38	0.58***	1.78	–	–	–	–	–0.20	0.82	0.65***	1.91
	(0.12)		(0.13)						(0.14)		(0.14)	
Following on Twitter	–	–	0.12	1.13	–	–	–0.18	0.84	–	–	0.84***	2.33
			(0.13)				(0.13)				(0.13)	
Tweeting about Politics	–	–	0.003	1.00	–	–	0.70***	2.01	0.94***	2.55	–	–
			(0.13)				(0.13)		(0.14)			
Offline Civic Engagement	0.14***	1.15	0.10***	1.10	0.13***	1.13	–0.01	0.99	0.03	1.03	0.08**	1.08
	(0.03)		(0.02)		(0.03)		(0.02)		(0.03)		(0.03)	
Issue Importance												
Economy	0.13	1.14	–0.35	0.71	0.15	1.16	0.27	1.31	–0.13	0.88	0.02	1.02
	(0.23)		(0.28)		(0.25)		(0.24)		(0.25)		(0.25)	
Education	–0.32	0.73	0.09	1.09	0.08	1.08	0.61**	1.84	–0.06	0.95	–0.04	0.96
	(0.23)		(0.27)		(0.26)		(0.26)		(0.27)		(0.28)	
Energy	0.15	1.17	0.42*	1.52	–0.16	0.86	–0.10	0.91	–0.17	0.84	–0.13	0.88
	(0.20)		(0.20)		(0.23)		(0.19)		(0.20)		(0.21)	
College Financing	0.12	1.12	0.10	1.10	0.09	1.09	–0.49**	0.61	0.23	1.26	0.16	1.17
	(0.18)		(0.21)		(0.21)		(0.20)		(0.22)		(0.23)	
Health Care	–0.02	0.98	0.11	1.12	–0.22	0.80	–0.30	0.74	–0.29	0.75	–0.08	0.92
	(0.18)		(0.20)		(0.20)		(0.19)		(0.18)		(0.20)	
Environment	–0.03	0.97	0.11	1.11	0.10	1.10	–0.24	0.79	0.17	1.19	0.11	1.12
	(0.19)		(0.19)		(0.22)		(0.18)		(0.19)		(0.21)	
Abortion	–0.08	0.92	–0.16	0.86	–0.15	0.86	0.11	1.12	0.14	1.15	–0.03	0.97
	(0.14)		(0.13)		(0.16)		(0.13)		(0.14)		(0.14)	
Immigration	–0.01	0.99	–0.0002	1.00	0.12	1.13	0.19	1.21	0.10	1.11	–0.16	0.85
	(0.15)		(0.15)		(0.16)		(0.15)		(0.15)		(0.15)	
Same Sex Marriage	0.18	1.20	–0.22	0.80	0.17	1.19	0.27*	1.31	–0.27*	0.76	0.003	1.00
	(0.13)		(0.14)		(0.15)		(0.14)		(0.15)		(0.15)	

Information Consumption												
Internet News	0.20	1.22	–0.02	0.98	–0.29*	0.75	0.30*	1.36	0.29*	1.33	–0.088	0.92
	(0.13)		(0.18)		(0.17)		(0.16)		(0.17)		(0.17)	
Political Blogs	–0.01	0.99	0.06	1.06	1.07***	2.92	0.12	1.13	–0.02	0.98	0.04	1.04
	(0.13)		(0.12)		(0.15)		(0.12)		(0.13)		(0.13)	
Respondent Characteristics												
Peer Civic	0.02	1.02	0.05	1.05	–0.07	0.93	–0.03	0.98	0.06	1.06	–0.05	0.95
Experiences	(0.07)		(0.06)		(0.07)		(0.06)		(0.06)		(0.06)	
Political Science	0.83	2.29	–0.25	0.78	–1.27*	0.28	–0.05	0.95	–0.89	0.41	–1.09	0.34
Major	(0.69)		(0.70)		(0.68)		(0.71)		(0.76)		(0.83)	
Military	–0.19	0.83	–0.52	0.60	–1.45*	0.24	0.31	1.36	0.17	1.19	-17.65	2.17*10-8
	(0.53)		(1.03)		(0.69)		(0.85)		(0.84)		(1252.90)	
Interest in Politics	0.21	1.23	0.51*	1.67	–0.52*	0.60	0.07	1.08	0.71**	2.04	0.19	1.21
	(0.21)		(0.28)		(0.24)		(0.26)		(0.27)		(0.27)	
Liberal	0.14	1.15	0.43	1.54	–0.08	0.93	0.26	1.29	0.06	1.06	–0.93**	0.39
	(0.33)		(0.34)		(0.37)		(0.33)		(0.35)		(0.37)	
Conservative	0.64	1.90	0.35	1.42	–0.40	0.67	–0.17	0.85	–0.29	0.75	0.31	1.36
	(0.40)		(0.44)		(0.43)		(0.42)		(0.43)		(0.44)	
Obama Supporter	1.20***	3.31	–0.50	0.61	–0.49	0.62	0.04	1.04	0.22	1.21	0.53	1.71
	(0.37)		(0.37)		(0.39)		(0.35)		(0.37)		(0.39)	
Strong Partisan	0.62*	1.86	0.82**	2.28	0.32	1.38	–0.09	0.92	0.65*	1.92	0.58*	1.78
	(0.29)		(0.31)		(0.32)		(0.32)		(0.32)		(0.33)	
Cut Point One	4.04***		3.48**		1.28		2.34*		2.67*		1.86	
	(1.36)		(1.17)		(1.51)		(1.08)		(1.15)		(1.15)	
Cut Point Two	4.72***		4.54***		2.37		3.57**		3.48**		2.90**	
	(1.37)		(1.18)		(1.52)		(1.09)		(1.15)		(1.16)	
Cut Point Three	5.78***		6.19***		3.79*		5.08***		5.04***		4.19***	
	(1.38)		(1.22)		(1.53)		(1.11)		(1.18)		(1.19)	
Cut Point Four	7.22***		7.20***		4.39***		6.31***		6.30***		5.63***	
	(1.41)		(1.25)		(1.54)		(1.14)		(1.21)		(1.22)	
N	278		243		278		243		243		243	
Log Likelihood	–317.96		–261.07		–254.17		–283.95		–260.58		–242.63	
Pseudo R-Squared	0.189		0.227		0.262		0.212		0.254		0.280	
Chi-Square	148.28		153.05		180.32		152.68		177.58		188.76	
Prob>Chi-Square	<0.0001		<0.0001		<0.0001		<0.0001		<0.0001		<0.0001	

Notes: The coefficients are ordered logistic regression coefficients and the values in parenthesis are standard errors. *denotes $p < .05$, **denotes $p < .01$, and ***denotes $p < .001$, all one-tailed tests.

Our primary independent variables in these models are the remaining online forms of civic activity. In our blogging model, for instance, the primary independent variables are friending and joining activity, following on Twitter and Tweeting. In all of the models in Table 6.3, another key independent variable is offline civic engagement, as our aim is to clarify the extent to which online and offline civic activity relate to one another.

Table 6.3, displays our results. In accord with the results obtained in Chapters 3 through 5, we discover inconsistent evidence for the importance of issues in fostering online civic activity. In most cases, we discover no evidence that suggests that issue importance drives online civic engagement. When we found evidence that issues matter, they did so in 2012, but never in 2008. In particular, we discovered that the importance of energy favored higher levels of friending and joining activity, and that the importance of same sex marriage also was connected with odds that favor higher levels of blogging. However, college financing was associated with odds that favor lower levels of blogging, as well as, odds that favor lower levels of following political Twitter feeds.

In addition, we found that, after controlling for offline activity and other online activities, information consumption through the internet is unrelated to friending and joining activity, but is related to other forms of online civic activity, albeit in somewhat inconsistent ways. In particular, the evidence is inconsistent with respect to the effects of internet news viewership and blogging. In 2008, we discover that each unit increase in reading internet news is connected with a 25.5% decrease in the odds that favor higher levels of blogging. Yet, in 2012, we find that a one unit increase in reading internet-based news is associated with a 35.6% increase in the odds that favor higher levels of blogging. That said, the effects of internet-based news manifest themselves most strongly when we examine following political Twitter feeds, as each unit increase in reading this form of news is connected with a 33.4% increase in the odds that favor higher levels of following activity.

In most cases, when controlling for offline activity, reading political blogs is unconnected with any change in online civic activity. The only exception to this finding occurs in 2008, when each unit increase in political blog readership is associated with a 192% increase in the odds that favor higher levels of blogging.

We also discovered some evidence that respondent characteristics affect the propensity with which college students engage in a variety of online civic activities, albeit in very inconsistent ways. Our strongest finding is that strong partisans experienced odds that favored higher levels of friending and joining activity (in 2008 and 2012), as well as, following on Twitter and tweeting about politics. In addition, political science majors or current/former members of the military were less likely to have engaged in blogging in 2008, but otherwise do not systematically differ from those who majored in something else. Further, we found that each unit increase in interest in politics was connected with odds that favor higher levels of following political Twitter feeds (in 2012) and friending and joining activity (in 2012, but not in 2008), but lower levels of blogging (in 2008, but not in 2012). In addition, we discovered that self-identifying as a liberal was associated with a decrease in the odds that favored higher levels of tweeting about politics. Interestingly, the civic experiences of one's peers do not appear to drive online civic activity. Also, political conservatives are no more likely to engage in any form of online civic activity than the rest of the population.

We find evidence that higher levels of offline civic activity are connected with increases in online civic engagement. In particular, we discover that each unit increase in pre-election civic engagement is associated with an increase in the odds that favor friending and joining activity by between 15% (2008) and 10% (2012). In addition, we found that each unit increase in pre-election civic activity was connected with a 13.3% increase in the odds that favor high levels of blogging. Finally, we discover that a one unit increase in offline, pre-election civic activity is associated with an 8.1% increase in the odds that favor higher levels of tweeting about politics.

We discovered that higher levels of blogging are connected with heightened friending and joining activity, as each unit increase in blogging increases the odds that favor higher levels of friending and joining by between 38.1% (2008) and 78.2% (2012). We also found that higher levels of friending and joining activity are connected with higher levels of blogging, as the odds that favor higher levels of blogging increase by between 37.4% (2008) and 67.1% (2012) for each unit increase in friending and joining activity.

Beyond the reciprocal relationship between friending and joining activity and blogging, increases in blogging are associated with higher levels of tweeting. Each unit increase in tweeting heightens the odds that favor higher levels of friending by 90.5%. In addition, higher levels of tweeting about politics are connected with higher levels of blogging in 2012, and following on Twitter. More specifically, each unit increase in tweeting about politics is connected with increased odds that favor higher levels of blogging (in 2012) by 101.3%, and higher levels of following on Twitter by 155.4%. Also, each unit increase in friending and joining activity is associated with higher odds that favor increased levels of following political Twitter feeds by 25.3%

In addition, following political feeds on Twitter and tweeting about politics are inexorably connected. More specifically, higher levels of following on Twitter are associated with higher levels of tweeting about politics, as each unit increase in following increases the odds that favor an increased propensity to tweet about politics by 155.4%. However, each unit increase in tweeting is positively connected with the odds that favor higher levels of following political Twitter feeds by 132.6%.

CONCLUSION

Each form of online engagement we considered—whether passive activities like friending or joining or following on twitter or expressive activities like blogging and tweeting—provides a relatively low-cost entry point for young adults to engage in politics. While we agree with proponents of slacktivism about the low-cost nature of these activities, our findings contradict the main tenet of slacktivism—that these low-cost activities have little to no meaningful impact (Morozov 2009)—and do not lead to other forms of engagement. We found consistent evidence that one form of passive online participation—friending or joining—leads directly to engaging in greater levels of engagement offline. The connections formed with candidates or political groups and the invitations and information provided there encourage young adults to venture out more into the costlier world of offline engagement.

We also discover that higher levels of blogging were associated with increased levels of offline civic activity in 2008, but not in 2012. Toward this end, we found evidence that blogging was connected with higher levels of offline engagement in both 2008 and 2012 when examined by itself. Interestingly, though, we discovered that tweeting was connected with higher levels of offline engagement in 2012. When considered together, students who took the risk of expressing their political views online became willing to pay the costs of engaging in offline activities at least some of the time.

The results from this chapter seemingly indicate that online activities can lead to offline engagement, and vice versa. Further, some of the online forms of activity seem to lead to engagement in others. By themselves, these findings are important because individual online and offline activities are often analyzed in isolation. When we analyze these findings separately, as is common in the literature and as we did in Chapters 2 through 5, we discover that we may miss some of the nuanced ways in which these participatory forms relate with one another. In Chapter 7, we explore the nuanced ways in which the differing online and offline participatory forms are interrelated in a web of participation.

NOTES

1. We did not ask whether respondents had "been asked online to work for or contribute money to a candidate, political party, or any other organization that supports candidates" in 2008.

2. We have no way to verify this assumption, as there were fewer than 5 people who took the Student Election Survey in 2008 who also took it in 2012. Because of the small number of people, we are unable to perform such a comparison in a way that would yield any generalizable conclusion.

Chapter 7

Causality, Endogeneity, and the Complex Web of Participation

If college students were simply engaged in slacktivism, their participation would likely be limited to a single form of online engagement. Instead, the relationships between online and offline forms of engagement create a complex web of political participation. The results from Chapter 6 suggest that online activities can lead to offline engagement, and vice versa. Thus, the causal arrows, at least in part, may flow in both directions. If true, then this both undermines charges of slacktivism and indicates that both direct and indirect effects may be present. Moreover, this indicates that endogeneity issues are likely.

In this chapter, we unravel these relationships. To begin, we examine the relationship between online civic activity and offline civic engagement. We do this by utilizing data from some respondents in the 2008 and 2012 Student Election Surveys who completed a post-election survey. This dataset allows us to partly examine endogeneity issues and the likely direction of causality. Then, we take a closer look at the results in Table 6.3, to discover some indirect statistical relationships that may exist between offline and online participatory forms, as well as, relationships between varying online civic activities. Once we uncover these potential relationships, we utilize a series of mediation analyses to discover whether they exist, and if so, the magnitude of these relationships relative to their more direct counterparts. These analyses provide a fuller and more complex portrait of how involvement in one activity leads to engagement in others.

POST-ELECTION OFFLINE ENGAGEMENT AND ONLINE CIVIC ACTIVITIES

To this point, we have established that several forms of online civic activity are connected with offline engagement. Yet, the data that has been presented to this point does not allow us to make any causal or quasi-causal claims. If we left the analysis at that point, there would be more questions than answers about the ways in which offline and online civic activities interrelate.

Fortunately, some respondents in the 2008 and 2012 Student Election Surveys completed a brief post-election survey. This survey allows us partly to address endogeneity issues and furnishes additional evidence that online civic activity sparks further offline engagement. To do this, we compared civic engagement levels reported in the post-election survey (T2) across the different levels of each online civic activity reported in our pre-election survey (T1). If an online activity sparks greater offline civic engagement, online activity at T1 should yield higher offline engagement levels at T2. To investigate whether this occurs, we performed a series of difference in means tests. The results of these tests also tell us whether the results that we discover are statistically significant or are due to random sampling error (see Kmenta 1997).

To begin, we generated an index of *offline* civic engagement that was constructed based on our post-election survey ($\alpha = 0.77$, 2008; $\alpha = 0.73$, 2012).[1] We then computed the mean level of each level of online civic activity among those students who had never engaged in this activity, and compared it with those who rarely did so, sometimes did so, regularly engaged in this activity, and did so very often. Tables 7.1 and 7.2 provide the results of this comparison.

When we investigate blogging, we discover that those who never blogged had mean civic engagement scores of about 3.0 (in 2008) and 2.0 (in 2012). In 2008, those who rarely blogged had a mean civic engagement score of 4.2 activities, sometimes blogged averaged approximately 4.4 activities, regularly blogged averaged 4.3 activities, and blogged very often averaged 5.5 activities. In 2012, those who rarely blogged had a mean civic engagement score of three activities, sometimes blogged averaged approximately 3.3 activities, regularly blogged averaged 4.6 activities, and blogged very often averaged five activities. With one exception, these differences in mean civic engagement activities at T2 between those who never blogged at T1 and those who engaged in varying levels of blogging at T1 are statistically significant. In general, the more one blogs about politics at T1, the greater his or her offline engagement is at T2.

Those who never friended at T1 had mean offline civic engagement scores at T2 of roughly 2.8 (in 2008) and 2.0 (in 2012). By comparison in 2008,

Table 7.1 Differences in Post-Election Civic Engagement by Levels of Pre-Election Online Activities

	2008					*2012*				
Comparison	*Never Activity Mean Civic Engagement*	*Comparison Group Mean Civic Engagement*	*T-Test*	*Degrees of Freedom*	*P-Value*	*Never Activity Mean Civic Engagement*	*Comparison Group Mean Civic Engagement*	*T-Test*	*Degrees of Freedom*	*P-Value*
Friending and Joining Activity										
Never Friend vs. Rarely Friend	2.78	4.00	2.94	113	0.002	1.95	3.07	4.39	215	<0.0001
Never Friend vs. Sometimes Friend	2.78	4.40	4.15	121	<0.0001	1.95	4.07	7.64	216	<0.0001
Never Friend vs. Regularly Friend	2.78	4.06	3.06	114	0.001	1.95	4.73	7.67	192	<0.0001
Never Friend vs. Friend Very Often	2.78	5.86	7.06	118	<0.0001	1.95	4.89	9.76	197	<0.0001
Blogging Activity										
Never Blog vs. Rarely Blog	3.01	4.19	2.57	133	0.01	1.95	3.02	3.94	194	0.0001
Never Blog vs. Sometimes Blog	3.01	4.42	2.86	131	0.01	1.95	3.34	5.42	180	<0.0001
Never Blog vs. Regularly Blog	3.01	4.25	1.82	120	0.07	1.95	4.61	7.55	160	<0.0001
Never Friend vs. Blog Very Often	3.01	5.53	5.51	131	<0.0001	1.95	4.97	8.67	157	<0.0001

Notes: Analyses of Civic Engagement by Levels of Pre-Election Online Activities in 2008 reprinted by Permission of SAGE Publications, Inc.

Sources: Friending and Joining Activity figures in 2008 are from analyses in the Student Election Survey Data in Rice, Moffett, and Madupalli (2013). All other figures in this table come from the Student Election Survey data.

Table 7.2 Differences in Post-Election Civic Engagement by Levels of Pre-Election Twitter-Based Activities

Comparison	*Never Activity Mean Civic Engagement*	*Comparison Group Mean Civic Engagement*	*T-test*	*Degrees of Freedom*	*P-Value*
Following Tweets					
Never Follow vs. Rarely Follow	2.09	2.71	1.50	95	0.138
Never Follow vs. Sometimes Follow	2.09	3.22	2.81	101	0.006
Never Follow vs. Regularly Follow	2.09	5.19	6.29	95	<0.0001
Never Follow vs. Follow Very Often	2.09	4.41	5.81	103	<0.0001
Tweeting					
Never Tweet vs. Rarely Tweet	2.23	3.54	2.94	112	0.004
Never Tweet vs. Sometimes Tweet	2.23	3.50	2.88	106	0.005
Never Tweet vs. Regularly Tweet	2.23	4.00	4.03	108	0.0001
Never Tweet vs. Tweet Very Often	2.23	4.96	6.57	112	<0.0001

Source: Moffett and Rice, Student Election Survey.

those who rarely friended had a mean offline civic engagement score of 4.0, those who did so sometimes had mean scores of 4.4, those who did so regularly had mean scores of 4.1, and those who did so very often had mean scores of 5.9. All of these represent significant differences from the offline civic engagement scores of those who never friended. In 2012, those who rarely friended had a mean offline civic engagement score of 3.1, those who did so regularly had mean scores of 4.1, those who did so regularly had mean scores of 4.7, and those who did so very often had mean scores of 4.9. Once again, all of these represented statistically significant differences from those who never friended. The evidence is clear—those who friend at some level go on to engage in greater levels of offline activities than those who never friend.

When we examine online civic activity via Twitter, similar trends emerge. More specifically, when we examine following, we find that those who never followed had mean civic engagement scores of about 2.1. Those who rarely followed had a mean civic engagement score of 2.7 activities, sometimes followed averaged approximately 3.2 activities, regularly followed averaged 5.2 activities, and followed very often averaged 4.4 activities. In three of four cases, these differences in mean civic engagement activities at T2 between those who never followed on Twitter at T1 and those who engaged in varying levels of following on Twitter activity at T1 are statistically significant. Generally, the more one follows political twitter feeds at T1, the more they participate offline at T2.

When we investigate tweeting, we find that those who never tweeted had mean civic engagement scores of about 2.2. Those who rarely tweeted had a mean civic engagement score of approximately 3.5 activities, sometimes tweeted averaged 3.5 activities, regularly tweeted averaged four activities, and tweeted very often averaged five activities. In all instances, these differences in mean civic engagement activities at T2 between those who never tweeted at T1 and those who engaged in varying levels of tweeting at T1 are statistically significant. The more one tweets about politics at T1, the more one participates offline at T2.

In sum, these results provide some evidence that engaging in a variety of online civic activities during the pre-election survey timespan yielded higher reported levels of civic engagement in the post-election survey. This provides support for our theories about each form of online political activity leading to greater offline activity. That said, they do not eliminate the possibility that higher levels of offline civic activities also lead to increased occurrences of online forms of civic engagement. Our theoretical arguments do not address this possibility nor preclude that the causal arrow points in both directions, they only require that online activity lead to greater offline activity.

If online civic activity leads to higher levels of offline civic engagement, then those who engaged in an online civic activity for the first time after the pre-election survey should engage in higher levels of offline activities than those who never engaged in any of the forms of online activities that we examine here. To consider this possibility, each respondent was asked whether s/he has engaged in friending or joining activity, blogging, tweeting about politics, or following candidates, parties, or politically oriented groups on Twitter since October 1 of the relevant election year. For example, if a respondent had tweeted since October 1, 2012, but reported not having done so in the pre-election survey, then we generated a dichotomous variable, *late tweeter*, that is coded one for those in this situation, and zero otherwise. If that same respondent had not tweeted since October 1, 2012, and reported never having done this activity in the pre-election survey, we generated a dummy variable, *never tweeter*, that is coded one for those in this situation and zero otherwise. We perform similar comparisons between late and never frienders and joiners, late and never bloggers, and late and never followers on Twitter.

To compare levels of civic engagement between late and never frienders, late and never bloggers, late and never followers on Twitter, and late and never tweeters, we computed the mean levels of pre-election and post-election survey civic engagement for those respondents who never engaged in a particular online civic activity (e.g., following on Twitter) in either administration of our survey instrument. Then, we computed the mean levels of pre-election and post-election survey offline civic engagement for those respondents who engaged in a particular online civic activity late in the game (e.g., following on Twitter). Through Tables 7.3 and 7.4, we perform our comparison.

When we examine blogging, following on Twitter, and tweeting in Tables 7.3 and 7.4, the relationship between doing these forms of activity late as opposed to not at all and higher levels of offline civic activity at T2 is not always statistically significant. In three of every four statistical tests, we discover no evidence that statistically significant differences in offline engagement exist between late bloggers and never bloggers, late followers and never followers, and late tweeters and never tweeters. We do, however, discover two noteworthy relationships that are statistically significant. We discover a statistically significant difference between the post-election civic engagement of never and late bloggers in 2008, as the mean level of activity among never bloggers is 2.8 while late bloggers average 4.5. Meanwhile, these two groups did not differ substantially in their pre-election civic engagement. This provides strong suggestive evidence that blogging about politics in 2008 caused greater offline participation. That said, we do not discover a similar relationship in 2012. Second, we discover that never followers on Twitter and late followers differ with respect to their pre-election civic activity levels, as never followers averaged a 6.3 (on a 60 point scale), while late followers averaged approximately 8.6 on that same scale. However, they did not significantly differ in their post-civic engagement levels. This might suggest that offline engagement sparked following rather than the other way around. Comparing the civic activity among late and never followers, tweeters, and bloggers provides limited evidence that these activities cause greater offline engagement. Among these, only blogging about politics in 2008 appears to have clearly sparked greater offline engagement.

That said, Table 7.3 provides stronger evidence that engaging in campaign-related friending increases offline civic engagement. More specifically, those who never friended a candidate in 2008 had a pre-election civic engagement score of about 6.1 out of a 60 point scale, while late frienders averaged approximately 7.2 on this same measure. This difference was not, however, statistically significant. The picture changes when we examine levels of post-election civic engagement. Those who never friended in 2008 had an average post-election civic engagement score of approximately 2.8 on a 14-point scale, while late frienders averaged approximately 3.7 on this index. This difference is significant. This provides strong support that engaging in friending leads to greater offline participation (and not the other way around).

In 2012, though, those who never friended a candidate had a pre-election civic engagement score of approximately 6.1 while late frienders averaged

Table 7.3 Differences in Civic Engagement Levels between Late and Never Performers of Activities by Pre-and Post-Election Levels of Civic Engagement

	2008					*2012*				
Comparison	*Never Activity Mean Civic Engagement*	*Late Activity Mean Civic Engagement*	*T-Test*	*Degrees of Freedom*	*P-Value*	*Never Activity Mean Civic Engagement*	*Late Activity Mean Civic Engagement*	*T-Test*	*Degrees of Freedom*	*P-Value*
Friending and Joining Activity										
Never Friend vs. Late Friend (Precivic Engagement Levels)	6.07	7.23	1.08	99	0.14	6.12	8.59	2.32	224	0.02
Never Friend vs. Late Friend (Postcivic Engagement Levels)	2.78	3.67	1.87	108	0.03	2.09	4.18	5.33	228	<0.0001
Blogging Activity										
Never Blog vs. Late Blog (Precivic Engagement Levels)	6.45	8.29	1.56	119	0.12	5.93	6.48	0.52	175	0.61
Never Blog vs. Late Blog (Postcivic Engagement Levels)	2.83	4.50	3.06	112	0.003	1.96	2.50	1.52	176	0.13

Notes: Analyses of Civic Engagement by Levels of Pre-Election Online Activities in 2008 reprinted by Permission of SAGE Publications, Inc.
Sources: Friending and Joining Activity figures in 2008 are from analyses in the Student Election Survey data in Rice, Moffett, and Madupalli (2013). All other figures in this table come from the Student Election Survey data.

Table 7.4 Differences in Post-Election Civic Engagement by Levels of Pre-Election Twitter-Based Activities

Comparison	*Never Activity Mean Civic Engagement*	*Late Activity Mean Civic Engagement*	*T-Test*	*Degrees of Freedom*	*P-Value*
Following Tweets					
Never Follow vs. Late Follow (Precivic Engagement Levels)	6.26	8.56	1.98	109	0.05
Never Follow vs. Late Follow (Postcivic Engagement Levels)	2.18	2.53	0.83	111	0.41
Tweeting					
Never Tweet vs. Late Tweet (Precivic Engagement Levels)	6.91	8.00	0.77	126	0.44
Never Tweet vs. Late Tweet (Postcivic Engagement Levels)	2.36	2.56	0.45	124	0.66

Source: Moffett and Rice, Student Election Survey.

roughly 8.6 on this same scale. This difference is statistically significant and so is their post-election offline civic engagement. Never frienders averaged a post-election civic engagement score of approximately 2.1 while late frienders averaged roughly 4.2 on this same scale. Thus, in 2012, we have evidence that friending candidates or joining groups yields higher levels of offline engagement (while not ruling out the possibility that higher levels of offline engagement also produces greater levels of friending).

RELATIONSHIP BETWEEN ONLINE FORMS OF CIVIC ACTIVITY

Through the models in Table 6.3, we find substantial evidence that online forms of civic activity are connected with one another in a positive direction. We discovered that higher levels of blogging are connected with heightened friending and joining activity. In addition, we found that higher levels of friending and joining activity are connected with higher levels of blogging. Moreover, increases in blogging are connected with higher levels of tweeting about politics, and higher levels of tweeting is connected with higher levels of blogging. Additionally, higher levels of friending and joining activity are associated with higher odds that favor increased levels of following Twitter feeds. Finally, following political feeds on Twitter and tweeting about politics are inexorably connected, as higher levels of following on Twitter are connected with higher levels of tweeting about politics, and vice versa.

When we put these results together, we get a clearer picture of the relationship between the different forms of online engagement and offline engagement. Through Figure 7.1, we map these relationships out based on the statistical results in Tables 6.2 and 6.3. We note several things about this figure. First, an arrow in one direction shows a statistically significant relationship between the independent variable and the dependent variable to which the arrow points. For instance, there is a line that starts at friending and joining activity and ends at following on Twitter. The presence of this line indicates that friending and joining activity affects following activity on Twitter. However, it does not indicate that following activity on Twitter affects friending and joining activity.

Second, a two-way arrow indicates that both variables have a statistically significant effect on each other. For example, there is a two-way arrow between pre-election offline civic engagement and friending and joining activity. This arrow indicates that pre-election offline civic engagement has a statistically significant relationship with friending and joining activity, and that friending and joining activity has a statistically significant relationship with offline civic engagement. Finally, solid lines denote statistically significant relationships in the 2012 surveys, while the sole dashed lines signify a statistically significant relationship in the 2008, but not in the 2012 surveys.

This figure illustrates the complexity of the relationships that exist between differing forms of online civic engagement. In particular, it illustrates that

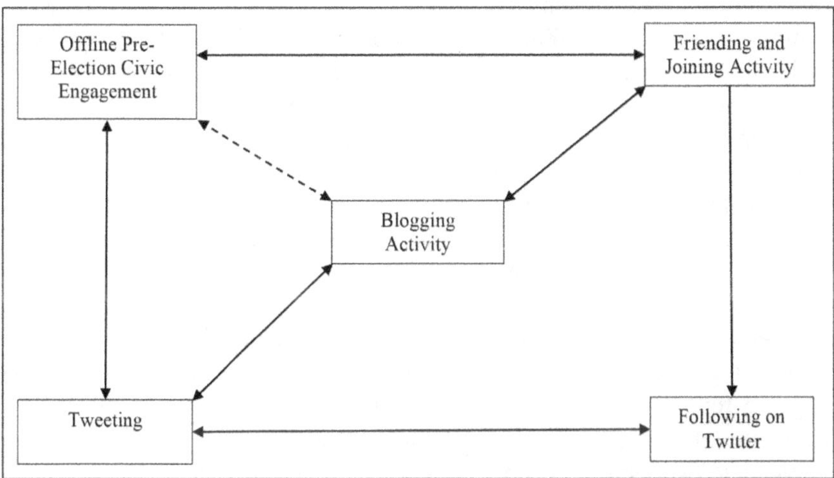

Figure 7.1 Mapping out Pre-Election Civic Engagement Relationships with Other Online Variables. *Source*: Moffett and Rice, Student Election Survey

a number of direct relationships between these forms of engagement exist. For example, there are two-way relationships between friending and joining activity, and blogging activity; between following on Twitter and tweeting; and between pre-election offline civic engagement and friending and joining activity.

More interesting are four one-way, indirect relationships that are uncovered by this figure that may exist: friending may affect tweeting about politics through blogging; friending may influence tweeting about politics through following political Twitter feeds; following political Twitter feeds may affect blogging through tweeting; and blogging may influence following political Twitter feeds through friending and joining activity. If these relationships exist, then we have uncovered additional insights about the relationships between varying forms of online civic activities that otherwise would have gone undiscovered. We analyze these one-way, indirect relationships through a mediation analysis to determine whether they exist, and if so, their magnitude. Mediation analyses allow us to demonstrate whether an independent variable has an effect on a dependent variable through a third, mediating factor (MacKinnon 2008). Thus, mediation analyses estimate the direct effect of the independent variable on the dependent variable *and* the indirect effect of the mediating variable on the dependent variable that exerts itself through the independent variable (MacKinnon 2008).

To perform this mediation analysis, we utilize seemingly unrelated regression (SUR) models. These models improve the efficiency of coefficient estimation when the error terms for two regression equations are correlated (Pindyck and Rubenfeld 1991, 208; Wilkins and Keiser 2004). These correlated residual terms happen when two outcomes of interest are the product of common factors that are imperfectly incorporated into the regression equation (Wilkins and Keiser 2004, 96). For instance, the relationship between friending and tweeting is the product of many common independent variables, including blogging. We use SUR models to estimate our models because the differing forms of online engagement require substantially similar activities and are carried out by the same members of the population. Thus, it is highly likely that the residuals from separate regression equations are correlated (Wilkins and Keiser 2004, 96).

Table 7.5 displays our results. There are four SUR models in this table: 1) friending on tweeting through blogging, 2) friending on tweeting through following political Twitter feeds, 3) following political Twitter feeds on blogging through tweeting, and 4) blogging on following political Twitter feeds through friending and joining activity. In each of these SUR models, we estimate two models. When we examine the first model, we estimate two equations: one to explain the variation in blogging activity, and the second to explain the variation in tweeting. When we use our second model, we estimate two equations: one to explain the variation in following political Twitter feeds, and the second to explain the variation in tweeting. In our third model, we estimate two equations: one to explain variation in tweeting, and the second to explain variance in blogging. With our fourth and final model, we estimate two equations: one to explain the variation in friending and joining activity, and the second to explain the variation in following political Twitter feeds.

Models One and Two furnish several insights. First, friending activity affects blogging activity, as the coefficients for each are positive and statistically significant at all levels. When one friends rarely, the odds that favor higher levels of blogging increase by 68.88%. They increase by 82.21% when one sometimes friends, 98.97% when one regularly friends, and 336.23% when one friends very often. Interestingly, friending appears to have little effect on following activity, as three of the four coefficients that correspond to the varying levels of friending are not statistically significant. Relatedly, friending has no statistically significant relationship with tweeting, as the coefficients that correspond to friending are not statistically significant in Models One or Two.

That said, blogging and following political feeds are positively connected with higher levels of tweeting. More specifically, each unit increase in blogging is connected with a 39.51% increase in the odds that favor higher levels of tweeting. Moreover, each unit increase in blogging are connected with increases in the odds that favor higher levels of following political Twitter feeds by 13.66%. Similarly, each unit increase in following political Twitter feeds is associated with a 56.67% increase in the odds that favor higher levels of tweeting about politics. Additionally, a one unit increase in following political twitter feeds is connected with an 11.29% increase in the odds that favor higher levels of blogging. Finally, each unit increase in pre-election civic activity is associated with an increase in the odds that favor: (1) higher levels of following political Twitter feeds by 13.66% and (2) higher levels of tweeting about politics by 2.63%.

Through Model Three, we learn that following political Twitter feeds is positively connected with tweeting about politics, but is largely unconnected with blogging. More specifically, the odds that favor higher levels of tweeting increase by 56.36% among those who rarely follow political Twitter feeds, 42.9% among those who sometimes follow political Twitter feeds, 362.74% among those who follow political Twitter feeds regularly, and by 798% among those who follow political Twitter feeds very often. In addition, each unit increase in friending and joining activity increases the odds that favor higher levels of tweeting by 11.74%, and higher levels of blogging by 32.71%. Moreover, each unit increase in tweeting about politics is associated with heightened odds that favor higher levels of blogging by 47.7%. Finally,

Table 7.5 Mediation Analysis of Indirect Effects of Online Variables in the 2012 Student Election Surveys

	Friending on Tweeting about Politics through Blogging (Model One)		*Friending on Tweeting about Politics through Following Political Twitter Feeds (Model Two)*		*Following Political Twitter Feeds on Blogging through Tweeting (Model Three)*		*Blogging on Following Political Twitter Feeds through Friending (Model Four)*	
Independent Variable	*Blogging*	*Tweeting*	*Following*	*Tweeting*	*Tweeting*	*Blogging*	*Friending*	*Following*
Level of Mediated Civic Activity								
Friending								
Friend Rarely	0.52**	0.14	0.12	0.14	–	–	–	–
	(0.20)	(0.18)	(0.22)	(0.18)				
Friend Sometimes	0.60**	–0.11	0.40*	–0.11	–	–	–	–
	(0.21)	(0.19)	(0.23)	(0.19)				
Friend Regularly	0.69*	0.31	0.33	0.31	–	–	–	–
	(0.30)	(0.27)	(0.33)	(0.27)				
Friend Very Often	1.47***	–0.20	0.19	–0.20	–	–	–	–
	(0.28)	(0.27)	(0.32)	(0.27)				
Following Political Twitter Feeds								
Follow Rarely	–	–	–	–	0.45*	–0.22	–	–
					(0.20)	(0.21)		
Follow Sometimes	–	–	–	–	0.36*	0.14	–	–
					(0.18)	(0.19)		
Follow Regularly	–	–	–	–	1.53***	–0.19	–	–
					(0.24)	(0.26)		
Follow Very Often	–	–	–	–	2.20***	–0.52*	–	–
					(0.24)	(0.28)		
Blogging Activity								
Blog Rarely	–	–	–	–	–	–	–0.11	–0.08
							(0.18)	(0.19)
Blog Sometimes	–	–	–	–	–	–	0.40*	–0.32
							(0.19)	(0.20)
Blog Regularly	–	–	–	–	–	–	0.35	–0.21
							(0.26)	(0.27)
Blog Very Often	–	–	–	–	–	–	1.38***	–0.18
							(0.26)	(0.28)

Other Civic Activities								
Friending and Joining	–	–		–	0.11*	0.28***	–	0.07
					(0.06)	(0.06)		(0.07)
Blogging	–	0.33***	0.13*	0.33***	–	–	–	–
		(0.06)	(0.07)	(0.06)				
Following on Twitter	0.11*	0.45***	–	0.45***	–	–	–	–
	(0.06)	(0.05)		(0.05)				
Tweeting about Politics	–	–	–	–	–	0.39***	0.05	0.51***
						(0.06)	(0.06)	(0.06)
Pre-Election Civic Activity	0.01	0.03*	0.13*	0.03*	0.02*	0.0001	0.06***	0.02
	(0.01)	(0.01)	(0.07)	(0.01)	(0.01)	(0.01)	(0.01)	(0.01)
Issue Importance								
Economy	0.22*	0.45***	–0.17	0.45***	0.09	0.18	–0.13	–0.13
	(0.13)	(0.05)	(0.14)	(0.05)	(0.12)	(0.12)	(0.12)	(0.12)
Education	0.38**	–0.01	0.002	–0.01	0.12	0.31**	0.04	–0.02
	(0.14)	(0.12)	(0.15)	(0.12)	(0.13)	(0.13)	(0.13)	(0.13)
Energy	–0.10	–0.05	–0.06	–0.05	–0.07	–0.06	0.17*	–0.03
	(0.10)	(0.09)	(0.11)	(0.09)	(0.10)	(0.10)	(0.09)	(0.10)
College Financing	–0.31**	0.07	0.23*	0.07	–0.02	–0.28**	0.03	0.14
	(0.11)	(0.10)	(0.12)	(0.10)	(0.10)	(0.10)	(0.10)	(0.10)
Health Care	–0.21*	–0.03	–0.15	–0.03	–0.08	–0.18*	0.02	–0.11
	(0.10)	(0.09)	(0.11)	(0.09)	(0.09)	(0.09)	(0.09)	(0.10)
Environment	–0.01	0.01	0.05	0.01	–0.03	–0.09	0.01	0.05
	(0.10)	(0.09)	(0.10)	(0.09)	(0.09)	(0.09)	(0.09)	(0.09)
Abortion	0.05	–0.03	0.01	–0.03	–0.01	0.06	–0.04	0.03
	(0.07)	(0.06)	(0.08)	(0.06)	(0.07)	(0.06)	(0.06)	(0.07)
Immigration	0.08	–0.10	0.04	–0.10	0.02	0.06	0.03	0.04
	(0.07)	(0.07)	(0.08)	(0.07)	(0.07)	(0.07)	(0.07)	(0.07)
Same Sex Marriage	0.17**	0.01	–0.13	0.01	0.10	0.13*	–0.10	–0.11
	(0.07)	(0.07)	(0.08)	(0.07)	(0.07)	(0.07)	(0.07)	(0.08)
Information Consumption								
Internet News	0.19*	–0.08	0.05	–0.08	0.02	0.17*	–0.03	0.07
	(0.09)	(0.08)	(0.10)	(0.08)	(0.08)	(0.08)	(0.08)	(0.08)
Political Blogs	0.09	0.08	0.04	0.08	0.09	0.07	0.03	–0.01
	(0.07)	(0.06)	(0.07)	(0.06)	(0.06)	(0.06)	(0.06)	(0.06)

(Continued)

Table 7.5 Mediation Analysis of Indirect Effects of Online Variables in the 2012 Student Election Surveys (continued)

	Friending on Tweeting about Politics through Blogging (Model One)		*Friending on Tweeting about Politics through Following Political Twitter Feeds (Model Two)*		*Following Political Twitter Feeds on Blogging through Tweeting (Model Three)*		*Blogging on Following Political Twitter Feeds through Friending (Model Four)*	
Independent Variable	*Blogging*	*Tweeting*	*Following*	*Tweeting*	*Tweeting*	*Blogging*	*Friending*	*Following*
Respondent Characteristics								
Peer Civic Experiences	–0.02	–0.02	0.03	–0.02	–0.04	0.003	0.02	0.03
	(0.03)	(0.03)	(0.03)	(0.03)	(0.03)	(0.03)	(0.03)	(0.03)
Political Science Major	–0.004	–0.22	–0.84*	–0.22	–0.13	–0.05	–0.06	–0.58
	(0.38)	(0.34)	(0.41)	(0.34)	(0.35)	(0.35)	(0.35)	(0.36)
Military	–0.29	–0.86*	–0.56	–0.86*	–1.04**	0.11	0.11	0.10
	(0.45)	(0.40)	(0.49)	(0.40)	(0.42)	(0.42)	(0.42)	(0.43)
Interest in Politics	–0.005	0.07	0.53***	0.07	0.002	–0.005	0.24*	0.40***
	(0.13)	(0.12)	(0.14)	(0.12)	(0.12)	(0.12)	(0.12)	(0.12)
Liberal	–0.02	–0.40**	–0.30	–0.40**	–0.33*	0.09	0.17	–0.04
	(0.18)	(0.16)	(0.19)	(0.16)	(0.17)	(0.17)	(0.17)	(0.17)
Conservative	–0.20	0.01	–0.33	0.01	0.12	–0.23	0.08	–0.26
	(0.22)	(0.20)	(0.24)	(0.20)	(0.21)	(0.21)	(0.20)	(0.21)
Obama Supporter	0.13	0.23	0.24	0.23	0.30*	–0.01	–0.16	0.09
	(0.18)	(0.16)	(0.20)	(0.16)	(0.17)	(0.17)	(0.17)	(0.17)
Strong Partisan	0.18	0.29*	0.70***	0.29*	0.29*	0.04	0.48***	0.37*
	(0.17)	(0.15)	(0.18)	(0.15)	(0.16)	(0.16)	(0.15)	(0.16)
Constant	–0.45	–0.05	–0.36	–0.05	–0.13	–0.35	–0.44	–0.17
	(0.56)	(0.50)	(0.61)	(0.50)	(0.52)	(0.52)	(0.51)	(0.53)
N	243	243	243	243	243	243	243	243
R-Squared	0.44	0.60	0.43	0.60	0.57	0.51	0.51	0.56
Chi-Squared	191.90	362.69	181.25	362.69	320.27	253.43	255.44	304.75
Prob>Chi-Squared	<0.0001	<0.0001	<0.0001	<0.0001	<0.0001	<0.0001	<0.0001	<0.0001

Notes: The coefficients are seemingly unrelated regression coefficients and the values in parenthesis are standard errors. * denotes $p < 0.05$, ** denotes $p < 0.01$, and *** denotes $p < 0.001$, all one-tailed tests.
Source: Moffett and Rice, Student Election Survey.

a one unit increase in pre-election civic activity is associated with an increase in the odds that favor higher levels of tweeting by 2.12%.

Model Four furnishes a few more insights. In particular, blogging is somewhat connected with higher levels of friending, but is completely unconnected with following political Twitter feeds. More specifically, the odds that favor higher levels of friending and joining activity increase by 49.18% among those who sometimes blog, and by 297.49% among those who blog very often. Further, tweeting about politics is associated with higher levels of following political Twitter feeds, as each unit increase in tweeting yields a 66.53% increase in the odds that favor higher levels of following. Finally, pre-election offline civic activity is connected with higher levels of friending and joining activity, as each unit increase in offline civic activity yields a 5.76% increase in the odds that favor higher levels of friending.

While these models illustrate a number of interesting trends with respect to the relationships between differing online civic activities, we have yet to discuss whether the direct and indirect effects are statistically significant. Preacher and Hayes (2008) provide a method by which we can compute

Table 7.6 Total Direct and Indirect Effects

	Coefficient	*Percentage of Effect*
Friending on Tweeting through Blogging (Model One)		
Direct Effect of Friending	0.14 (0.62)	11.62%
Indirect Effect of Friending (through Blogging)	1.09*** (0.30)	88.38%
Friending on Tweeting through Following Political Twitter Feeds (Model Two)		
Direct Effect of Friending	0.14 (0.65)	29.51%
Indirect Effect of Friending (through Following Political Twitter Feeds)	0.34 (0.27)	70.49%
Following Political Twitter Feeds on Blogging through Tweeting (Model Three)		
Direct Effect of Following Political Twitter Feeds	–0.79 (0.66)	30.94%
Indirect Effect of Following Political Twitter Feeds (through Tweeting)	1.77*** (0.37)	69.06%
Blogging on Following Political Twitter Feeds through Friending (Model Four)		
Direct Effect of Blogging	–0.20 (0.70)	58.46%
Indirect Effect of Blogging (through Friending)	0.14 (0.14)	41.54%

Notes: The coefficients are ordered logistic regression coefficients and the values in parenthesis are standard errors. * denotes $p < 0.05$, ** denotes $p < 0.01$, and *** denotes $p < 0.001$, all one-tailed tests.
Source: Moffett and Rice, Student Election Survey.

whether the magnitude of the direct effects at varying levels of our primary independent variable on our primary dependent variable are statistically significant. Their method also allows us to estimate the magnitude of the indirect effects at varying levels of our primary independent variable, and ascertain whether these effects are statistically significant (Preacher and Hayes 2008). Once we perform both steps, we can easily determine which percentage of the overall effect of our mediated civic activity is direct, or alternatively, indirect. Through Table 7.6 this is the task to which we now turn.

This table displays two noteworthy findings. First, friending does not exert a direct effect on tweeting, but does exert positive, indirect effects through blogging, but no such effects exist through following political Twitter feeds. More specifically, the indirect effect of friending on tweeting through blogging accounts for more than 88% of the overall effect. Second, following political Twitter feeds does not exert a direct effect on blogging, but does exert a positive, statistically significant effect on blogging through tweeting. In fact, this effect accounts for slightly more than 69% of the overall effect. Based on these results, we can conclude that online activities exert indirect effects on other online activities in some cases. Thus, models that only examine direct effects through a straightforward regression analysis might miss some of the true effects that online forms of civic activities have on one another.

CONCLUSION

Through the analyses in this chapter, we have a clearer picture of the ways in which offline and online forms of civic activity connect with one another. One of our most important and robust findings in the previous chapters is that friending and joining activity is consistently connected with higher levels of offline civic engagement. In this chapter, we have unearthed substantial evidence that supports an underlying causal connection between friending and joining activity and civic engagement. Higher levels of friending and joining activity during the pre-election period (T1) produce higher levels of offline activity at T2. Further, those who engage in friending activity late in the game are still more likely to engage in higher levels of offline activity than those who never friend. This lends strong support to our argument that friending serves as a low-cost entry point for political participation and, rather than serving as a form of slacktivism, that it leads to engagement in other, costlier offline activity.

However, the causal connections between other forms of online civic activity and offline engagement are less clear. Previously, we found that blogging or posting about politics was associated with higher levels of offline engagement in 2008 but not 2012. In this chapter, we uncovered that higher levels of blogging or posting about politics at T1 in both 2008 and 2012 generally resulted in greater levels of offline civic engagement at T2. However, we found that the difference in offline civic engagement between those who chose to blog late in the game and those who did not blog at all was much less clear. Late bloggers only had significantly higher offline engagement scores at T2 than those who never blogged in 2008. In 2012, there was no significant difference in these two groups' offline engagement levels at T2.

Tweeting about politics at higher levels at T1 was generally associated with higher offline civic engagement levels at T2. However, when we performed a comparison between late and never tweeters with respect to offline pre-election and post-election engagement, we uncovered no relationship between tweeting and offline engagement. Likewise, greater levels of following at T1 were generally associated with higher levels of offline engagement at T2. However, late followers and never followers only differed significantly in their pre-election offline civic engagement, not in their civic engagement at T2. With the evidence that currently exists, we cannot conclude anything about a causal relationship between tweeting and offline civic activity. However, since tweeting is a relatively new form of expression, it may be too early to make a definitive, authoritative statement regarding whether twitter usage increases offline engagement.

The story becomes more complex when we examine the varying forms of online civic activity, and how they relate to one another. The clearest stories that emerge are that blogging and friending and joining activities are inexorably linked to one another, as are tweeting and following on Twitter, and blogging and tweeting. These linkages occur in such a way that we cannot conclusively determine which one causes the other. Thus, it is possible, and even probable that reciprocal causality exists between these variables. Given the currently available methods, we are unable to definitively tease this out.

It is clear that engaging in one online activity leads to engaging in others. This suggests that even those online activities that do not directly lead to engaging in greater offline engagement still could indirectly do so via other online forms. We tested whether these indirect effects existed, and uncovered two notable findings. First, we uncovered strong evidence that friending exerts an indirect effect on tweeting through blogging, but does not exert a direct effect on tweeting by itself. When viewed in light of the findings in Table 6.3, it makes sense that the initial evidence suggested no direct effect between friending and tweeting. This initial evidence was an artifact of examining whether this direct effect occurs, with no consideration of any indirect effect. Thus, it makes sense that approximately 88% of the overall effect is this indirect, positive effect.

Second, we discovered that following political Twitter feeds exerts an indirect effect on blogging through tweeting, but does not exert a direct effect on blogging by itself. When viewed with the other online models, it makes sense that the initial evidence suggested no direct effect between following and blogging. When we investigated the existence of an indirect effect of following political Twitter feeds on blogging through tweeting, we found ample evidence that suggests that the effect is primarily indirect. More specifically, slightly more than 69% of the overall effect of blogging on following political Twitter feeds happens through tweeting.

Both of these indirect effects are significant, as online forms of civic activity do not operate in isolation. An increasing number of people are using social media, and in particular, multiple platforms. When viewed in this light, we should expect that some forms of online civic activity exert strong direct effects on other forms of online activity, like friending and joining activity, and to a lesser extent, blogging. Yet, these forms of activity also affect one another, especially when we include Twitter into the equation.

We also found strong evidence that engaging in one online activity, whether it be passive or expressive, leads to engaging in others. The mediation analyses demonstrate that both of the more passive forms of engagement lead to engaging in expressive forms of online participation, albeit sometimes by an indirect route. Whether young adults begin their foray into politics via Facebook, blogs, or Twitter, their participation is highly unlikely to stop there. Engaging in any one of these forms of participation leads to engaging in others and friending or joining in particular opens doors to offline engagement that young adults routinely choose to enter.

In Chapter 8, we consider how our different findings across different chapters with respect to the effects of issues, respondent characteristics, information consumption, and other forms of civic activity come together. We then provide evidence that our main results are generalizable to a broader population. We also address what our results as a whole suggest about the future of political participation.

NOTE

1. This scale was constructed based on answers to each appendage to this phrase: "Since October 1, 2008, have you…": (1) "Worn a campaign button or shirt, put a campaign sticker on your car, or placed a sign in your window or in front of your residence;" (2) "Tried to talk to people and explain why they should vote for or against one of the parties or candidates;" (3) "Contacted a newspaper, radio, or TV talk show to express your opinion on an issue;" (4) "Watched a presidential debate;" (5) "Watched the vice presidential debate;" (6) "Attended a nonpartisan election or campaign-related event on campus;" (7) "Attended any political meetings rallies, speeches, dinners, or things like that in support of a particular candidate;"

(8) "Participated in political activities such as protests, marches, or demonstrations;" (9) "Contributed money to a Republican candidate or political party;" (10) "Contributed money to a Democratic candidate or political party;" (11) "Worked or volunteered on a political campaign for a candidate or party;" (12) "Contacted or visited someone in government who represents your community;" (13) "Worked with a group to solve a problem in a community;" and (14) "Made a purchasing decision based on the conduct or values of a company." For each activity, the response choices were yes, no, or don't know. Each respondent received one point for each activity in which s/he participated.

Chapter 8

College Students and the Future of Political Participation

As political campaigns ventured online, they altered the cost calculus of young adults for getting involved in politics. Already technologically savvy and blessed with easy internet access, college students faced little cost and almost no learning curve to engage in these new forms of participation. As presidential campaigns first capitalized on blogs in 2004, Facebook in 2008, and Twitter in 2012, it was they who faced steep learning curves and an uncertain payoff. These venues were disproportionately populated by young adults, an age group who had generally been disinclined to participate in politics. Yet, as we have seen in this book, substantial percentages of college students embraced these new political uses of already familiar online tools.

In Chapter 1, we elaborated two primary objectives of this book: to investigate what shapes both the online and offline civic activity of college students; and to provide insight into how online engagement opens the door to offline engagement. For instance, we examined how the importance of particular political issues to college students might shape their online participation in Chapter 2. In Chapters 3 through 5 we expanded our analysis to a host of other respondent characteristics in order to provide a fuller picture of what drives various forms of online and offline engagement. Then, we turned to how offline and online civic activities affect one another. Numerous findings emerge through the analyses in Chapters 2 through 7.

As we review these findings, we will discuss the ways in which they confirm portions of the extant literature, depart from this literature, and provide important building blocks on which other analyses can proceed. Then, we utilize data from Pew surveys taken in 2008 and 2012 to discover the extent to which these findings are generalizable to the broader population of young people and whether they are confined to young adults or hold true across ages. Finally, we will discuss the implications of our discoveries for social scientists, political campaigns, and the broader public policy community in 2016 and beyond. It is to these tasks that we now turn.

POLITICAL ISSUES AND CIVIC ENGAGEMENT

In Chapter 2, we argued that the importance of political issues may encourage civic activity for three main reasons. First, issues exert an effect on elections at least for some time, even though the effect may be inconsistent across elections (Macdonald, Rabinowitz, and Listhaug 1995; Hawley 2013). Second, different presidential elections bring about a diverse set of issues that can vary by election. Third, many researchers have found that the state of the economy is the one issue that consistently encourages participation in that a bad economy encourages those dissatisfied with its state to vote for nonincumbent candidates or parties (see e.g., Blais 2000; Godbout and Belanger 2007; Lewis-Beck 1990; Lewis-Beck, Martini, and Kiewiet 2013; Whitten and Palmer 1999). The economy has a unique effect on college students, as good jobs become increasingly difficult to obtain as the economy worsens. Students may face a tougher time getting a job to support their educational expenses, higher tuition rates in response to state budget cuts to higher education, and lower levels of grant support to finance educational expenses.

In Chapter 2, we investigated how college students' issue priorities led to engaging in a wide variety of online forms of civic activity. To do so, we gathered data on the level of importance to which students assigned nine different issues immediately prior to the 2008 and 2012 presidential elections.[1] Then, in Chapter 3, we looked at how the importance of these same issues shaped offline civic activity, while adding controls for additional independent variables that might also shape participation. The analysis in Chapters 4 and 5 provide insight into how issues drive online participation once we control for these other variables.

When we did this, we discover that issue priorities have a differential effect on *online* civic activity in 2008 and 2012, but have very little effect on offline civic engagement in either 2008 or 2012. This effect depends on the issue, the form of civic activity being investigated, and the year in which it is being examined.[2] The only issue for which we found any consistent evidence concerns the importance of the economy, which shaped participation for several forms of online activity in 2012. Once we controlled for respondent characteristics in later chapters, though, views on the economy lost their significance.

At the same time, there are other issues such as education, same sex marriage, and energy policy, on which levels of importance did not correspond to a consistent positive effect on a particular form of civic activity. Meanwhile, some issues such as health care and the environment actually led to decreases in some forms of participation, especially in 2012.

We found links between the importance of same sex marriage, immigration, energy policy, education, and health care and at least one form of civic activity across model specifications, especially in 2012. While these findings are somewhat limited in that they apply to a particular form of engagement, and almost always for a single year, they are consistent with prior literature's inconsistent and sometimes contradictory findings on issues and political behavior. When viewed on a broader level, there is enough evidence to indicate that a majority of issues do have an effect on college students' offline and online civic activity at least occasionally.

ONLINE ACTIVITIES, RESPONDENT ATTRIBUTES, AND CIVIC ACTIVITY

In Chapter 3, we turned to an investigation of young adults' offline engagement. While they may be underrepresented in the offline political world, they do participate. We examined how well traditional predictors of civic activity explain the offline activities of young adults. We introduced measures that examine the extent to which students engage in online activities, like reading blogs and consuming online news. We also introduced a variety of measures that examine the attributes of individual respondents in our survey: individual-level interest in politics, strong self-identification with one of the political parties, the civic experiences of one's peers, whether each is a political science major, whether each is a current or former member of the military, ideology, and being a supporter of Barack Obama. When we examine these covariates, the results suggest that some factors have a stronger effect on civic activities than others. Then, in Chapters 4 and 5, we considered how these activities and attributes shape a variety of forms of online engagement.

The "usual suspects" that explain political participation only partially apply to college students. Our results suggest that among college students, strong partisanship is a more consistent spur to greater participation than interest in politics. Students who self-identify strongly with one of the political parties are more likely to engage in higher levels of friending and joining activities in both 2008 and 2012. In addition, strong partisans are more likely to engage in higher levels of following political Twitter feeds, and tweeting about politics. Similarly, each unit increase in interest in politics is associated with higher levels of following political Twitter feeds and tweeting about politics. However, interest in politics had inconsistent relationships with other forms of civic activity. For example, higher interest in politics was actually associated with less offline engagement in 2008 although in some specifications it was associated with greater offline engagement in 2012. These characteristics traditionally associated with greater political participation only sometimes drove the political participation of college students and did so only for certain activities. This suggests a different process is at work driving young adults' engagement.

We found some connections between the extent to which students engage in online information consumption and civic engagement. Higher levels of online news consumption lead to increases in offline political activity (in 2008, but not in 2012) and blogging (in 2012, but not in 2008). In addition, increases in the frequency with which a student reads blogs are connected with higher levels of blogging about politics (in 2008, but not consistently in 2012). In fact, the frequency of blog reading has a positive relationship with every form of civic activity (save following political Twitter feeds) in at least one model specification.

In a similar vein, we also find some connection between self-identifying as a liberal and tweeting about politics, and between friending and joining activity and being a supporter of Barack Obama. Interestingly, we discovered that students who self-identified as liberals in 2012 were associated with lower levels of tweeting about politics. Also, students who supported Barack Obama's bid for the presidency in 2008 were connected with higher levels of friending and joining activities in 2008 (but not in 2012). In addition, political science majors and those with more civically engaged peers engaged in higher levels of offline engagement but not all forms of online engagement.

We can safely conclude that strong partisanship affects the civic activity of college students. In this respect, college students who participate more resemble the population as a whole that is more likely to participate. Interest in politics was a less consistent predictor of participation. It was associated with increases in some forms of activity and decreases in others. Yet strong partisans and those with higher levels of interest in politics do not fill the universe of the college students who participate. We found in Chapters 4 and 5 that those lacking strong partisanship and who had average levels of interest in politics and online information consumption still had a significant likelihood of engaging in each of the forms of online participation. Further, even complete political novices had nonzero, albeit small, probabilities of being drawn in to engage in each activity. Online forms of participation have helped expand who participates.

ONLINE AND OFFLINE FORMS OF CIVIC ACTIVITY

Online forms of participation also help expand how college students participate. In Chapters 6 and 7, we investigated the ways in which the varying forms of online engagement connect to one another, as well as, with offline civic activity, while controlling for the effects of issue importance, online information consumption, and respondent attributes. These were some of the strongest and most consistent effects we uncovered. Two main findings result from this investigation. First, online forms of civic activity are connected with offline civic activity, and to some extent, the other way around. We discovered that friending and joining activities are associated with higher levels of offline civic activity, and that higher levels of offline civic engagement are connected with increases in friending and joining activities. Also, we found that increases in offline civic activity are connected with higher levels of tweeting about politics. Finally, we found strong connections that suggest causal relationships between higher levels of friending and joining activity and offline engagement, and between higher levels of tweeting about politics and offline engagement.

Second, we discover a substantial connection between differing forms of online engagement. More specifically, we find that increases in friending and joining activity are connected with higher levels of blogging about politics, and vice versa. We also find that increases in blogging are associated with higher levels of tweeting about politics, and vice versa. In addition, we unearth evidence that higher levels of tweeting about politics are connected with increases in following political Twitter feeds. Further, we find that higher levels of friending and joining activities are associated with higher levels of following political Twitter feeds.

When we put these trends together, they produce a picture that might indicate the presence of some indirect effects across various online forms of civic activity. We found that friending and joining activities positively affect tweeting through blogging. We also discovered that following political Twitter feeds has a positive, statistically significant connection with blogging through tweeting about politics.

Readers should take three main points away from these analyses. First, a variety of online forms of participation lead to greater offline participation. Second, online forms of civic engagement are connected with one another, and in many cases, in mutually reinforcing ways that are difficult to disentangle. Third, and equally interesting, online participation spurs additional participation in other online civic activities through indirect mechanisms as well. Regardless of how college students first foray into politics, their participation is highly likely to spread to other forms. Thus, any analysis that only examines direct effects misses a part of the puzzle.

YOUNG ADULTS AND CIVIC ACTIVITY

While these findings are compelling, there is one potential limitation: they are based on surveys that were performed at a single university. In Chapter 1, we established that students at this university are reflective of college students as a whole on a number of measures. Still, a logical question proceeds as follows: to what extent are these findings generalizable across all young people? Further, are these effects confined to young adults or do they hold true for all adults regardless of age? We tackle these questions by utilizing data from national surveys taken by the Pew Internet Projects before the 2008 and 2012 elections on offline and online forms of civic activity. The 2008 version of this survey was administered from August 12 through September 3 and surveyed a random sample of 2,250 adults via random digit dialing. The 2012 variant of this survey was administered from July 16 through August 7 and surveyed a random sample of 2,250 adults via random digit dialing. Of the 2012 participants, 1,350 were surveyed by landlines while 900 were surveyed by cellular telephones. Princeton Survey Research Associates International administered both surveys on behalf of the Pew Internet and American Life project.

Our dependent variables were offline engagement, friending and joining activities and online political expression. We measured offline engagement through an additive index of seven items ($\alpha = 0.77$, 2008; $\alpha = 0.67$, 2012).[3] Each respondent was asked whether s/he had performed the particular activity sometime in the past twelve months. Because this dependent variable is a count, we utilized a negative binomial regression, as this technique is the one that is most suitable, given the type of data that we analyze (Hilbe 2011). In this case, OLS models are not appropriate because they generate predicted values of the dependent variable that are less than zero (Osgood 2000). Thus, a linear specification, like OLS, distorts the true relationship between our dependent and independent variables (see Hilbe 2011; Osgood 2000).

To measure friending and joining activity in each survey, respondents were asked a set of complementary questions that differed slightly between 2008 and 2012. These questions asked whether a respondent has performed any of a set of activities related to friending and joining activity, like friending any candidates on social networking websites or following elected officials or candidates for office on a social networking website. This variable was coded one for respondents who had performed any of these activities and zero otherwise. Because this dependent variable is binary, we utilized logistic regression. OLS is not the preferred technique to use with binary variables because it neither generates efficient parameter estimates nor always provides predicted values that lie within the bounds of the binary dependent variable (Maddala 1983). On the other hand, logistic regression generates efficient parameter estimates and generates predicted values that lie within the bounds of the dichotomous dependent variable (Maddala 1983).

To measure whether respondents had engaged in any form of online political expression, respondents were asked a set of differing, but complementary questions in the 2008 and 2012 administrations of this survey instrument. In 2008, respondents were asked whether they had posted comments, pictures, video, or had written a blog about a political or social issue. In 2012, respondents were asked whether they had posted links to political stories or articles, posted their own thoughts or comments about political issues, among other activities. For both administrations of this survey, this variable was coded one if a respondent had reported performing any of these activities and zero otherwise. We used logistic regression to test our theoretical expectations with this dependent variable because it is binary. A complete list of the exact questions that were used from the 2008 and 2012 administrations of the Pew survey are available in Appendix B.

We utilize five variables that are coded in a similar fashion to measure some of the concepts about which we theorize earlier in this book. First, we measure the effects of online news consumption through a question that asked respondents in 2008 and 2012 whether they had gotten their news online. This variable is coded one for those who reported having done so, and zero otherwise. Second, we measure the effects of being a supporter of Barack Obama's bid for the presidency (or reelection in 2012) through a question that asked each respondent who they would support if the election were held today. This variable is coded one for those who replied that they would have supported Barack Obama, and zero for those who reported that they would have supported some other candidate. Third, we utilize a question in the 2012 surveys that asked each person to describe his or her political views on a five-point scale that ranged from very conservative to very liberal.[4] From here, we generated two binary variables: one for self-identified liberals (coded one for liberals and zero otherwise), and the other for self-identified conservatives (coded one for conservatives and zero otherwise).[5] We measured the effects of being a young adult (aged 18–25) by generating a binary that is coded one for those who reported their age within this bracket, and zero otherwise.[6] We interacted this variable with each of our independent variables, including the remaining forms of civic activity that are not a dependent variable in a particular specification.

The creation of these interaction terms allows us to conduct several important tests. They allow us to establish the extent to which the relationships we uncovered throughout the book are generalizable. First, they enable us to test whether these effects are confined to college students (or to the students at the university we surveyed) or whether they extend to all 18- to 25-year-olds. Second, they enable us to test whether these effects are limited to 18- to 25-year-olds or whether they extend to all adults. Third, they enable us to test whether these effects are amplified among 18- to 25-year-olds. If neither the engagement variables themselves nor the interactions between engagement and age were significant, it would call the generalizability of our results into serious question. If only the interaction terms are significant, that would indicate these effects only occur among those aged 18 to 25. If the variables themselves are significant but their interactions with age are not significant, this indicates that the effect holds true across age groups. While it includes 18- to 25-year-olds, there is no unique impact among this age. Finally, if both the individual variables and the interaction terms are significant, that would indicate that these variables have an effect across ages but it is amplified (or diminished, depending on the sign) among those aged 18 to 25.

Table 8.1 displays the results. This table contains three sets of models: one for offline engagement, a second for friending and joining activity, and a third for online political expression. There are two models within each set of models: one for the particular activity (e.g., offline engagement) in 2008, and a second one for that same activity in 2012. We interpret the results in this table in a slightly different fashion than that which we used in previous chapters.[7] To interpret the results in this table, we used the margins command in STATA, which allows us to compute the change in the number of predicted activities for negative binomial regressions, and the change in predicted probability for logistic regression models.[8]

We begin by discussing those results that are less central to our core argument. These models furnish some evidence that political context affects civic activity among the entire population, but relatively little evidence that political context has much of an effect specific to 18- to 25-year-olds. The most consistent impact of political context across forms of engagement we uncovered was for online news consumption. In 2012, we discovered that those members of the population who acquired news from online sources were connected with an average of 0.6 additional offline activities, and an increase in the probabilities of friending and joining and online political expression of 28.1% and 10.9%, respectively. However, in 2008, online news consumption failed to exert a significant effect on any civic activity. Online news consumption sometimes results in higher participation and when it does it does so across ages. The Pew data reveals that acquiring news from online sources was not connected with significantly higher or lower levels of civic activity specifically among younger people. Young adults may consume less news but when they do so online, it yields the same positive impact that it does among all adults. These findings are somewhat consistent with the findings about online news consumption in earlier chapters regarding young adults. For example, we found that greater online news consumption was associated with higher levels of blogging and posting about politics in 2012 but not in 2008.

Once we deviate from acquiring news from online sources, political context variables play an even less consistent role in influencing participation. For instance, being an Obama supporter was connected with 0.15 additional offline activities in 2008, and 0.56 additional activities in 2012. However, Obama supporters were no more likely to engage in friending and joining or online political expression than those who supported some other candidate.

In general, Obama supporters between the ages of 18- to 25-year-old were no more likely to engage in higher levels of civic activity than Obama supporters as a whole. However, young Obama supporters were, all else equal, less likely to participate offline as supporters of Obama in this age group exhibited a 0.32 decrease in offline civic activity in 2008 compared to Obama supporters as a whole. Clearly, support for Obama alone was not enough to mobilize young adults. These results, too, are consistent with the limited and inconsistent evidence in previous chapters that support for Obama had any impact on young adults' participation.

In addition, self-identifying as a liberal or conservative is not connected with changes in civic activity most of the time. When we discovered any change, we found a 5.9% increase in the probability of expressing oneself online when a respondent self-identified as a liberal, and a 0.37 increase in the number of offline activities when a respondent identified him or herself as a conservative. Beyond this, we discovered no evidence that 18- to 25-year-olds who self-identified as liberals changed their level of civic activity simply on account of their ideological leaning. This finding mirrors the findings in earlier chapters, which have consistently found little evidence that links ideology and civic activity. However, in 2012 young conservatives were even more likely to engage in offline activity than conservatives as a whole. They had a 0.196 increase in civic engagement above and beyond the 0.369 increase by conservatives as a whole.

The key part of the analysis, though, rests in the effects of participatory forms on one another. We find compelling evidence that participating by one route is connected with a higher likelihood that one participates by other routes. A one standard deviation increase in offline engagement was connected with a 7.5% increase in the predicted probability of friending and joining in 2008, and a 12.5% increase in this predicted probability in 2012. In addition, this same increase in offline engagement is connected with a 10.9% increase in the probability of online political expression in 2008, and a 10.0% increase in this predicted probability in 2012. Moreover, friending and joining was associated with a 0.83 increase in offline civic activity in 2008, and a 0.72 increase in this activity in 2012. Also, when one engaged in friending and joining activity, the predicted probability of engaging in online political expression increases by 33.0% in 2008, and 29.6% in 2012. Additionally, engaging in online political expression is connected with a 0.82 point increase in offline activity in 2008, and a 0.75 point increase in this activity in 2012. Finally, engaging in online political expression increases the predicted probability of friending and joining activity by 23.6% increase in 2008, and 30.5% in 2012. These results indicate that the mobilizing effects of friending, joining, and online expression that we uncovered in this book are not confined to young adults. They extend to anyone that uses them. Further,

Table 8.1 Civic Engagement Models (Pew Data) for 2008 and 2012

	Offline Engagement				*Friending and Joining*				*Online Political Expression*			
Independent Variable	*2008 Model*	*Change in Predicted Number of Activities (2008)*	*2012 Model*	*Change in Predicted Number of Activities (2012)*	*2008 Model*	*Change in Predicted Probability (2008)*	*2012 Model*	*Change in Predicted Probability (2012)*	*2008 Model*	*Change in Predicted Probability (2008)*	*2012 Model*	*Change in Predicted Probability (2012)*
Offline Engagement	–	–	–	–	0.349**	0.075	0.370***	0.125	0.291**	0.109	0.444***	0.100
					(0.116)		(0.066)		(0.101)		(0.087)	
Friending and Joining	0.504**	0.831	0.467***	0.723	–	–	–	–	1.713***	0.330	2.181***	0.296
	(0.168)		(0.079)						(0.412)		(0.354)	
Online Political Expression	0.447**	0.822	0.563***	0.750	1.724***	0.236	2.202***	0.305	–	–	–	–
	(0.147)		(0.103)		(0.409)		(0.350)					
Political Context												
Online News	0.127	0.118	0.678***	0.597	–0.117	0.025	2.757***	0.281	–0.068	–0.035	0.580*	0.109
	(0.134)		(0.182)		(0.416)		(0.785)		(0.339)		(0.299)	
Obama Supporter	0.269*	0.145	0.379***	0.558	0.234	0.037	–0.061	–0.023	–0.357	–0.045	0.053	0.025
	(0.135)		(0.083)		(0.412)		(0.240)		(0.349)		(0.211)	
Liberal	–	–	–0.014	–0.036	–	–	0.321	0.036	–	–	0.433*	0.059
			(0.092)				(0.257)				(0.259)	
Conservative	–	–	0.186*	0.368	–	–	0.330	0.011	–	–	0.060	0.019
			(0.097)				(0.263)				(0.222)	
Age 18–25	–0.110	–0.298	-1.435**	–0.338	0.217	0.090	2.221	0.137	0.322	0.080	–0.069	–0.141
	(0.310)		(0.615)		(0.923)		(1.447)		(0.623)		(0.679)	
Age and Political Context												
Age 18–25 * Offline Engagement	–	–	–	–	0.040	0.027	0.390*	0.093	0.248	0.065	1.047*	0.025
					(0.198)		(0.161)		(0.206)		(0.486)	

Age 18–25 * Friending and Joining	0.060	0.464	0.403*	0.423	–	–	–	–	–0.312	–0.382	–0.399	–0.362
	(0.272)		(0.190)						(0.713)		(0.671)	
Age 18–25 * Online Political Expression	0.338	0.609	1.087*	0.373	–0.333	–0.337	–0.546	0.445	–	–	–	–
	(0.280)		(0.509)		(0.718)		(0.665)					
Age 18–25 * Online News	–0.124	–0.181	–0.365	–0.328	0.783	0.119	–0.886	0.423	–0.415	–0.041	0.352	0.247
	(0.284)		(0.514)		(0.731)		(1.245)		(0.628)		(0.656)	
Age 18–25 * Obama Supporter	–0.532*	–0.315	0.173	0.236	0.160	0.135	–0.322	–0.095	0.196	0.040	0.648	0.192
	(0.295)		(0.181)		(0.703)		(0.503)		(0.662)		(0.564)	
Age 18–25 * Liberal	–	–	0.191	0.214	–	–	–0.412	–0.143	–	–	–0.358	–0.168
			(0.199)				(0.522)				(0.569)	
Age 18–25 * Conservative	–	–	0.349*	0.196	–	–	–1.048*	–0.076	–	–	0.371	0.175
			(0.210)				(0.514)				(0.618)	
Constant	–0.087		–1.195***		-3.061***		-6.004***		-1.743***		-0.904**	
	(0.125)		(0.190)		(0.506)		(0.870)		(0.331)		(0.314)	
N	377		964		377		964		377		964	
F-Statistic	7.36		18.56		6.01		10.68		6.06		8.50	
Prob> F	<0.0001		<0.0001		<0.0001		<0.0001		<0.0001		<0.0001	

Notes: The coefficients are negative binomial regression coefficients for the offline engagement model, and logistic regression coefficients for the friending and joining, and the online political expression models. Further, the values in parenthesis are standard errors. * denotes $p < 0.05$, ** denotes $p < 0.01$, and *** denotes $p < 0.001$, all one-tailed tests.

Source: Surveys from the Pew Research Center (2008 and 2012).

across ages, engaging in one form of participation, whether online or offline, leads to engaging in others. One can safely conclude that online and offline participatory forms are interconnected, as are friending and joining and online political expression.

The plot thickens when we examine whether these activities also have an additional impact that is unique to 18- to 25-year-olds. In 2008, we observed no evidence that offline engagement, friending and joining, and online political expression were connected with any additional increase in online or offline civic activities among 18- to 25-year-olds. In 2012, however, we uncover evidence of several linkages between offline and online forms of civic activity specific to this age group. First, among 18- to 25-year-olds, friending and joining is connected with engaging in 1.15 additional offline civic activities, while the rest of the population experienced an increase of only 0.72 points. Second, 18- to 25-year-olds who engaged in online political expression participated in 1.12 additional offline activities, compared with 0.75 additional activities for the population. Third, a one standard deviation increase in offline engagement among 18- to 25-year-olds was associated with an increase in the predicted probability of friending and joining of 21.8% (compared with a 12.5% increase in this predicted probability among the remainder of the population). Finally, a one standard deviation increase in offline engagement among 18- to 25-year-olds was connected with an increase in the predicted probability of online political expression of 12.5% (compared with a 10% increase in this predicted probability among the rest of the population).

Altogether, this set of results suggests that there are some systematic differences between the ways in which offline and online forms of civic activity fosters engaging in other forms of such activity among 18- to 25-year-olds than it does among the rest of the population. In 2008, the results indicate that friending, joining, online political expression, and offline engagement have a mobilizing effect among all who engage in them. This impact was no smaller or greater among 18- to 25-year-olds than it was for anyone else. Yet, online activity still leveled the participatory playing field in 2008, simply because so many more young people were politically active online. Toward this end, Smith, Schlozman, Verba, and Brady (2009, 51) note the following about the 2008 Pew Research Center survey:

> those under age 35 represent 28% of the respondents in our survey but make up fully 72% of those who make political use of social networking sites, and 55% of those who post comments or visual material about politics on the Web. The youngest members of this group—those under age 25—constitute just 10% of our survey respondents but make up 40% of those who make political use of social networking sites and 29% of those who post comments or visual material about politics online.

While these activities generated no greater impact among young adults than they did among other ages, young adults were so much more likely to engage in online activities that Schlozman, Verba, and Brady (2012, 508) suggest that "the generational digital divide may have the consequence of reducing the participatory underrepresentation of the young." They noted, however, that more study is needed as the Obama campaign may have resulted in 2008 being an anomalous year (Schlozman, Verba, and Brady 2012).

The analysis presented here reveals that in 2012, the story changes. First of all, the age gaps in the online use of political tools shrunk in 2012 relative to 2008. Young adults still had an advantage, but not as great as that in the previous election. Still, we found that online activities continue to be associated with greater offline engagement. Those aged 18 to 25 return to being less likely to participate offline, all else equal, than other age groups, as those in this age group participate in approximately 0.34 fewer activities (perhaps because there was less effort to involve them than there was in 2008). Yet, online activities have an amplified impact on offline activities among young adults in 2012. Thus, we find strong support that online activities help level the participatory playing field for young adults in both years, just via slightly different mechanisms.

OUR RESULTS IN CONTEXT

Throughout this book, we have investigated civic engagement in its varying forms, and as a collective whole. Figure 8.1 provides a snapshot just of college students' campaign-related participation in 2008 and 2012. Not surprisingly, the percent engaged in online campaign-related activities generally eclipses the percent engaged in offline campaign-related activities. After all, these activities tend to carry lower cost to college students. However, candidates have used Facebook and Twitter to extend invitations to participate in other ways and our findings suggest a number of college students respond favorably to these invitations. The percent reported engaging in each of the offline campaign activities might be far lower if not for students' decisions to join, friend, or like candidates.

The findings from this book fit neatly with portions of the literature on civic engagement. For instance, a number of researchers have found a strong link between strong partisanship and a wide variety of civic activities (see e.g., Campbell et al. 1960; Flavin and Griffin 2009; Rosenstone and Hansen 1993; Verba et al. 1995). This is not surprising in that political parties and their affiliated organizations play critical roles in mobilizing people to vote and perform other, mostly offline, civic activities. These organizations can much more easily mobilize those who strongly believe in their cause at the outset.

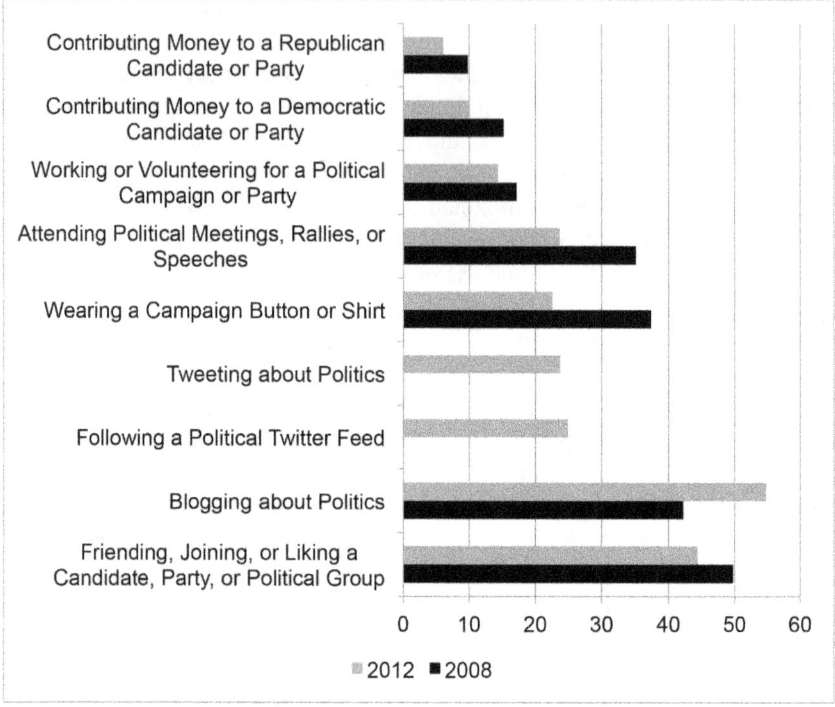

Figure 8.1 Percentage of Students Reporting Engaging in Campaign-Related Activities During the Pre-Election Period. *Source*: Moffett and Rice, Student Election Survey

We have also discovered evidence that interest in politics plays a pivotal role in fostering several online and offline civic activities. As with strong partisanship, this is not too surprising, since many forms of civic activity require high levels of commitment. In addition, the decision to participate in friending and joining activities, as well as following political Twitter feeds requires some sort of public commitment to a particular cause and a willingness to accept any consequences that come from having participated in the political process by that route. However, interest in politics is also associated with lower levels of some forms of activity, such as offline engagement in 2008.

Moreover, we found a two-way relationship between offline civic activity and at least two forms of online civic engagement: friending and joining activity (in 2008 and 2012) and tweeting about politics (2012). Thus, engaging in activity online fosters participatory activity in the offline world. This finding is particularly important because young people are disproportionate users of Facebook and Twitter, the primary outlets for friending and joining activity, as well as tweeting about politics, respectively (Duggan and Brenner 2013). Facebook and Twitter open a door to opportunities for offline participation that a significant percentage of young adults choose to engage. Conversely, participating in civic activity away from the internet also encourages participation in the online world. To a degree, participation begets participation.

Further, we found that a complex, somewhat interrelated web exists between different forms of online participatory activity. This suggests that each online entry point for participation leads to engaging in others and can eventually spill over to the offline world. For instance, we discovered two-way relationships between; (1) friending and joining activity and blogging about politics, (2) blogging about politics and tweeting about politics, and (3) tweeting about politics and following political Twitter feeds. This third finding should not be too surprising, since tweeting and following political Twitter feeds exist within the same social media platform. In this way, it is reasonable that Twitter-related participatory forms are mutually interrelated. However, this finding has important implications for one subgroup of the population: African Americans, as members of this group are more apt to utilize Twitter as a forum of expression compared with members of other racial groups. The complex web of online participation we uncovered suggests their participation is unlikely to stop there. Participation that begins on Twitter soon extends beyond it and encompasses other platforms and routes by which young people can engage the political process. Finally, we found that 18- to 25-year-olds systematically differ from their older counterparts with respect to the relationship between offline civic engagement and online civic activity. In this way, engaging in online forms of civic activity stacks the deck in favor of other online and offline forms of civic activity, especially among young adults.

On the one hand, discovering that online forms of political participation are interrelated is a breakthrough in its own right, as much of the research about online forms of political participation only examines one particular platform, or a single route by which to politically participate. While these studies contribute substantially to what we know about political participation, they left a gap in what we know: what is the relationship between different online forms of political participation? The findings in this book help bridge that gap in two ways. First, we discover that these forms of participation are interrelated in direct and indirect ways. Second, we have unraveled this relationship, in at least a small way. We find that these forms of participation are related in ways that are simultaneously seemingly obvious, and considerably less so.

IMPLICATIONS FOR SOCIAL SCIENTISTS

Our results suggest that scholars tempted to dismiss online forms of participation as slacktivism that is inconsequential or of limited importance do so at their peril. Significant in their own right, many of these forms of online participation also lead young adults both to other forms of online participation and to the traditional political activities long valued in political behavior research. As the online world of political activity continues to change and develop, it belongs at the center, rather than the periphery of such research endeavors.

Our findings provide at least two routes by which others could build upon the framework that we utilize here. Our research was limited in part by currently available statistical methods. It is clear that more work is necessary to further unpack the relationships between friending and joining activity, blogging, following political Twitter feeds, and tweeting about politics. To fully perform this task, one could utilize more sophisticated statistical methodology that allows these relationships to be further explored in a way that is not currently possible. Experimental methodology could also potentially be used to isolate the effects of particular forms of online participation on each other and on offline engagement in a way that survey-based research does not allow.

In addition, researchers might create new surveys to investigate to what extent our findings hold among young adults as a whole rather than college students in particular. While the analysis of Pew Research Center surveys shows that a number of our results are generalizable both beyond 18- to 25-year-olds attending a particular university and beyond 18- to 25-year-old college students, more remains left to uncover regarding how the participation of young adult college students differs from young adults as a whole. Gaps in their levels of internet access have evaporated. As of 2013, only 2% of 18- to 25-year-olds reported that they do not use the internet (Pew 2015). While large percentages of this age group use both Facebook and Twitter, these percentages may mask differences by education level. For example, among the population as a whole users of Twitter and LinkedIn tend to have higher education levels while gaps in usage by education levels for Facebook are quite small (Duggan et al. 2015). In addition, education has been a strong predictor of traditional forms of offline civic activity (see e.g., Verba et al. 1995); this may or may not carry over to young adults and the online world.

IMPLICATIONS FOR POLITICAL CAMPAIGNS

The ability of Howard Dean's Blog for America to build support and raise money helped contribute to a rush of candidates developing online presences. Barack Obama's successful use of Facebook and Twitter inspired campaigns of every ideological persuasion to invest heavily in developing a strong social media presence. These pioneering efforts demonstrated that such investments can have large payoffs. Today, politicians are seeking to successfully exploit more and more new platforms. They create Facebook pages, Twitter handles, and LinkedIn profiles and fill them with content. No one wants to miss the potential gains offered by "the next big thing."

As potential presidential candidates began declaring their intent to run in 2016, they began a rush to image-based Pinterest and Instagram. Pundits began to ask if 2016 would be the first "Instagram Election"—after all, one time favorite for the Republican nomination Jeb Bush announced the creation of his Super PAC aimed at the 2016 presidential election with a video via Instagram. (Schwarz 2015). Although his campaign stumbled, this rush may not be ill-founded—in 2014 usage of Pinterest, Instagram, and LinkedIn have all surpassed Twitter among the population as a whole (Duggan et al. 2015). Pew reports that 18- to 29-year-olds use Instagram, 37% of that age group uses Twitter, 34% uses Pinterest, and 23% uses LinkedIn—they lead the way in usage of Twitter, Instagram, and Pinterest but lag behind on LinkedIn. (Duggan et al. 2015). While Instagram and Pinterest may not offer candidates the same opportunities as other social networking sites, visuals can be powerful in politics, and potential presidential candidates rushed to figure out how to marshal them for their benefit. Hillary Clinton posted old family photos on Instagram and Marco Rubio posted a photo on the bumper cars with his kids at the Iowa State Fair in efforts to connect with voters. Meanwhile, Donald Trump used Instagram to help escalate his Twitter attacks against Jeb Bush, and Bush attempted to fend these off with visual-based attacks of his own (Frumin 2015).

Candidates trying to win their party's nomination for president in 2016 also began rushing to Snapchat to share campaign news and make users feel like they are a part of the campaign. Jeb Bush became the first candidate to officially partner with Snapchat—he did so on the same day he officially launched his campaign, sharing an inside glimpse of the kick off to his campaign with snapchat users as it happened (Smith 2015). Likewise, Hillary Clinton's first official campaign rally was brought to the feeds of 100 million snapchat users (Chittal 2015). Many other candidates opened their own snapchat accounts that they used to share content with their followers. Campaigns began pioneering new efforts to use Snapchat to try and woo supporters. John Kasich became the first campaign to air a time-synchronized geo-filtered ad on Snapchat, wishing residents of New Hampshire good morning with an image of the Kasich campaign logo made out of bacon (Miller 2015). Bernie Sanders became one of the first candidates to extend the social media race to Periscope and Meerkat, with a presence on nearly every major online social network currently in existence (Brenner 2015).

Ted Cruz's campaign also incorporated Periscope into their social media strategy to bring campaign events to those who could not be at one in person (Chittal 2015). While a number of candidates have subreddits devoted to them on Reddit, the Sanders for President subreddit has generated several hundred thousand comments and has been successfully used for grassroots organizing (Barthel et al. 2016). In fact, Sanders' supporters were active on Reddit even before he officially announced his candidacy (Lapowsky 2015). Other campaigns followed suit, seeking to use a number of social media platforms to their advantage.

The brief history of web 2.0 applications suggests that some of these efforts may be wasted. Their popularity can be fleeting. In 2008, MySpace had more users than Facebook—it may have seemed a more likely source for mobilizing supporters. Yet it was Facebook, not MySpace that was leveraged successfully. Today MySpace is only a dim memory in American culture. When new platforms and applications emerge on the scene, they must fight for attention. Sometimes they face a field of competitors trying to become the next online focal point. Some are slow to achieve a critical mass—others never live up to their potential. Both Barack Obama and John McCain were on Twitter in 2008 but Obama could not quite manage 120,000 followers and McCain had less than 5,000 (Dutta and Fraser 2008). In an election where only 9% of internet-connected American adults reporting using Twitter (Lenhart and Fox 2009) its potential was limited. Four years later, the percentage of Americans on Twitter grew significantly and Obama's followers on Twitter swelled to over 20 million (Felix 2012). Twitter went from an inconsequential campaign aside to a crucial part of campaign efforts in four short years.

While not every effort will pay off, sitting a platform out entirely or minimizing a presence on it may pose too big a risk. Our research makes clear that campaigns who use social media effectively can draw in young adults and leverage their energy for other important campaign activities both online and offline. Online efforts that will reach predominantly young adults are far from wasted and should not dissuade campaigns from investing in them.

While virtually all the contenders for president in 2016 have used a variety of social media platforms in their campaigns, perhaps none has better illustrated the main points of this book than the Bernie Sanders campaign. His campaign addresses issues of high importance or interest to young adults. He campaigned that college should be free and that marijuana should be legal. The latter position is supported by over 70% of those aged 18 to 34 (Jones 2015) while the former would make a college education accessible to all young adults without taking on a crushing load of student loans. These issues have helped make him particularly popular with young adults. In addition, his campaign has actively sought to reach out and engage young adults on a wide range of social media platforms. Young adults kept up to date with the Sanders campaign through their Snapchat feeds and shared opportunities to get involved on subreddits. His combination of reaching out to young adults on the social media platforms they already populate and speaking about issues of high importance to young adults, earned him a large and passionate group of young adult supporters who helped campaign for him and supported him in the polls. In New Hampshire, exit polls showed 83% of voters between the ages of 18 and 29 voted for Sanders (Bradner and Merica 2016). As the primary schedule marched on, he continued to garner large shares of the young adult vote.

Bernie Sanders also brought his message directly to college campuses on the campaign trail. One of those campuses was the one at the focus of our Student Election Survey: Southern Illinois University Edwardsville (SIUE). The news of his visit first broke on the Twitter handle @SIUE at 12:27 p.m. on March 2, 2016. While it would not be confirmed by the campaign until the following day, students were abuzz about his visit by the time one of us taught a 1:30 p.m. class on March 2. Students spread the news through a variety of social media platforms. When requests for volunteers went out on e-mail, Facebook, and Twitter, students enthusiastically responded. While the call time for some of the volunteers began at 6:00 a.m. on March 4, some students told local media they began lining up to the attend the rally at 1:30 a.m. By 7:00 a.m., the line stretched so long that the gymnasium where the rally would be held was not visible from the line's end. Enthusiastic student volunteers walked up and down the line looking for anyone who might need special assistance and asking people to sign up to volunteer for the campaign. Meanwhile, once inside, a campaign worker went through the crowd reminding people that liking Sanders on Facebook isn't voting, attending a rally isn't voting, volunteering isn't voting, only voting is voting.

While people had come from miles around to hear Bernie Sanders and a variety of ages were represented, much of the crowd was made up of young adults, many of whom were students. His calls for free college were met by particularly long and loud cheers. The gymnasium where the rally was held was packed to capacity at 4,700 while another estimated 1,000 waited outside and were briefly greeted by Sanders (Donald 2016). Once he left, SIUE Students for Bernie continued its efforts on Facebook and other social media platforms to organize students to vote. While Hillary Clinton narrowly won Illinois less than two weeks later, Bernie Sanders carried Madison County, where SIUE is located, by just over a ten point margin. Meanwhile, in Edwardsville's 21st precinct, whose polling place is at SIUE, Bernie Sanders won 91.4% of the vote. Clearly, when candidates reach out to students where they are, both via social media and in person, with issues they care about, students respond.

IMPLICATIONS FOR STUDENTS AND THOSE WHO WISH TO INCREASE YOUNG ADULTS' PARTICIPATION

As web developers and programmers continue to create new web 2.0 applications and campaigns continue to try to convert them into effective tools for campaigning, young adults remain best positioned to take advantage of most efforts on the cutting edge of political participation. As the internet and mobile usage of children and teenagers make clear, each new cohort of college students for the foreseeable future will face a technological advantage. And, as this book uncovers, when campaigns use online tools to offer opportunities for involvement, a sizeable portion of young adults respond.

Encouraging young people in their online civic endeavors yields very real, tangible benefits away from the internet. Further, emphasizing issues of great concern to young adults may encourage them to become more involved and engaged. However, based on the results here, predicting which form of involvement they may choose as a result might prove difficult.

Those concerned over young adults' low levels of participation in traditional forms of offline civic engagement would do well to invest in online outreach. As our research shows, when college students get involved in one form of online participation, they become more likely to branch out into others. Helping young adults leverage their online political power can have important offline consequences as well.

Voting is the gold standard of political participation for good reason yet it is not the only form of political participation of consequence. When young adults engage in seemingly passive activities like friending or liking a candidate or political group on Facebook or following them on Twitter, they also become more likely to engage in expressive forms of political participation, like blogging or tweeting about politics. Thus, encouraging students to invite politics into their social networks provides a pathway to raising their voices and venturing into less familiar and costlier forms of offline participation.

NOTES

1. These issues were the economy, education, energy, college financing, health care, environment, abortion, immigration, and same sex marriage.

2. In sum, there was at least one model specification in which each issue had an effect on some form of civic engagement. However, there are few specifications in which college financing or abortion affected any form of civic activity. When we found any evidence concerning college financing or abortion, it was inconsistent at best. Thus, these issues appear to have little to no effect on online or offline civic activities.

3. These seven items are as follows: (1) Attended a political rally or speech; (2) Attended an organized protest of any kind; (3) Attended a political meeting on local, town or school affairs; (4) Worked or volunteered for a political party or candidate; (5) Been an active member of any group that tries to influence public policy or government, not including a political party; (6) Worked with fellow citizens to solve a

problem in your community; and (7) Contacted a national, state, or local government official in person, by phone, or by letter about an issue that is important to you.

4. Regrettably, ideology was not queried in the 2008 Pew surveys.

5. For both variables, political moderates act as the relevant comparison category.

6. There are fewer independent variables in these tables as compared with the models in previous chapters. The primary reason for the difference that we observe here is that several key theoretical constructs that were central parts of earlier chapters were not asked in both surveys. More specifically, strength of partisanship, the importance of issues, unique questions about Twitter-based activities (that were not embedded in other social networking questions), blog readership, major in college, or interest in politics were not asked about in either the 2008 and 2012 administrations of this survey. With these caveats in mind, we proceed with using the Pew surveys because they are the only surveys that asked a nationally representative sample in 2008 and 2012 about offline and online civic activities.

7. In previous chapters, we used the CLARIFY routines to perform this task. These routines do not work in this case, because the Pew survey data are weighted, and the CLARIFY routines do not allow for weighted data to be used.

8. By default, this command sets all binary variables equal to zero, continuous variables at their mean, and binary variables at zero. To compute the predicted change in the number of activities, for instance, we changed each binary variable from zero to one, while holding all other binaries and interactives at zero, and continuous variables at their mean. For continuous variables, we changed the value for these variables from the mean to one standard deviation above it, while holding binaries and interactives at zero, and any other continuous variable at its mean. We performed analogous steps for the changes in predicted probability for the logistic regression models. When we examine interactive variables, we set the constitutive term (i.e., age binary) to one, and the interacted term at its mean (for a continuous variable) or one (for a binary variable).

Appendix A

Question Wording and Summary Statistics for Student Election Survey Variables

In this appendix, we identify the question wording for each of the variables included in this analysis, including all dependent and independent variables. Then, we give summary statistics for each variable used in our analysis. This appendix contains the complete list of variables from the surveys that we used in this book. In all parts of the survey, students had the option of declining to answer a question. For those variables in which alpha was less than .8, we report the correlation matrix for each of the items in the index.

DEPENDENT VARIABLES

Online Friending or Joining Activity

2008

During 2008, how often have you friended or joined a group related to a presidential candidate or political party on a social networking site such as MySpace or Facebook?

1) Never; 2) Rarely; 3) Sometimes; 4) Regularly; 5) Very Often

2012

During 2012, how often have you friended or joined a professional network related to a presidential candidate or political party on a social networking site such as Facebook or LinkedIn?

1) Never; 2) Rarely; 3) Sometimes; 4) Regularly; 5) Very Often

Blogging

During 2008 (2012), how often have you expressed your views about politics on a website, blog, or chatroom?

1) Never; 2) Rarely; 3) Sometimes; 4) Regularly; 5) Very Often

Following Political Tweets

During 2012, how often have you followed Twitter feeds of presidential candidates, political parties, or other politically-oriented groups?

4) Very Often; 3) Often; 2) Sometimes; 1) Rarely; 0) Not at All; 5) Don't Know or Do Not have a Twitter Account

Tweeting

During 2012, how often have you tweeted about any presidential candidate, political party, or other politically-oriented cause?

4) Very Often; 3) Often; 2) Sometimes; 1) Rarely; 0) Not at All; 5) Don't Know or Do Not have a Twitter Account

Offline Civic Engagement Activities

During 2008 (2012), how often have you…

a. Worn a campaign button or shirt, put a campaign sticker on your car, or placed a sign in your window or in front of your residence
b. Tried to talk to people and explain why they should vote for or against one of the parties or candidates
c. Contacted a newspaper, radio, or TV talk show to express your opinion on an issue
d. Attended any political meetings, rallies, speeches, dinners, or things like that in support of a particular candidate
e. Participated in political activities such as protests, marches, or demonstrations
f. Worked or volunteered on a political campaign for a candidate or party
g. Contacted or visited someone in government who represents your community
h. Worked with a group to solve a problem in a community
i. Made a purchasing decision based on the conduct or values of a company

j. Contributed money to a Republican candidate, political party, or affiliated organization
k. Contributed money to a Democratic candidate, political party, or affiliated organization
l. How frequently have you ever participated in any community service or volunteer activity? By volunteer activity, we mean actually working in some way to help others for no pay

Each question was asked using a scale of 0 to 4 with 0 equivalent to never and 4 equivalent to very often. Don't know option included.

Online Civic Engagement Index
Defined in Chapter 2.
Post-Election Offline Civic Engagement Index
Defined in Chapter 6.

INDEPENDENT VARIABLES

Issue Importance

How important are candidates' stances on each of the following issues in influencing your decision about who you will vote for?

a. Economy
b. Health care
c. Abortion
d. Same-sex marriage
e. Immigration
f. Energy
g. Environment
h. Education
i. College financing

Each question was asked using a scale of 0 to 4 with 0 equivalent to not at all important and 4 equivalent to very important.

Frequency of Political Blog Reading

In a typical week, how often do you read internet blogs about politics and current events?

4) Very Often; 3) Often; 2) Sometimes; 1) Rarely; 0) Not at All; 5) Don't Know

Frequency of Online News Reading

In a typical week, how often do you read news on the internet about politics and current events?

4) Very Often; 3) Often; 2) Sometimes; 1) Rarely; 0) Not at All; 5) Don't Know

Peer Civic Experiences

How much do you agree or disagree with the following statements?

a. My friends are active in volunteer work in their community
b. My friends vote in elections
c. My friends encourage me to express my opinions about politics and current events even if they are different from their views

Note: Each question was asked using a scale of 0 to 4 with 0 equivalent to strongly disagree and 4 equivalent to strongly agree. Don't know option included.

In 2008, the correlation between friends vote in elections and friends are active in volunteer work is .381, the correlation between friends encourage expression about politics and current events and friends are active in volunteer work is .350, and the correlation between friends encourage expression about politics and current events and friends vote in elections is .480. In 2012, the correlation between friends vote in elections and friends are active in volunteer work is .410, the correlation between friends encourage expression about politics and current events and friends are active in volunteer work is .315, and the correlation between friends encourage expression about politics and current events and friends vote in elections is .574.

Political Science Major

If you have declared a major(s), what is your area(s) of study? (check all that apply)

_____ Arts; _____ Architecture ; _____ Business; _____ Education; _____ Engineering; _____ Humanities; _____ Interdisciplinary; _____ Math and Sciences; _____ Nursing; _____ Political Science; _____ Social Sciences, other than Political Science; _____ Social Work; _____ Undeclared; _____ Other

Military

Have you ever served or are you currently serving in the U.S. military, the National Guard, military reserves, or in a ROTC program?

1) Yes; 2) No

Interest in Politics

How interested would you say you are in politics? Are you…

0) Not at all interested; 1) Not very interested; 2) Somewhat interested; 3) Very interested; 4) Don't Know

Ideology (Constructed from these Questions)

Generally speaking, how would you describe your political ideology?

1) Very conservative; 2) Conservative; 3) Moderate; 4) Liberal; 5) Very liberal; 6) Other ___________; 7) Don't know

If the respondent answered "moderate" or "don't know" for ideology, then s/he was asked the following question:

If you had to choose, would you consider yourself a liberal or a conservative?

1) Liberal; 2) Conservative

Intend to Vote for Obama

Who do you think you will vote for in the election for President? [randomize order]

2008 Options

1) John McCain; 2) Barack Obama; 3) Ralph Nader; 4) Bob Barr; 5) Undecided; 6) Other

2012 Options

1) Mitt Romney; 2) Barack Obama; 3) Jill Stein; 4) Gary Johnson; 5) Undecided; 6) Other

Strong Partisan

Generally speaking, do you usually think of yourself as a Republican, a Democrat, an Independent, or something else?

1) Republican; 2) Democrat; 3) Independent; 4) Other ________________

If the respondent answered "Republican," for partisan identification, then s/he was asked the following question:

Do you think of yourself as strongly Republican or not very strong?

1) Strong Republican; 2) Not very strong Republican

If the respondent answered "Democrat," for partisan identification, then s/he was asked the following question:

Do you think of yourself as strongly Democratic or not very strong?

1) Strong Democrat; 2) Not very strong Democrat

Table A1 Summary Statistics for Online and Offline Civic Engagement Variables

	2008					2012				
Variable	*Number of Observations*	*Mean*	*Standard Deviation*	*Minimum*	*Maximum*	*Number of Observations*	*Mean*	*Standard Deviation*	*Minimum*	*Maximum*
Dependent Variables										
Friending and Joining	358	1.25	1.46	0	4	575	0.93	1.25	0	4
Blogging	358	0.93	1.33	0	4	578	1.13	1.29	0	4
Following on Twitter	–	–	–	–	–	350	1.21	1.47	0	4
Tweeting about Politics	–	–	–	–	–	349	1.10	1.43	0	4
Offline Civic Engagement	349	8.75	6.05	0	36	600	8.36	6.79	0	44
Post-Election Offline Engagement	181	3.61	2.18	0	11	359	3.01	2.22	0	14
Online Civic Engagement Index	–	–	–	–	–	327	4.57	4.43	0	16
Issue Importance										
Economy	363	3.47	0.66	0	4	623	3.37	0.78	0	4
Education	362	3.31	0.80	0	4	624	3.48	0.71	0	4
Energy	362	3.10	0.89	0	4	622	2.70	0.97	0	4
College Financing	362	3.20	0.96	0	4	624	3.38	0.89	0	4
Health Care	362	3.10	0.86	0	4	624	3.16	0.89	0	4
Environment	361	2.89	0.97	0	4	621	2.68	1.00	0	4
Abortion	362	2.35	1.28	0	4	621	2.50	1.29	0	4
Immigration	362	2.27	1.00	0	4	622	2.42	1.09	0	4
Same Sex Marriage	362	1.97	1.30	0	4	625	2.43	1.33	0	4
Information Consumption										
Frequency of Blog Reading	349	1.29	1.22	0	4	620	1.43	1.33	0	4
Online News Consumption	350	2.46	1.22	0	4	618	2.29	1.26	0	4
Respondent Characteristics										
Peer Civic Experiences	313	7.84	2.15	0	12	546	7.16	2.48	0	12
Political Science Major	366	0.03	0.17	0	1	617	0.06	0.23	0	1
Military	352	0.05	0.22	0	1	621	0.03	0.17	0	1
Interest in Politics	364	2.99	0.77	0	3	621	1.79	0.86	0	3
Liberal	366	0.35	0.48	0	1	627	0.32	0.47	0	1
Conservative	366	0.22	0.41	0	1	627	0.22	0.41	0	1
Obama Supporters	344	0.58	0.50	0	1	574	0.49	0.50	0	1
Strong Partisan	366	0.38	0.49	0	1	626	0.32	0.47	0	1
African American	–	–	–	–	–	627	0.08	0.28	0	1

Source: Moffett and Rice, Student Election Survey.

Appendix B

Question Wording and Summary Statistics for 2008 and 2012 Pew Surveys Variables

In this appendix, we identify the question wording for each of the variables included in this analysis, including all dependent and independent variables based on the Pew data. Then, we give summary statistics for each variable used in our analysis. This appendix contains the complete list of variables from the surveys that we used in this book. In all parts of the survey, respondents had the option of declining to answer a question.

DEPENDENT VARIABLES

Offline Civic Engagement

Here's a list of activities some people do and others do not. For each, please tell me if you have done this in the past 12 months or not. In the past 12 months, have you:

a. Attended a political rally or speech
b. Attended an organized protest of any kind
c. Attended a political meeting on local, town or school affairs
d. Worked or volunteered for a political party or candidate
e. Been an active member of any group that tries to influence public policy or government, not including a political party
f. Worked with fellow citizens to solve a problem in your community
g. Contacted a national, state, or local government official in person, by phone, or by letter about an issue that is important to you

Friending and Joining Activity

2008

Thinking about what you have done on social networking sites like Facebook and MySpace, have you:

a. Gotten any campaign or candidate information on the sites?
b. Started or joined a political group, or group supporting a cause on a social networking site?
c. Signed up as a "friend" of any candidates on a social networking site?

2012

Do you currently:

a. belong to a group on a social networking site that is involved in political or social issues, or that is working to advance a cause
b. follow any elected officials, candidates for office or other political figures on a social networking site or on Twitter

Online Political Expression

2008

Now thinking about what some people do on the internet… In the past 12 months, have you:

a. Posted comments on a website or blog about a political or social issue
b. Posted PICTURES on the internet about a political or social issue
c. Posted VIDEO on the internet about a political or social issue
d. Written in your blog about a political or social issue

2012

Do you ever use social networking sites or Twitter to

a. Post links to political stories or articles for others to read
b. Post your own thoughts or comments on political or social issues
c. Encourage other people to take action on a political or social issue that is important to you
d. Repost content related to political or social issues that was originally posted by someone else
e. "Like" or promote material related to political or social issues that others have posted

INDEPENDENT VARIABLES

Online News

Please tell me if you ever use the internet to do any of the following things. Did you ever get news online?

This is coded 1 if the respondent replied yes, and zero otherwise.

Obama Supporter

If the 2008 (2012) election were being held today and the candidates were_____, who would you vote for?

1. Barack Obama
2. John McCain (2008)
3. Mitt Romney (2012)
4. Other Candidate
5. Would not vote
6. Don't Know
7. Refused to Answer

Ideology (2012 Only)

In general, would you describe your political views as:

1. Very conservative
2. Conservative
3. Moderate
4. Liberal
5. Very liberal
6. Don't know
7. Refused

Age 18–25

What is your age?

Table B1 Summary Statistics for Online and Offline Civic Engagement Variables (Pew Surveys)

	2008					2012				
Variable	*Number of Observations*	*Mean*	*Standard Deviation*	*Minimum*	*Maximum*	*Number of Observations*	*Mean*	*Standard Deviation*	*Minimum*	*Maximum*
Dependent Variables										
Friending and Joining	1,010	0.069	0.254	0	1	1,203	0.289	0.454	0	1
Blogging	1,501	0.131	0.337	0	1	1,198	0.655	0.475	0	1
Offline Civic Engagement	2,228	1.208	1.489	0	7	2,236	1.187	1.436	0	7
Political Context										
Online News Consumption	2,251	0.775	0.418	0	1	2,251	0.672	0.470	0	1
Obama Supporter	2,251	0.341	0.474	0	1	1,893	0.426	0.495	0	1
Liberal	–	–	–	–	–	2,069	0.233	0.423	0	1
Conservative	–	–	–	–	–	2,069	0.414	0.293	0	1
Age 18-25	2,198	0.064	0.245	0	1	2,215	0.121	0.326	0	1

Source: Moffett and Rice, Student Election Survey.

References

Abel, Jaison R., Richard Dietz and Yaqin Su 2014. "Are Recent College Graduates Finding Good Jobs?" *Current Issues in Economics and Finance* 20: 1–8. http://www.newyorkfed.org/research/current_issues/ci20–1.pdf.

Abramowitz, Alan I. 1992. "It's Abortion, Stupid: Policy Voting in the 1992 Presidential Election." *The Journal of Politics* 57(1): 176–86.

Altman, Alex 2011. "Public Workers Protest in Wisconsin." *Time.com.* February 16, 2011. http://swampland.time.com/2011/02/16/public-workers-protest-in-wisconsin.

Armstrong, Cory L. and Melinda J. McAdams 2011. "Blogging the Time Away? Young Adults' Motivations for Blog Use." *Atlantic Journal of Communication* 19(2): 113–28.

Barthel, Michael, Galen Stocking, Jesse Holcomb and Amy Mitchell. 2016. "In discussions about presidential candidates, Sanders mentioned far more than others." February 25, 2016. http://www.journalism.org/2016/02/25/in-discussions-about-presidential-candidates-sanders-mentioned-far-more-than-others/.

Baumgartner, Jody C. and Jonathan S. Morris 2010. "MyFaceTube Politics: Social Networking Websites and Political Engagement of Young Adults." *Social Science Computer Review* 28(1): 24–44.

Beck, Paul Allen and M. Kent Jennings 1979. "Political Periods and Political Participation." *American Political Science Review* 73(3): 737–50.

Bedolla, Lisa Garcia 2005. *Fluid Borders; Latino Power, Identity, and Politics in Los Angeles*. Berkeley, CA: University of California Press.

Bekafigo, Marija Anna and Allan McBride 2013. "Who Tweets About Politics?: Political Participation of Twitter Users During the 2011 Gubernatorial Elections." *Social Science Computer Review* 31(5): 625–43.

Bennett, Stephen E., Richard S. Flickinger and Staci L. Rhine 2000. "Political Talk Over Here, Over There, Over Time." *British Journal of Political Science* 30(1): 99–120.

Bereznak, Alyssa 2014. "A Q and A with the Teen Who Took the Photo of 'Alex from Target.'" November 13, 2014. https://www.yahoo.com/tech/a-q-a-with-the-teen-who-took-the photo-of-alex-from-101970340239.html.

Best, Samuel J. and Brian S. Krueger 2005. "Analyzing the Representativeness of Internet Political Participation." *Political Behavior* 27(2): 183–216.

Bilton, Nick 2014. "Alex from Target: The Other Side of Fame." November 13, 2014. http://www.nytimes.com/2014/11/13/style/alex-from-target-the-other-side-of-fame.html?_r=0.

Blais, Andre 2000. *To Vote or Not to Vote: The Merits and Limits of Rational Choice Theory*. Pittsburgh, PA: University of Pittsburgh Press.

Bloom, Joel 2003. "The Blogosphere: How a Once-Humble Medium Came to Drive Elite Media Discourse and Influence Public Policy and Elections." Paper presented at the annual meeting of the American Political Science Association, Philadelphia, PA.

Bond, Robert M., Christopher J. Fariss, Jason J. Jones, Adam D.I. Kramer, Cameron Marlow, Jaime E. Settle and James H. Fowler 2012. "A 61-Million-Person Experiment in Social Influence and Political Mobilization." *Nature* 489: 295–98.

Bradner, Eric and Dan Merica 2016. "Young Voters Abandon Hillary Clinton for Bernie Sanders." February 10, 2016. http://www.cnn.com/2016/02/10/politics/hillary-clinton-new-hampshire-primary/.

Brenner, Joanna 2015. "Tracking the 2016 Presidential Hopefuls on Social Media." August 10, 2015. http://www.newsweek.com/tracking-2016-presidential-hopefuls-social-media-361548.

Brenner, Joanna and Aaron Smith 2013. "72% of Online Adults are Social Networking Site Users." November 21, 2014. http://www.pewinternet.org/2013/08/05/72-of-online-adults-are-social-networking-site-users/.

Bruns, Axel, Jean Burgess, Kate Crawford and Frances Shaw 2012. "#qldfloods and @QPSMedia: Crisis Communication on Twitter in the 2011 South East Queensland Floods." Brisbane: ARC Centre of Excellence for Creative Industries and Innovation. Retrieved from, http://cci.edu.au/floodsreport.pdf.

Bruns, Axel, Tim Highfield and Jean Burgess 2013. "The Arab Spring and Social Media Audiences: English and Arabic Twitter users and their Networks." *American Behavioral Scientist* 57(7): 871–98.

Bryant, Ben 2012. "Four out of Five Young People Feel 'Lost' Without Internet." *The Guardian*, October 30, 2012. http://www.telegraph.co.uk/technology/internet/9643082/Four-out-of-five-young-people-feel-lost-without-internet.html.

Bureau of Labor Statistics 2014. "Volunteering in the United States, 2013." November 19, 2014. http://www.bls.gov/news.release/volun.nr0.htm.

Campbell, Andrea Louise 2003. "Participatory Reactions to Policy Threats: Senior Citizens and the Defense of Social Security and Medicare." *Political Behavior* 25(1): 29–49.

Campbell, Andrea Louise 2011. *How Policies Make Citizens: Senior Political Activism and the American Welfare State*. Princeton, NJ: Princeton University Press.

Campbell, Angus, Philip E. Converse, Warren E. Miller and Donald E. Stokes 1960. *The American Voter*. New York, NY: John Wiley and Sons, Inc.

Carmines, Edward G. and James A. Stimson 1980. "The Two Faces of Issue Voting." *American Political Science Review* 74(1): 78–91.

Carr, David 2008. "How Obama Tapped into Social Networks' Power." *The New York Times*. November 9, 2008.http://www.nytimes.com/2008/11/10/business/media/10carr.html?_r=0.

Center for Information and Research on Civic Learning and Engagement 2013. "The Youth Vote in 2012." November 19, 2014. http://www.civicyouth.org/wp-content/uploads/2013/05/CIRCLE_2013FS_outhVoting2012FINAL.pdf.

Cheng, Jiesi, Aaron Sun, Daning Hu and Daniel Zeng 2011. "An Information Diffusion-Based Recommendation Framework for Micro-Blogging." *Journal of the Association of Information Systems* 12(7): 463–86.

Cheong, France and Christopher Cheong 2011. "Social Media Data Mining: A Social Network Analysis of Tweets during the 2010–2011 Australian Floods." Proceedings of the Pacific Asia Conference on Information Systems, Paper 46. http://aisel.aisnet.org/pacis2011/46.

Chittal, Nisha 2015. "How Ted Cruz's Digital Team Wants to Win the Internet in 2016." May 9, 2015. http://www.msnbc.com/msnbc/how-ted-cruz-digital-team-wants-win-the-internet-2016

Chittal, Nisha 2015. "2016 Candidates Turn to Snapchat to Announce Their Campaigns." June 16, 2015. http://www.msnbc.com/msnbc/2016-candidates-turn-snapchat-announce-their-campaigns.

Converse, Philip 1964. "The Nature of Belief Systems in Mass Publics." In *Ideology and Discontent*. Ed. David E. Apter. New York, NY: Free Press, 206–61.

Curtis, Anthony R. 2014. "The Brief History of Social Media." December 3, 2014. http://www2.uncp.edu/home/acurtis/NewMedia/SocialMedia/SocialMediaHistory.html.

Dalton, Russell J. 2008. *The Good Citizen: How a Younger Generation is Reshaping American Politics*. Washington, DC: CQ Press.

Dawson, Michael C. 1995. *Behind the Mule: Race and Class in African-American Politics*. Princeton, NJ: Princeton University Press.

Dawson, Michael C. 2003. *Black Visions: The Roots of Contemporary African-American Political Ideologies*. Chicago, IL: University of Chicago Press.

De Zuniga, Homero Gil, Eulalia Puig-i-abril and Hernando Rojas. 2009. "Weblogs, Traditional Sources Online and Political Participation: An Assessment of how the Internet is Changing the Environment." *New Media and Society* 11(4): 553–74.

Delli Carpini, Michael X., Fay Lomax Cook and Lawrence R. Jacobs 2004. "Public Deliberations, Discursive Participation and Citizen Engagement: A Review of the Empirical Literature." *Annual Review of Political Science* 7(1): 315–44.

Donald, Elizabeth 2016. "Bernie Sanders at SIUE: 'We can create the nation we want to become." March 4, 2016. http://www.bnd.com/news/local/article63996377.html.

Downs, Anthony 1957. *An Economic Theory of Democracy*. New York, NY: Harper.

Dugan, Andrew 2013. "Democrats Enjoy 2–1 Advantage over GOP Among Hispanics. Gallup Politics. Released February 19." July 11, 2014. http://www.gallup.com/poll/160706/democrats-enjoy-advantage-gop-among-hispanics.aspx.

Duggan, Maeve and Joanna Brenner 2013. "The Demographics of Social Media Users-2012: Social Networking Site Users." November 21, 2014. http://www.pewinternet.org/2013/02/14/social-networking-site-users/.

Duggan, Maeve, Nicole B. Ellison, Cliff Lampe, Amanda Lenhart and Mary Madden 2015. "Social Media Update 2014." *Pew Research Center*. March 23, 2015http://www.pewinternet.org/2015/01/09/social-media-update-2014/.

Dunne, Aine, Margaret-Anne Lawlor and Jennifer Rowley 2010. "Young People's use of Online Social Networking Sites-A Uses and Gratifications Perspective." *Journal of Research in Interactive Marketing* 4(1): 46–58.

Dutta, Soumitra and Matthew Fraser. 2008. "Barack Obama and the Facebook Election." *US News and World Report.* November 19. http://www.usnews.com/opinion/articles/2008/11/19/barack-obama-and-the-facebook-election.

Ekdale, Brian, Kang Namkoong and Timothy K.F. Fung. 2010. "Why Blog? (then and now): Exploring the Motivations for Blogging by Popular American Political Bloggers." *New Media and Society* 12(2): 217–34.

Eltantawy, Nahed and Julie B. Wiest 2011. "Social Media in the Egyptian Revolution: Reconsidering Resource Mobilization Theory." *International Journal of Communication* 5(2011): 1207–24.

Felix, Samantha. 2012. "Side by Side: How Obama and Romney's Social Media Battle Stacks Up." *Business Insider.* September 23. http://www.businessinsider.com/winner-of-the-obamaromney-social-media-campaign-2012–9?op=1.

Finkel, Steven E. and Gregory Trevor 1986. "Reassessing Ideological Bias in Campaign Participation." *Political Behavior* 8(4): 374–90.

Flavin, Patrick and John D. Griffin 2009. "Policy, Preferences, and Participation: Government's Impact on Democratic Citizenship." *The Journal of Politics* 71(2): 544–59.

Fournier, Patrick, Andre Blais, Richard Nadeau, Elisabeth Gidengil and Neil Nevitte 2003. "Issue Importance and Performance Voting." *Political Behavior* 25(1): 51–67.

Fowler, James H. and Cindy D. Kam 2007 "Beyond the Self: Social Identity, Altruism, and Political Participation." *The Journal of Politics* 69(3): 813–27.

Frumin, Aliyah 2015. "The New 2016 Battleground: Instagram." *MSNBC*. September 6, 2015. http://www.msnbc.com/msnbc/the-new-2016-battleground-instagram

Fullerton, Andrew S. 2009. "A Conceptual Framework for Ordered Logistic Regression Models." *Sociological Methods and Research* 38(2): 306–47.

Gainous, Jason and Kevin M. Wagner 2014. *Tweeting to Power: The Social Media Revolution in American Politics*. Oxford, UK: Oxford University Press.

Godbout, Jean-Francois and Eric Belanger 2007. "Economic Voting and Political Sophistication in the United States: A Reassessment." *Political Research Quarterly* 60(3): 541–54.

Greene, William H. 2000. *Econometric Analysis*. 4th Ed. Upper Saddle River, NJ: Prentice Hall.

Groshek, Jacob and Ahmed Al-Rawi 2013. "Public Sentiment and Critical Framing in Social Media Content during the 2012 U.S. Presidential Campaign." *Social Science Computer Review* 31(5): 563–76.

Hargittai, Eszter and Eden Litt 2011. "The Tweet Smell of Celebrity Success: Explaining Variation in Twitter Adoption among a Diverse Group of Young Adults." *New Media Society* 13(5): 824–42.

Hargittai, Eszter, Jason Gallo and Matthew Kane 2008. "Cross-Ideological Discussions among Conservative and Liberal Bloggers." *Public Choice* 134(1–2): 67–86.

Hawley, George 2013. "Issue Voting and Immigration: Do Restrictionist Policies Cost Congressional Republicans Votes?" *Social Science Quarterly* 94(5): 1185–1206.

Hero, Rodney E. 2000. *Faces of Inequality: Social Diversity in American Politics*. New York, NY: Oxford University Press.

Herzog, A. Regula, Robert L. Kahn, James N. Morgan, James S. Jackson and Toni C. Antonucci 1989. "Age Differences in Productive Activities." *Journal of Gerontology* 44(4): S129–38.

Hilbe, Joseph M. 2011. *Negative Binomial Regression*. 2nd Ed. New York City, NY: Cambridge University Press.

Hutchings, Vincent L. and Nicholas A. Valentino 2004. "The Centrality of Race in American Politics." *Annual Review of Political Science* 7: 383–408.

Johnson, Thomas J. and Barbara K. Kaye 2004. "Wag the Blog: How Reliance on Traditional Media and the Internet Influence Credibility Perceptions of Weblogs among Blog Users." *Journalism and Mass Communication Quarterly* 81(3): 622–42.

Jones, Jeffrey M. 2015. "In U.S., 58% Back Legal Marijuana Use." October 21, 2015. http://www.gallup.com/poll/186260/back-legal-marijuana.aspx.

Jones, Sydney and Susannah Fox 2009. "Generations Online in 2009." January 28, 2009. http://www.pewinternet.org/2009/01/28/generations-online-in-2009/.

Keeter, Scott, Juliana Horowitz and Alec Tyson 2008. "Young Voters in the 2008 Election." November 13, 2008. http://www.pewresearch.org/2008/11/13/young-voters-in-the-2008-election/.

Kenski, Kate and Natalie Jomini Stroud 2006. "Connections between Internet Use and Political Efficacy, Knowledge, and Participation." *Journal of Broadcasting and Electronic Media* 50(2): 173–192.

Kerbel, Matthew R. and Joel D. Bloom 2005. "Blog for America and Civic Involvement." *The Harvard International Journal of Press/Politics* 10(4): 3–27.

Kiley, Jocelyn 2014. "61% of Young Republicans Favor Same-sex Marriage." Fact Tank: News in the Numbers. Pew Research Center. March 10, 2014. http://www.pewresearch.org/fact-tank/2014/03/10/61-of-young-republicans-favor-same-sex-marriage.

King, Gary, Michael Tomz and Jason Wittenberg 2000. "Making the Most of Statistical Analyses: Improving Interpretation and Presentation." *American Journal of Political Science* 44(2): 347–61.

Kmenta, Jan 1997. *Elements of Econometrics*. 2nd Ed. Ann Arbor, MI: University of Michigan Press.

Lapowsky, Issie 2015. "Social Media Pwned the Presidential Primaries." *Wired* December 24, 2015. http://www.wired.com/2015/12/the-year-the-crowd-stole-control-from-presidential-hopefuls/

Lawless, Jennifer 2012. "Twitter and Facebook: New Ways for Members of Congress to Send the Same Old Messages" In *iPolitics: Citizens, Elections, and Governing in the New Media Era*. Ed. Richard L. Fox and Jennifer M. Ramos, 206–32. New York, NY: Cambridge University Press.

Lawrence, Eric, John Sides and Henry Farrell 2010. "Self-Segregation or Deliberation? Blog Readership, Participation, and Polarization in American Politics." *Perspectives on Politics* 8(1): 141–57.

Lenhart, Amanda and Suzannah Fox 2006. "Bloggers: A Portrait of the Internet's New Storytellers." January 5, 2015. http://www.pewinternet.org/files/old-media/Files/Reports/2006/PIP%20Bloggers%20Report%20July%2019%202006.pdf.

Lenhart, Amanda, Kristen Purcell, Aaron Smith and Kathryn Zickuhr 2010. "Social Media and Internet Use Among Teens and Young Adults." November 21, 2014. http://www.pewinternet.org/files/old-media//Files/Reports/2010/PIP_Social_Media_and_Young_Adults_Report_Final_with_toplines.pdf.

Lewis, Mitzi 2011. "An Analysis of the Relationship between Political Blog Reading, Online Political Activity, and Voting During the 2008 Presidential Campaign." *The International Journal of Interdisciplinary Social Sciences* 6(3): 11–28.

Lewis-Beck, Michael S. 1990. *Economics and Elections: The Major Western Democracies*. Ann Arbor, MI: University of Michigan Press.

Lewis-Beck, Michael S., Nicholas F. Martini and D. Roderick Kiewiet 2013. "The Nature of Economic Perceptions in Mass Publics." *Electoral Studies* 32(3): 524–28.

Lewis-Beck, Michael S., William G. Jacoby, Helmut Norpoth and Herbert F. Weisberg 2008. *The American Voter Revisited*. Ann Arbor, MI: University of Michigan Press.

Lin, Nan 1999. "Building a Network Theory of Social Capital." *Connections* 22(1): 28–51.

Macafee, Timothy and J.J. De Simone. 2012. "Killing the Bill Online? Pathways to Young People's Protest Engagement via Social Media." *Cyberpsychology, Behavior, and Social Networking* 15(11): 579–84.

Macdonald, Stuart Elaine, George Rabinowitz and Ola Listhaug 1995. "Political Sophistication and Models of Issue Voting." *British Journal of Political Science* 25(4): 453–83.

MacKinnon, David P. 2008. *Introduction to Statistical Mediation Analysis*. New York City, NY: Routledge Press.

Maddala, G.S. 1983. *Limited-Dependent and Qualitative Variables in Econometrics*. New York City, NY: Cambridge University Press.

Madden, Mary 2010. "Older Adults and Social Media." August 27, 2010. http://www.pewinternet.org/2010/08/27/older-adults-and-social-media/.

Mansbridge, Jane 1990. "Self-Interest in Political Life." *Political Theory* 18(1): 132–53.

Marinucci, Carla 2014. "Signs of Donor Fatigue at Obama's Bay Area Fundraisers." *San Francisco Chronicle*. July 24, 2014. http://www.sfgate.com/politics/article/Signs-of-donor-fatigue-at-Obama-s-Bay-Area-5642285.php.

McClurg, Scott D. 2003. "Social Networks and Political Participation: The Role of Social Interaction in Explaining Political Participation." *Political Research Quarterly* 56(4): 449–64.

Menchik, Paul L. and Burton A. Weisbrod 1987. "Volunteer Labor Supply." *Journal of Public Economics* 32(2): 159–83.

Meraz, Sharon 2013. "The Democratic Contribution of Weakly Tied Political Networks: Moderate Political Blogs as Bridges to Heterogeneous Information Pools." *Social Science Computer Review* 31(2): 191–207.

Milbrath, Lester and M. Lal Goel 1977. *Political Participation*. Chicago, IL: Rand McNally.

Miller, Warren E. and J. Merrill Shanks 1996. *The New American Voter*. Cambridge, MA: Harvard University Press.

Miller, Zeke J. 2015. "John Kasich Takes Presidential Campaign to Snapchat with Bacon Filter Ad." September 2, 2015. http://time.com/4019684/john-kasich-2016-election-campaigns-snapchat-bacon/.

Min, Seong-Jae 2007. "Online vs. face-to-face deliberation: Effects on Civic Engagement." *Journal of Computer-Mediated Communication* 12(4): 1369–87.

Morozov, Evgeny 2009. "Iran: Downside to the 'Twitter Revolution.'" *Dissent* Fall 2009: 10–14.

Nielsen 2008. "Twitter Grows Fastest, MySpace Still the Social King." *Nielsenwire*. October 23.

Norris, Pippa 1998. "Virtual Democracy." *Harvard International Journal of Press/Politics* 3(3): 1–5.

Olson, Mancur, Jr. 1965. *The Logic of Collective Action*. Cambridge, MA: Harvard University Press.

Osgood, D. Wayne 2000. "Poisson-Based Regression Analysis of Aggregate Crime Rates." *Journal of Quantitative Criminology* 16(1): 21–43.

Ozymy, Joshua 2012. "The Poverty of Participation: Self-Interest, Student Loans, and Student Activism." *Political Behavior* 34(1): 103–16.

Pantoja, Adrian D., Ricardo Ramirez and Gary M. Segura 2001. "Citizens by Choice, Voters by Necessity: Patterns in Political Mobilization by Naturalized Latinos." *Political Research Quarterly* 54(4): 729–50.

Parmelee, John H. and Shannon L. Bichard 2012. *Politics and the Twitter Revolution: How Tweets Influence the Relationship between Political Leaders and the Public*. Lanham, MD: Lexington Books.

Peterson, Rolfe Daus 2012. "To Tweet or Not to Tweet: Exploring the Determinants of Early Adoption of Twitter by House Members in the 111th Congress." *Social Science Journal* 49(4): 430–38.

Petrocik, John R. 1996. "Issue Ownership in Presidential Elections, with a 1980 Case Study." *American Journal of Political Science* 40(3): 825–50.

Petrocik, John R., William L. Benoit and Glenn J. Hansen. 2003/2004. "Issue Ownership and Presidential Campaigning, 1952–2000." *Political Science Quarterly* 118(4): 599–626.

Pew Research Center for the People and the Press 2010. "Americans Spending More Time Following the News." September 12, 2010. http://www.people-press.org/2010/09/12/section-2-online-and-digital-news/.

Pew Research Center for the People and the Press 2012. "In Changing News Landscape, Even Television is Vulnerable." September 27, 2012. http://www.people-press.org/2012/09/27/section-1-watching-reading-and-listening-to-the-news-3/.

Pew Internet Project 2013a. "Teens and Technology." March 13, 2013. http://www.pewinternet.org/2013/03/13/main-findings-5/.

Pew Internet Project 2013b. "Social Media Update 2013." December 30, 2013. http://www.pewinternet.org/2013/12/30/social-media-update-2013/.

Pew Internet Project 2014a. "Social Networking Fact Sheet." November 13, 2014. http://www.pewinternet.org/fact-sheets/social-networking-fact-sheet/.

Pew Internet Project 2014b. "Internet User Demographics." November 21, 2014. http://www.pewinternet.org/data-trend/internet-use/latest-stats/.

Pew Internet Project 2015. "Offline Adults." March 23, 2015. http://www.perwinternet.org/data-trend/internet-use/offline-adults/.

Pindyck, Robert S. and Daniel L. Rubinfeld 1991. *Econometric Models and Economic Forecasts*. 3rd Ed. New York, NY: McGraw Hill, Inc.

Preacher, Kristopher J. and Andrew F. Hayes 2008. "Asymptotic and Resampling Strategies for Assessing and Comparing Indirect Effects in Multiple Mediator Models." *Behavior Research Methods* 40(3): 879–91.

Rice, Laurie, Kenneth W. Moffett and Ramana Madupalli 2013. "Campaign-Related Social Networking and the Political Participation of College Students." *Social Science Computer Review* 31(3): 251–79.

Rosenstone, Steven and John Mark Hansen 1993. *Mobilization, Participation and Democracy in America*. New York, NY: Macmillan Press.

Saad, Lydia 2012. "Conservatives Remain the Largest Ideological Group in U.S." *Gallup Politics*. January 12, 2012. http://www.gallup.com/poll/152021/conservatives-remain-largest-ideological-group.aspx.

Sarkesian, Sam C. 1981. "Military Professionalism and Civil-Military Relations in the West." *International Political Science Review* 2(3): 283–97.

Scherer, Michael 2012. "Friended: How the Obama Campaign Connected with Young Voters." *Time Magazine*, November 20, 2012. http://swampland.time.com/2012/11/20/friended-how-the-obama-campaign-connected-with-young-voters/.

Schlozman, Kay Lehman, Sydney Verba and Henry E. Brady 2012. *The Unheavenly Chorus: Unequal Political Voice and the Broken Promise of American Democracy*. Princeton, NJ: Princeton University Press.

Schoenberg, Sandra Perlman 1980. "Some Trends in the Community Participation of Women in Their Neighborhoods." *Signs: Journal of Women in Culture and Society* 5(3): S261–68.

Schwarz, Hunter 2015. "2016 May Yet Be the First 'Instagram election.'" *The Washington Post*. January 5, 2015. http://www.washingtonpost.com/blogs/post-politics/wp/2015/01/06/2016-may-yet-be-the-first-instagram-election/.

Shah, Dhavan V., Nojin Kwak and R. Lance Holbert 2001. "'Connecting' and 'Disconnecting' With Civic Life: Patterns of Internet Use and the Production of Social Capital." *Political Communication* 18(2): 141–62.

Shah, Dhavan V., Jaeho Cho, William P. Eveland, Jr. and Nojin Kwak 2005. "Information and Expression in a Digital Age: Modeling Internet Effects on Civic Participation." *Communication Research* 32(5): 531–65.

Sharp, Adam 2012a. "#DNC2012 Night 3: Obama's speech sets records." February 25, 2014.https://blog.Twitter.com/2012/dnc2012-night-3-obamas-speech-sets-records.

Sharp, Adam 2012b. "Dispatch from the Denver Debate." February 25, 2014. https://blog.Twitter.com/2012/dispatch-from-the-denver-debate.

Sharp, Adam 2012c. "Election Night 2012." February 25, 2014. https://blog.Twitter.com/2012/election-night-2012.

Sides, John and Andrew Karch 2008. "Messages that Mobilize? Issue Publics and the Content of Campaign Advertising." *The Journal of Politics* 70(2): 466–76.

Simpson, John 2013. "A Heads Up for the June 2013 OED release." February 25, 2014. http://public.oed.com/the-oed-today/recent-updates-to-the-oed/june-2013-update/a-heads-up-for-the-june-2013-oed-release.

Smith, Aaron 2013. "Civic Engagement in the Digital Age." *Pew Research Center Report*, April 25, 2013. http://www.pewinternet.org/2013/04/25/civic-engagement-in-the-digital-age/.

Smith, Aaron, Key Lehman Schlozman, Sidney Verba and Henry Brady 2009. "The Internet and Civic Engagement." *Pew Research Center Report*. September 2009. http://www.pewinternet.org/files/old-media//Files/Reports/2009/ The%20Internet%20and%20Civic%20Engagement.pdf.

Smith, Candace 2015. "Here's What the 2016 Presidential Campaign Looks Like on Snapchat." September 30, 2015. http://abcnews.go.com/Politics/heres-2016-presidential-campaign-snapchat/story?id=32191260.

Smith, Justin Davis 1999. "Poor Marketing or the Decline of Altruism? Young People and Volunteering in the United Kingdom." *International Journal of Nonprofit and Voluntary Sector Marketing* 4(4): 372–77.

Sobieraj, Sarah and Jeffrey M. Berry 2011. "From Incivility to Outrage: Political Discourse in Blogs, Talk Radio, and Cable News." *Political Communication* 28(1): 19–41.

Sorenson, Adam 2011. "Republicans Close the Social Media Gap." *Time Magazine*, January 27, 2011. http://swampland.time.com/2011/01/27/republicans-close-the-social-media-gap/.

Southern Illinois University Edwardsville 2009 and 2013. *Fact Book*, November 4, 2014. http://www.siue.edu.

Steinfield, Charles, Nicole B. Ellison and Cliff Lampe 2008. "Social Capital, Self-Esteem and the Use of Online Social Network Sites: A Longitudinal Analysis." *Journal of Applied Developmental Psychology* 29(6): 434–45.

Stokes, Atiya Kai 2003. "Latino Group Consciousness and Political Participation." *American Politics Research* 31(4): 361–78.

Sullivan, Harry S. 1953. *The Interpersonal Theory of Psychiatry*. New York, NY: Norton.

Teixeira, Ruy 1987. *Why Americans Don't Vote*. New York, NY: Greenwood Press.

Thompson, Clive. 2006. "The Early Years." *New York Magazine*, September 1, 2013. http://nymag.com/news/media/15971.

Tolbert, Caroline J. and Ramona S. McNeal 2003. "Unraveling the Effects of the Internet on Political Participation?" *Political Research Quarterly* 56(2): 175–85.

Towner, Terri L. and David A. Dulio 2011. "The Web 2.0 Election: Does the Online Medium Matter?" *The Journal of Political Marketing* 10(1–2): 165–88.

Towner, Terri L. 2013. "All Political Participation is Socially Networked?: New Media and the 2012 Election." *Social Science Computer Review* 31(5): 527–41.

Tumasjan, Andranik, Timm O. Sprenger, Philipp G. Sandner and Isabell M. Welpe 2011. "Election Forecasts with Twitter: How 140 Characters Reflect the Political Landscape." *Social Science Computer Review* 29(4): 402–18.

Twitter 2015. "Barack Obama." January 9, 2015. https://biz.Twitter.com/success-stories/barack-obama.

U.S. Census Bureau 2014. "Illinois Quick Facts from the U.S. Census Bureau." November 4, 2014. http://quickfacts.census.gov/qfd/states/17000.html.

U.S. Department of Education 2011. "Enrollment in Postsecondary Institutions, Fall 2009, Graduation Rates, 2003 and 2006 Cohorts and Financial Statistics, Fiscal Year 2009." November 4, 2014. http://nces.ed.gov/pubs2011/2011230.pdf.

U.S. Department of Education 2013. "Projections of Education Statistics to 2021." November 4, 2014. http://nces.ed.gov/pubs2013/2013008.pdf.

U.S. Department of Education 2014. "Characteristics of Postsecondary Students." November 4, 2014. http://nces.ed.gov/programs/coe/indicator_csb.asp.

Verba, Sidney and Norman H. Nie 1972. *Participation in America: Political Democracy and Social Equality*. New York, NY: Harper and Row.

Verba, Sidney, Henry E. Brady and Kay L. Schlozman 1995. *Voice and Equality: Civic Voluntarism in American Democracy*. Cambridge, MA: Harvard University Press.

Vitak, Jessica, Paul Zube and Andrew Smock, Caleb T. Carr, Nicole Ellison and Cliff Lampe 2011. "It's Complicated: Facebook Users' Political Participation in the 2008 Election." *CyberPsychology, Behavior, and Social Networking* 14(3): 107–14.

Wallsten, Kevin 2007. "Agenda Setting and the Blogosphere: An Analysis of the Relationship between Mainstream Media and Political Blogs." *Review of Policy Research* 24(6): 567–87.

Walton, Hanes Jr. 1985. *Invisible Politics: Black Political Behavior*. Albany, NY: SUNY Press.

Wattenberg, Marvin P. 2011. *Is Voting for Young People?* 3rd Ed. New York, NY: Pearson Longman.

Whitten, Guy D. and Harvey D. Palmer 1999. "Cross-National Analyses of Economic Voting." *Electoral Studies* 18(1): 49–67.

Wilkins, Vicki M. and Lael R. Keiser 2006. "Linking Passive and Active Representation by Gender: The Case of Child Support Agencies." *Journal of Public Administration Research and Theory* 16(1): 87–102.

Wilkinson, David and Mike Thelwall. 2012. "Trending Twitter Topics in English: An International Comparison." *Journal of the American Society for Information Science and Technology* 63(8): 1631–46.

Wilson, John 2000. "Volunteering." *Annual Review of Sociology* 26(1): 215–40.

Wortham, Jenna 2012. "The Presidential Campaign on Social Media." February 25, 2014. http://www.nytimes.com/interactive/2012/10/08/technology/campaign-social-media.html?_r=0.

Zhang, Weiwu, Trent Seltzer and Shannon L. Bichard 2013. "Two Sides of the Coin: Assessing the Influence of Social Network Site Use during the 2012 U.S. Presidential Campaign." *Social Science Computer Review* 31(5): 542–51.

Zukin, Cliff, Scott Keeter, Molly Andolina, Krista Jenkins and Michael X. Delli Carpini 2006. *A New Engagement? Political Participation, Civic Life, and the Changing American Citizen*. New York, NY: Oxford University Press.

Index

About the Authors

Kenneth W. Moffett is Associate Professor of Political Science at Southern Illinois University Edwardsville. His research interests include political participation, American political institutions, civic engagement, and public policy. His research has been published in *American Politics Research, Climatic Change, Congress and the Presidency, Legislative Studies Quarterly, Party Politics, Social Science Quarterly, Social Science Computer Review*, among other outlets. Moffett received his B.A. from California State University, Fresno and his master's and doctorate degrees from The University of Iowa.

Laurie L. Rice is Associate Professor of Political Science at Southern Illinois University Edwardsville. Her research interests include political communication, the presidency, presidential elections, and civic engagement. Her research on these topics appears in journals such as *Congress and the Presidency, Presidential Studies Quarterly, Social Science Computer Review, and Social Science Quarterly*. Rice received her B.A. from University of Redlands and her master's and doctorate degrees from University of California San Diego.

www.ingramcontent.com/pod-product-compliance
Lightning Source LLC
Chambersburg PA
CBHW051239050326
40689CB00007B/988

* 9 7 8 1 4 9 8 5 3 8 5 9 6 *